CURRICULUM FOR GIFTED AND TALENTED STUDENTS

ESSENTIAL READINGS IN GIFTED EDUCATION

SERIES EDITOR

SALLY M. REIS

Joyce VanTassel-Baska

EDITOR

CURRICULUM FOR
GIFTED AND TALENTED
STUDENTS

A Joint Publication of Corwin Press and the National Association for Gifted Children

ESSENTIAL READINGS IN GIFTED EDUCATION
Sally M. Reis, SERIES EDITOR

CORWIN PRESS
A Sage Publications Company
Thousand Oaks, California

For information:

Corwin Press
A Sage Publications Company
2455 Teller Road
Thousand Oaks, California 91320
www.corwinpress.com

Sage Publications Ltd.
6 Bonhill Street
London EC2A 4PU
United Kingdom

Sage Publications India Pvt. Ltd.
B-42, Panchsheel Enclave
Post Box 4109
New Delhi 110 017 India

Printed in the United States of America

Library of Congress Cataloging-in-Publication Data

Curriculum for gifted and talented students / Joyce VanTassel-Baska [editor].
    p. cm. — (Essential readings in gifted education ; v. 4)
Includes bibliographical references and index.
ISBN 0-7619-8874-2 (pbk.: alk. paper)
    1. Gifted children—Education—Curricula—United States.
2. Curriculum planning—United States. I. VanTassel-Baska, Joyce.
II. Series.
LC3993.9 .C89 2004
371.95—dc22   2003020158

This book is printed on acid-free paper.

04   05   06   10   9   8   7   6   5   4   3   2

Acquisitions Editor:	Kylee Liegl
Editorial Assistant:	Jaime Cuvier
Typesetter:	C&M Digitals (P) Ltd.
Cover Designer:	Tracy E. Miller
Graphic Designer:	Lisa Miller

Contents

About the Editors

Sally M. Reis is a professor and the department head of the Educational Psychology Department at the University of Connecticut where she also serves as principal investigator of the National Research Center on the Gifted and Talented. She was a teacher for 15 years, 11 of which were spent working with gifted students on the elementary, junior high, and high school levels. She has authored more than 130 articles, 9 books, 40 book chapters, and numerous monographs and technical reports.

Her research interests are related to special populations of gifted and talented students, including: students with learning disabilities, gifted females and diverse groups of talented students. She is also interested in extensions of the Schoolwide Enrichment Model for both gifted and talented students and as a way to expand offerings and provide general enrichment to identify talents and potentials in students who have not been previously identified as gifted.

She has traveled extensively conducting workshops and providing professional development for school districts on gifted education, enrichment programs, and talent development programs. She is co-author of *The Schoolwide Enrichment Model, The Secondary Triad Model, Dilemmas in Talent Development in the Middle Years*, and a book published in 1998 about women's talent development titled *Work Left Undone: Choices and Compromises of Talented Females*. Sally serves on several editorial boards, including the *Gifted Child Quarterly*, and is a past president of the National Association for Gifted Children.

Joyce VanTassel-Baska is The Jody and Layton Smith Professor of Education and Executive Director of the Center for Gifted Education at the College of William and Mary in Virginia where she has developed a graduate program and a research and development center in gifted education. Formerly she initiated and directed the Center for Talent Development at Northwestern University. She has also served as the state director of gifted programs for Illinois, as a regional director of a gifted service center in the Chicago area, as coordinator of gifted programs for the

Toledo, Ohio, public school system, and as a teacher of gifted high school students in English and Latin. She has worked as a consultant on gifted education in all 50 states and for key national groups, including the U.S. Department of Education, National Association of Secondary School Principals, and American Association of School Administrators. She has consulted internationally in Australia, New Zealand, Hungary, Jordan, Singapore, and the United Arab Emirates. She is past president of The Association for the Gifted of the Council for Exceptional Children, and the Northwestern University Chapter of Phi Delta Kappa. She is currently president-elect of the National Association for Gifted Children.

Dr. VanTassel-Baska has published widely including 15 books and over 275 refereed journal articles, book chapters, and scholarly reports. Recent books include: *Designing and Utilizing Evaluation for Gifted Program Improvement* (in press) (with Annie Feng), *Content-based Curriculum for Gifted Learners* (2003) (with Catherine Little) and *Curriculum Planning and Instructional Design for Gifted Learners* (2003). She also serves as the editor of *Gifted and Talented International*, a publication of the World Council on Gifted and Talented.

Dr. VanTassel-Baska has received numerous awards for her work, including the National Association for Gifted Children's Early Leader Award in 1986, the State Council of Higher Education in Virginia Outstanding Faculty Award in 1993, the Phi Beta Kappa faculty award in 1995, and the National Association of Gifted Children's Distinguished Scholar Award in 1997. She has received awards from five states – Ohio, Virginia, Colorado, South Carolina, and Illinois – for her contribution to the field of gifted education in those states. She was selected as a Fulbright Scholar to New Zealand in 2000 and a visiting scholar to Cambridge University in England in 1993. Her major research interests are on the talent development process and effective curricular interventions with the gifted. She holds B.A., M.A., M. Ed., and Ed.D. degrees from the University of Toledo.

Series Introduction

Sally M. Reis

The accomplishments of the last 50 years in the education of gifted students should not be underestimated: the field of education of the gifted and talented has emerged as strong and visible. In many states, a policy or position statement from the state board of education supports the education of the gifted and talented, and specific legislation generally recognizes the special needs of this group. Growth in our field has not been constant, however, and researchers and scholars have discussed the various high and low points of national interest and commitment to educating the gifted and talented (Gallagher, 1979; Renzulli, 1980; Tannenbaum, 1983). Gallagher described the struggle between support and apathy for special programs for gifted and talented students as having roots in historical tradition—the battle between an aristocratic elite and our concomitant belief in egalitarianism. Tannenbaum suggested the existence of two peak periods of interest in the gifted as the five years following Sputnik in 1957 and the last half of the decade of the 1970s, describing a valley of neglect between the peaks in which the public focused its attention on the disadvantaged and the handicapped. "The cyclical nature of interest in the gifted is probably unique in American education. No other special group of children has been alternately embraced and repelled with so much vigor by educators and laypersons alike" (Tannenbaum, 1983, p. 16). Many wonder if the cyclical nature to which Tannenbaum referred is not somewhat prophetic, as it appears that our field may be experiencing another downward spiral in interest as a result of current governmental initiatives and an increasing emphasis on testing and standardization of curriculum. Tannenbaum's description of a valley of neglect may describe current conditions. During the late 1980s, programming flourished during a peak of interest and a textbook on systems and models for gifted programs included 15 models for elementary and secondary programs (Renzulli, 1986). The Jacob Javits Gifted and Talented Students Education Act passed by Congress in 1988 resulted in the creation of the National Research Center on the Gifted and Talented, and dozens of model programs were added to the collective knowledge in the field in areas related to underrepresented populations and successful practices. In the 1990s, reduction or elimination of gifted programs occurred, as budget pressures exacerbated by the lingering recession in the late 1990s resulted in the reduction of services mandated by fewer than half of the states in our country.

Even during times in which more activity focused on the needs of gifted and talented students, concerns were still raised about the limited services provided to these students. In the second federal report on the status of education for our nation's most talented students entitled *National Excellence, A Case for Developing America's Talent* (Ross, 1993), "a quiet crisis" was described in the absence of attention paid to this population: "Despite sporadic attention over the years to the needs of bright students, most of them continue to spend time in school working well below their capabilities. The belief espoused in school reform that children from all economic and cultural backgrounds must reach their full potential has not been extended to America's most talented students. They are underchallenged and therefore underachieve" (p. 5). The report further indicates that our nation's gifted and talented students have a less rigorous curriculum, read fewer demanding books, and are less prepared for work or postsecondary education than the most talented students in many other industrialized countries. Talented children who come from economically disadvantaged homes or are members of minority groups are especially neglected, the report also indicates, and many of them will not realize their potential without some type of intervention.

In this anniversary series of volumes celebrating the evolution of our field, noted scholars introduce a collection of the most frequently cited articles from the premiere journal in our field, *Gifted Child Quarterly*. Each volume includes a collection of thoughtful, and in some cases, provocative articles that honor our past, acknowledge the challenges we face in the present, and provide hopeful guidance for the future as we seek the optimal educational experiences for all talented students. These influential articles, published after a rigorous peer review, were selected because they are frequently cited and considered seminal in our field. Considered in their entirety, the articles show that we have learned a great deal from the volume of work represented by this series. Our knowledge has expanded over several decades of work, and progress has been made toward reaching consensus about what is known. As several of the noted scholars who introduce separate areas explain in their introductions, this series helps us to understand that some questions have been answered, while others remain. While we still search for these answers, we are now better prepared to ask questions that continue and evolve. The seminal articles in this series help us to resolve some issues, while they highlight other questions that simply refuse to go away. Finally, the articles help us to identify new challenges that continue to emerge in our field. Carol Tomlinson suggests, for example, that the area of curriculum differentiation in the field of gifted education is, in her words, an issue born in the field of gifted education, and one that continues to experience rebirth.

Some of the earliest questions in our field have been answered and time has enabled those answers to be considered part of our common core of knowledge. For example, it is widely acknowledged that both school and home experiences can help to develop giftedness in persons with high potential and that a continuum of services in and out of school can provide the greatest likelihood that this development will occur. Debates over other "hot" issues such as grouping and acceleration that took place in the gifted education community 30 years ago are now largely unnecessary, as Linda Brody points out in her introduction to a series of articles in this area. General agreement seems to have been reached, for example, that grouping, enrichment and acceleration are all necessary to provide appropriate educational opportunities for gifted and talented learners. These healthy debates of the past helped to strengthen our field but visionary and reflective work remains to be done. In this series, section editors summarize what has been learned and raise provocative questions about the future. The questions alone are some of the most thoughtful in our field, providing enough research opportunities for scholars for the next decade. The brief introductions below provide some highlights about the series.

DEFINITIONS OF GIFTEDNESS (VOLUME 1)

In Volume 1, Robert Sternberg introduces us to seminal articles about definitions of giftedness and the types of talents and gifts exhibited by children and youth. The most widely used definitions of gifts and talents utilized by educators generally follow those proposed in federal reports. For example, the Marland Report (Marland, 1972) commissioned by the Congress included the first federal definition of giftedness, which was widely adopted or adapted by the states.

The selection of a definition of giftedness has been and continues to be the major policy decision made at state and local levels. It is interesting to note that policy decisions are often either unrelated or marginally related to actual procedures or to research findings about a definition of giftedness or identification of the gifted, a fact well documented by the many ineffective, incorrect, and downright ridiculous methods of identification used to find students who meet the criteria in the federal definition. This gap between policy and practice may be caused by many variables. Unfortunately, although the federal definition was written to be inclusive, it is, instead, rather vague, and problems caused by this definition have been recognized by experts in the field (Renzulli, 1978). In the most recent federal report on the status of gifted and talented programs entitled *National Excellence* (Ross, 1993), a newer federal definition is proposed based on new insights provided by neuroscience and cognitive psychology. Arguing that the term *gifted* connotes a mature power rather than a developing ability and, therefore, is antithetic to recent research findings about children, the new definition "reflects today's knowledge and thinking" (p. 26) by emphasizing talent development, stating that gifted and talented children are children and youth with outstanding talent performance or show the potential for performing at remarkably high levels of accomplishment when compared with others of their age, experience, or environment. These children and youth exhibit high performance capability in intellectual, creative, and/or artistic areas, possess an unusual leadership capacity, or excel in specific academic fields. They require services or activities not ordinarily provided by the schools. Outstanding talents are present in children and youth from all cultural groups, across all economic strata, and in all areas of human endeavor. (p. 26)

Fair identification systems use a variety of multiple assessment measures that respect diversity, accommodate students who develop at different rates, and identify potential as well as demonstrated talent. In the introduction to the volume, Sternberg admits, that just as people have bad habits, so do academic fields, explaining, "a bad habit of much of the gifted field is to do research on giftedness, or worse, identify children as gifted or not gifted, without having a clear conception of what it means to be gifted." Sternberg summarizes major themes from the seminal articles about definitions by asking key questions about the nature of giftedness and talent, the ways in which we should study giftedness, whether we should expand conventional notions of giftedness, and if so, how that can be accomplished; whether differences exist between giftedness and talent; the validity of available assessments; and perhaps most importantly, how do we and can we develop giftedness and talent. Sternberg succinctly summarizes points of broad agreement from the many scholars who have contributed to this section, concluding that giftedness involves more than just high IQ, that it has noncognitive and cognitive components, that the environment is crucial in terms of whether potentials for gifted performance will be realized, and that giftedness is not a single thing. He further cautions that the ways we conceptualize giftedness greatly influences who will have opportunities to develop their gifts and reminds readers of our responsibilities as educators. He also asks one of the most critical questions in our field: whether gifted and talented individuals will use their knowledge to benefit or harm our world.

IDENTIFICATION OF
HIGH-ABILITY STUDENTS (VOLUME 2)

In Volume 2, Joseph Renzulli introduces what is perhaps the most critical question still facing practitioners and researchers in our field, that is how, when, and why should we identify gifted and talented students. Renzulli believes that conceptions of giftedness exist along a continuum ranging from a very conservative or restricted view of giftedness to a more flexible or multi-dimensional approach. What many seem not to understand is that the first step in identification should always be to ask: identification for what? For what type of program or experience is the youngster being identified? If, for example, an arts program is being developed for talented artists, the resulting identification system must be structured to identify youngsters with either demonstrated or potential talent in art.

Renzulli's introductory chapter summarizes seminal articles about identification, and summarizes emerging consensus. For example, most suggest, that while intelligence tests and other cognitive ability tests provide one very important form of information about one dimension of a young person's potential, mainly in the areas of verbal and analytic skills, they do not tell us all that we need to know about who should be identified. These authors do not argue that cognitive ability tests should be dropped from the identification process. Rather, most believe that (a) other indicators of potential should be used for identification, (b) these indicators should be given equal consideration when it comes to making final decisions about which students will be candidates for special services, and (c) in the final analysis, it is the thoughtful judgment of knowledgeable professionals rather than instruments and cut-off scores that should guide selection decisions.

Another issue addressed by the authors of the seminal articles about identification is what has been referred to as the distinction between (a) convergent and divergent thinking (Guilford, 1967; Torrance, 1984), (b) entrenchment and non-entrenchment (Sternberg, 1982), and (c) schoolhouse giftedness versus creative/productive giftedness (Renzulli, 1982; Renzulli & Delcourt, 1986). It is easier to identify schoolhouse giftedness than it is to identify students with the potential for creative productive giftedness. Renzulli believes that progress has been made in the identification of gifted students, especially during the past quarter century, and that new approaches address the equity issue, policies, and practices that respect new theories about human potential and conceptions of giftedness. He also believes, however, that continuous commitment to research-based identification practices is still needed, for "it is important to keep in mind that some of the characteristics that have led to the recognition of history's most gifted contributors are not always as measurable as others. We need to continue our search for those elusive things that are left over after everything explainable has been explained, to realize that giftedness is culturally and contextually imbedded in all human activity, and most of all, to value the value of even those things that we cannot yet explain."

ACCELERATION AND GROUPING, CURRICULUM, AND CURRICULUM DIFFERENTIATION (VOLUMES 3, 4, 5)

Three volumes in this series address curricular and grouping issues in gifted programs, and it is in this area, perhaps, that some of the most promising practices have been implemented for gifted and talented students. Grouping and curriculum interact with each other, as various forms of grouping patterns have enabled students to work on advanced curricular opportunities with other talented students. And, as is commonly known now about instructional and ability grouping, it is not the way students are grouped that matters most, but rather, it is what happens within the groups that makes the most difference.

In too many school settings, little differentiation of curriculum and instruction for gifted students is provided during the school day, and minimal opportunities are offered. Occasionally, afterschool enrichment programs or Saturday programs offered by museums, science centers, or local universities take the place of comprehensive school programs, and too many academically talented students attend school in classrooms across the country in which they are bored, unmotivated, and unchallenged. Acceleration, once a frequently used educational practice in our country, is often dismissed by teachers and administrators as an inappropriate practice for a variety of reasons, including scheduling problems, concerns about the social effects of grade skipping, and others. Various forms of acceleration, including enabling precocious students to enter kindergarten or first grade early, grade skipping, and early entrance to college are not commonly used by most school districts.

Unfortunately, major alternative grouping strategies involve the reorganization of school structures, and these have been too slow in coming, perhaps due to the difficulty of making major educational changes, because of scheduling, finances, and other issues that have caused schools to substantially delay major change patterns. Because of this delay, gifted students too often fail to receive classroom instruction based on their unique needs that place them far ahead of their chronological peers in basic skills and verbal abilities and enable them to learn much more rapidly and tackle much more complex materials than their peers. Our most able students need appropriately paced, rich and challenging instruction, and curriculum that varies significantly from what is being taught in regular classrooms across America. Too often, academically talented students are "left behind" in school.

Linda Brody introduces the question of how to group students optimally for instructional purposes and pays particular concern to the degree to which the typical age-in-grade instructional program can meet the needs of gifted students – those students with advanced cognitive abilities and achievement that may already have mastered the curriculum designed for their age peers. The articles about grouping emphasize the importance of responding to the learning needs of individual students with curricular flexibility, the need for educators to be flexible when assigning students to instructional groups, and the need to modify those groups when necessary. Brody's introduction points out that the debate about grouping gifted and talented learners together was one area that brought the field together, as every researcher in the field supports some type of grouping option, and few would disagree with the need to use grouping and accelerated learning as tools that allow us to differentiate content for students with different learning needs. When utilized as a way to offer a more advanced educational program to students with advanced cognitive abilities and achievement levels, these practices can help achieve the goal of an appropriate education for all students.

Joyce VanTassel-Baska introduces the seminal articles in curriculum, by explaining that they represent several big ideas that emphasize the values and relevant factors of a curriculum for the gifted, the technology of curriculum development, aspects of differentiation of a curriculum for the gifted within core subject areas and without, and the research-based efficacy of such curriculum and related instructional pedagogy in use. She also reminds readers of Harry Passow's concerns about curriculum balance, suggesting that an imbalance exists, as little evidence suggests that the affective development of gifted students is occurring through special curricula for the gifted. Moreover, interdisciplinary efforts at curriculum frequently exclude the arts and foreign language. Only through acknowledging and applying curriculum balance in these areas are we likely to be producing the type of humane individual Passow envisioned. To achieve balance, VanTassel-Baska recommends a full set of curriculum options across domains, as well as the need to nurture the social-emotional needs of diverse gifted and talented learners.

Carol Tomlinson introduces the critical area of differentiation in the field of gifted education that has only emerged in the last 13 years. She believes the diverse nature of the articles and their relatively recent publication suggests that this area is indeed, in her words, "an issue born in the field of gifted education, and one that continues to experience rebirth." She suggests that one helpful way of thinking about the articles in this volume is that their approach varies, as some approach the topic of differentiation of curriculum with a greater emphasis on the distinctive mission of gifted education. Others look at differentiation with a greater emphasis on the goals, issues, and missions shared between general education and gifted education. Drawing from an analogy with anthropology, Tomlinson suggests that "splitters" in that field focus on differences among cultures while "lumpers" have a greater interest in what cultures share in common. Splitters ask the question of what happens for high-ability students in mixed-ability settings, while lumpers question what common issues and solutions exist for multiple populations in mixed-ability settings.

Tomlinson suggests that the most compelling feature of the collection of articles in this section—and certainly its key unifying feature—is the linkage between the two areas of educational practice in attempting to address an issue likely to be seminal to the success of both over the coming quarter century and beyond, and this collection may serve as a catalyst for next steps in those directions for the field of gifted education as it continues collaboration with general education and other educational specialties while simultaneously addressing those missions uniquely its own.

UNDERREPRESENTED AND TWICE-EXCEPTIONAL POPULATIONS AND SOCIAL AND EMOTIONAL ISSUES (VOLUMES 6, 7, 8)

The majority of young people participating in gifted and talented programs across the country continue to represent the majority culture in our society. Few doubts exist regarding the reasons that economically disadvantaged, twice-exceptional, and culturally diverse students are underrepresented in gifted programs. One reason may be the ineffective and inappropriate identification and selection procedures used for the identification of these young people that limits referrals and nominations and eventual placement. Research summarized in this series indicates that groups that have been traditionally underrepresented in gifted programs could be better served if some of the following elements are considered: new constructs of giftedness, attention to cultural and contextual variability, the use of more varied and authentic assessments, performance-based identification, and identification opportunities through rich and varied learning opportunities.

Alexinia Baldwin discusses the lower participation of culturally diverse and underserved populations in programs for the gifted as a major concern that has forged dialogues and discussion in *Gifted Child Quarterly* over the past five decades. She classifies these concerns in three major themes: *identification/selection*, *programming*, and *staff assignment and development*. Calling the first theme **Identification/Selection**, she indicates that it has always been the Achilles heel of educators' efforts to ensure that giftedness can be expressed in many ways through broad identification techniques. Citing favorable early work by Renzulli and Hartman (1971) and Baldwin (1977) that expanded options for identification, Baldwin cautions that much remains to be done. The second theme, **Programming**, recognizes the abilities of students who are culturally diverse but often forces them to exist in programs designed "for one size fits all." Her third theme relates to **Staffing and Research,** as she voices concerns about the diversity of teachers in these programs as well as the attitudes or mindsets of researchers who develop theories and conduct the research that addresses these concerns.

Susan Baum traces the historical roots of gifted and talented individuals with special needs, summarizing Terman's early work that suggested the gifted were healthier, more popular, and better adjusted than their less able peers. More importantly, gifted individuals were regarded as those who could perform at high levels in all areas with little or no support. Baum suggests that acceptance of these stereotypical characteristics diminished the possibility that there could be special populations of gifted students with special needs. Baum believes that the seminal articles in this collection address one or more of the critical issues that face gifted students at risk and suggest strategies for overcoming the barriers that prevent them from realizing their promise. The articles focus on three populations of students: twice-exceptional students—gifted students who are at risk for poor development due to difficulties in learning and attention;

gifted students who face gender issues that inhibit their ability to achieve or develop socially and emotionally, and students who are economically disadvantaged and at risk for dropping out of school. Baum summarizes research indicating that each of these groups of youngsters is affected by one or more barriers to development, and the most poignant of these barriers are identification strategies, lack of awareness of consequences of co-morbidity, deficit thinking in program design, and lack of appropriate social and emotional support. She ends her introduction with a series of thoughtful questions focusing on future directions in this critical area.

Sidney Moon introduces the seminal articles on the social and emotional development of and counseling for gifted children by acknowledging the contributions of the National Association for Gifted Children's task forces that have examined social/emotional issues. The first task force, formed in 2000 and called the Social and Emotional Issues Task Force, completed its work in 2002 by publishing an edited book, *The Social and Emotional Development of Gifted Children: What Do We Know?* This volume provides an extensive review of the literature on the social and emotional development of gifted children (Neihart, Reis, Robinson, & Moon, 2002). Moon believes that the seminal studies in the area of the social and emotional development and counseling illustrate both the strengths and the weaknesses of the current literature on social and emotional issues in the field of gifted education. These articles bring increased attention to the affective needs of special populations of gifted students, such as underachievers, who are at risk for failure to achieve their potential, but also point to the need for more empirical studies on "what works" with these students, both in terms of preventative strategies and more intensive interventions. She acknowledges that although good counseling models have been developed, they need to be rigorously evaluated to determine their effectiveness under disparate conditions, and calls for additional research on the affective and counseling interventions with specific subtypes of gifted students such as Asian Americans, African Americans, and twice-exceptional students. Moon also strongly encourages researchers in the field of gifted education to collaborate with researchers from affective fields such as personal and social psychology, counseling psychology, family therapy, and psychiatry to learn to intervene most effectively with gifted individuals with problems and to learn better how to help all gifted persons achieve optimal social, emotional, and personal development.

ARTISTICALLY AND CREATIVELY TALENTED STUDENTS (VOLUMES 9, 10)

Enid Zimmerman introduces the volume on talent development in the visual and performing arts with a summary of articles about students who are talented in music, dance, visual arts, and spatial, kinesthetic, and expressive areas. Major themes that appear in the articles include perceptions by parents, students, and teachers that often focus on concerns related to nature versus nurture in arts talent development; research about the crystallizing experiences of artistically talented students; collaboration between school and community members about identification of talented art students from diverse backgrounds; and leadership issues related to empowering teachers of talented arts students. They all are concerned to some extent with teacher, parent, and student views about educating artistically talented students. Included also are discussions about identification of talented students from urban, suburban, and rural environments. Zimmerman believes that in this particular area, a critical need exists for research about the impact of educational opportunities, educational settings, and the role of art teachers on the development of artistically talented students. The impact of the standards and testing movement and its relationship to the education of talented students in the visual and performing arts is an area greatly in need of investigation. Research also is needed about students' backgrounds, personalities, gender orientations, skill development, and cognitive and affective abilities as well as cross-cultural contexts and the impact of global and popular culture on the education of artistically talented students. The compelling case study with which she introduces this volume sets the stage for the need for this research.

Donald Treffinger introduces reflections on articles about creativity by discussing the following five core themes that express the collective efforts of researchers to grasp common conceptual and theoretical challenges associated with creativity. The themes include **Definitions** (how we define giftedness, talent, or creativity), **Characteristics** (the indicators of giftedness and creativity in people), **Justification** (Why is creativity important in education?), **Assessment** of creativity, and the ways we **Nurture** creativity. Treffinger also discusses the expansion of knowledge, the changes that have occurred, the search for answers, and the questions that still remain. In the early years of interest of creativity research, Treffinger believed that considerable discussion existed about whether it was possible to foster creativity through training or instruction. He reports that over the last 50 years, educators have learned that deliberate efforts to nurture creativity are possible (e.g., Torrance, 1987), and further extends this line of inquiry by asking the key question, "What works best, for whom, and under what conditions?" Treffinger summarizes the challenges faced by educators who try to nurture the development of creativity through effective teaching and to ask which experiences will have the greatest impact, as these will help to determine our ongoing lines of research, development, and training initiatives.

EVALUATION AND PUBLIC POLICY (VOLUMES 11, 12)

Carolyn Callahan introduces the seminal articles on evaluation and suggests that this important component neglected by experts in the field of gifted education for at least the last three decades can be a plea for important work by both evaluators and practitioners. She divides the seminal literature on evaluation, and in particular the literature on the evaluation of gifted programs into four categories, those which (a) provide theory and/or practical guidelines, (b) describe or report on specific program evaluations; (c) provide stimuli for the discussion of issues surrounding the evaluation process; and (d) suggest new research on the evaluation process. Callahan concludes with a challenge indicating work to be done and the opportunity for experts to make valuable contributions to increased effectiveness and efficiency of programs for the gifted.

James Gallagher provides a call-to-arms in the seminal articles he introduces on public policy by raising some of the most challenging questions in the field. Gallagher suggests that as a field, we need to come to some consensus about stronger interventions and consider how we react to accusations of elitism. He believes that our field could be doing a great deal more with additional targeted resources supporting the general education teacher and the development of specialists in gifted education, and summarizes that our failure to fight in the public arena for scarce resources may raise again the question posed two decades ago by Renzulli (1980), looking toward 1990: "Will the gifted child movement be alive and well in 2010?"

CONCLUSION

What can we learn from an examination of our field and the seminal articles that have emerged over the last few decades? First, we must respect **the past** by acknowledging the times in which articles were written and the shoulders of those persons upon whom we stand as we continue to create and develop our field. An old proverb tells us that when we drink from the well, we must remember to acknowledge those who dug the well, and in our field the early articles represent the seeds that grew our field. Next, we must **celebrate the present** and the exciting work and new directions in our field and the knowledge that is now accepted as a common core. Last, we must **embrace the future** by understanding that there is no finished product when it comes to research on gifted and talented children and how we are best able to meet their unique needs. Opportunities abound in the work reported in this series, but many questions remain. A few things seem clear. Action in the future should be based on both qualitative and quantitative research as well as longitudinal studies, and what we have completed only scratches the surface regarding the many variables and issues that still need to be explored. Research is needed that suggests positive changes that will lead to more inclusive programs that recognize the talents and gifts of diverse students in our country. When this occurs, future teachers and researchers in gifted education will find answers that can be embraced by educators, communities, and families, and the needs of all talented and gifted students will be more effectively met in their classrooms by teachers who have been trained to develop their students' gifts and talents.

We also need to consider carefully how we work with the field of education in general. As technology emerges and improves, new opportunities will become available to us. Soon, all students should be able to have their curricular needs preassessed before they begin any new curriculum unit. Soon, the issue of keeping students on grade-level material when they are many grades ahead should disappear as technology enables us to pinpoint students' strengths. Will chronological grades be eliminated? The choices we have when technology enables us to learn better what students already know presents exciting scenarios for the future, and it is imperative that we advocate carefully for multiple opportunities for these students, based on their strengths and interests, as well as a challenging core curriculum. Parents, educators, and professionals who care about these special populations need to become politically active to draw attention to the unique needs of these students, and researchers need to conduct the experimental studies that can prove the efficacy of providing talent development options as well as opportunities for healthy social and emotional growth.

For any field to continue to be vibrant and to grow, new voices must be heard, and new players sought. A great opportunity is available in our field; for as we continue to advocate for gifted and talented students, we can also play important roles in the changing educational reform movement. We can continue to work to achieve more challenging opportunities for all students while we fight to maintain gifted, talented, and enrichment programs. We can continue our advocacy for differentiation through acceleration, individual curriculum opportunities, and a continuum of advanced curriculum and personal support opportunities. The questions answered and those raised in this volume of seminal articles can help us to move forward as a field. We hope those who read the series will join us in this exciting journey.

REFERENCES

Baldwin, A.Y. (1977). Tests do underpredict: a case study. *Phi Delta Kappan, 58,* 620-621.

Gallagher, J. J. (1979). Issues in education for the gifted. In A. H. Passow (Ed.), *The gifted and the talented: Their education and development* (pp. 28-44). Chicago: University of Chicago Press.

Guilford, J. E. (1967). *The nature of human intelligence.* New York: McGraw-Hill.

Marland, S. P., Jr. (1972). *Education of the gifted and talented: Vol. 1. Report to the Congress of the United States by the U.S. Commissioner of Education.* Washington, DC: U. S. Government Printing Office.

Neihart, M., Reis, S., Robinson, N., & Moon, S. M. (Eds.). (2002). *The social and emotional development of gifted children. What do we know?* Waco, TX: Prufrock.

Renzulli, J. S. (1978). What makes giftedness? Reexamining a definition. *Phi Delta Kappan, 60*(5), 180-184.

Renzulli, J. S. (1980). Will the gifted child movement be alive and well in 1990? *Gifted Child Quarterly, 24*(1), 3-9. **[See Vol. 12.]**

Renzulli, J. (1982). Dear Mr. and Mrs. Copernicus: We regret to inform you . . . *Gifted Child Quarterly, 26*(1), 11-14. **[See Vol. 2.]**

Renzulli, J. S. (Ed.). (1986). *Systems and models for developing programs for the gifted and talented.* Mansfield Center, CT: Creative Learning Press.

Renzulli, J. S., & Delcourt, M. A. B. (1986). The legacy and logic of research on the identification of gifted persons. *Gifted Child Quarterly, 30*(1), 20-23. **[See Vol. 2.]**

Renzulli J., & Hartman, R. (1971). Scale for rating behavioral characteristics of superior students. *Exceptional Children, 38,* 243-248.

Ross, P. (1993). *National excellence: A case for developing America's talent.* Washington, DC: U. S. Department of Education, Government Printing Office.

Sternberg, R. J. (1982). Nonentrenchment in the assessment of intellectual giftedness. *Gifted Child Quarterly, 26*(2), 63-67. **[See Vol. 2.]**

Tannenbaum, A. J. (1983). *Gifted children: Psychological and educational perspectives.* New York: Macmillan.

Torrance, E. P. (1984). The role of creativity in identification of the gifted and talented. *Gifted Child Quarterly, 28*(4), 153-156. **[See Vols. 2 and 10.]**

Torrance, E. P. (1987). Recent trends in teaching children and adults to think creatively. In S. G. Isaksen, (Ed.), *Frontiers of creativity research: Beyond the basics* (pp. 204-215). Buffalo, NY: Bearly Limited.

Introduction to Curriculum for Gifted and Talented Students: A 25-Year Retrospective and Prospective

Joyce VanTassel-Baska

The College of William and Mary

Curriculum for the gifted has been a major issue in the field over the past 25 years as attested to by the proliferation of books and articles on the subject. In preparation for writing this chapter, the author reviewed articles published in three journals as well as *Gifted Child Quarterly* to identify key trends and issues of note. Clearly, much space has been given to curriculum topics in *Gifted Child Quarterly* as well as other journals of note, including *Roeper Review, Journal for the Education of the Gifted*, and *Journal of Secondary Gifted Education*. The major emphasis of articles, regardless of source, across these years has been on (a) the values and relevance factors of a curriculum for the gifted, (b) the technology of curriculum development, (c) aspects of differentiation of a curriculum for the gifted within core subject areas and without, and (d) the research-based efficacy of such curriculum and related instructional pedagogy in use. Table 1 provides an overview of these emphases and the sources from which they come. Each of the seminal articles included in this volume are represented in the table along with selected articles from other journals.

Table 1   An Overview of Seminal Curriculum Studies, 1982-2002

Values and Relevance Factors in Gifted Education	Passow (1986)
	Renzulli (1992)
	Kirschenbaum (1998)
	Piirto (1999)
	Ford & Harris (2000)
The Technology of Curriculum Development for the Gifted	Kaplan (1982)
	Maker (1986)
	Jacobs & Borland (1986)
	Renzulli (1988)
	Johnson, Boyce, & VanTassel-Baska (1995)
	Purcell, Burns, Tomlinson, Imbeau, & Martin (2002)
Aspects of Differentiation for a Curriculum for the Gifted	Renzulli (1982)
	Wheatley (1983)
	VanTassel-Baska (1986)
Research-Based Efficacy of Differentiated Curriculum and Instruction for the Gifted	Gallagher, Stepien, & Rosenthal (1992)
	Lynch (1992)
	Sowell (1993)
	Gallagher & Stepien (1996)
	Ravaglia, Suppes, Stillinger, & Alper (1995)
	VanTassel-Baska, Johnson, Hughes, & Boyce (1996)
	Friedman & Lee (1996)
	VanTassel-Baska, Bass, Reis, Poland, & Avery (1998)
	VanTassel-Baska, Avery, Little, & Hughes (2000)
	VanTassel-Baska, Zuo, Avery, & Little (2002)

SPECIAL EARLY EMPHASES ON PROCESS AND CONTENT

The early articles in the *Gifted Child Quarterly* seminal pieces come from Kaplan (1982) on the need to provide multiple curriculum options based on the multiple prototypes of gifted learners and Wheatley (1983) on the need to focus 20% of the mathematics curriculum for the gifted on problem solving while distributing the rest of the emphases across the National Council for Teachers of Mathematics (NCTM) standards. His stated concern was that textbooks of the time overindulged in computational rules at the expense of higher order mathematical reasoning, a concern that has continued to plague the field. Even as late in the reform effort as 1995, in a review of commercial science materials, Johnson, Boyce, and VanTassel-Baska found a similar problem. Textbooks still represented a major source of use in schools yet contained very limited differentiated features for special populations of learners. The authors provided a checklist for schools to use in selecting appropriately differentiated materials for gifted students in science. More recently, Purcell, Burns, Tomlinson, Imbeau, and Martin (2002) have published a set of criteria for developing and evaluating curriculum regardless of subject area, a result of five years of NAGC curriculum division work.

SPECIAL ISSUE ON CURRICULUM IN 1986

A key set of the seminal articles on curriculum selected for this volume came from a special issue co-edited by A. Harry Passow and myself in 1986. We had come to believe that the field needed to take a stronger interest in the content of interventions for gifted learners as an antidote to the emphasis that had been placed on conceptions of giftedness, identification, and administrative arrangements. The issue was also timely for NAGC in that the Curriculum Division had just been formed. As its first chair, I focused our work on early projects to (a) develop scope and sequence models for the field and (b) develop model or exemplary units of study. The selected articles for this special issue of *Gifted Child Quarterly* then were highly pragmatic, attempting to provide guidance to practitioners for important "close to the ground" issues of curriculum.

Passow's article on secondary programming was laudatory in its insistence on a secondary program model for the gifted that was finely balanced between cognitive and affective areas. His insistence on a goal structure that called for concerns about self-understanding, service to others, and moral and ethical development around real-world issues alongside the emphasis on higher level thinking and problem-solving, a stress on the liberal arts, and specialized opportunities attested to his deep belief in developing gifted individuals who could and would help construct a better world. His notion about the need for balance between general and specialized development of abilities is also worth noting. While an advocate for Advanced Placement and International Baccalaureate programs, he also saw the need for more personalized interactions like mentorships, internships, and independent study. Passow saw clearly the role of good guidance practices in holding a secondary program together and worried about the limitations placed on holistic development of the gifted when such provisions were lacking.

Another pragmatic piece in this same issue was the Jacobs and Borland (1986) treatise on interdisciplinarity, a well-reasoned and thoughtful look at ways to think about creating interdisciplinary curriculum. Central to their argument for such curriculum for the gifted lay their deep understanding of the capacity of this type of learner to handle the complexity and abstract connections demanded of serious work across disciplines. Their stance on the teachers' need to know one discipline well before attempting to make meaningful connections to other disciplines is as true today as it was 18 years ago. Jacobs, of course, went on to write more deeply on her own about the key processes for developing such curriculum and worked with many teachers to accomplish the feat. The authors also offered their audience good examples of organizing approaches and examples of what an interdisciplinary curriculum might be like. Then, as now, little research evidence supports the efficacy of the approach although educators of the gifted still recommend it today as a key ingredient in effective curriculum structure (Tomlinson, et al., 2002; VanTassel-Baska & Little, 2003).

The Maker article on scope and sequence continues the pragmatic nature of articles from this special issue. Its down-to-earth presentation of definitions, rationale, development steps, and clear examples provided the field with a blueprint for such development as this area of macro curriculum development was beginning to evolve as an important consideration in programs. The middle to late 1980s saw a major increase in scope and sequence projects, not unlike the increase in curriculum development unit projects today. The Maker article remains contemporary in its approach; moreover, the need for such work has not abated as attested to by a current meta-evaluation of gifted programs (VanTassel-Baska, in press).

The VanTassel-Baska piece in the 1986 issue focused on the need for employing complementary approaches to developing curriculum for the gifted, based on research of effectiveness to date. While the number of curriculum studies has increased subsequent to this article, none refute the basic premise of the need to accelerate curriculum in all relevant subject areas for gifted learners, the need to focus on the high level process skills of thinking, problem-solving, and research that may result in a high-quality product, and the need for a concept or thematic emphasis that is both intra- and interdisciplinary. This article ultimately marked the beginning of the Integrated Curriculum Model (ICM) that evolved into the William and Mary curriculum work in all subject areas at elementary and secondary levels (VanTassel-Baska & Little, 2003). The thinking in the 1986 article, however, had not yet integrated the three curriculum emphases, but rather saw them as parallel curriculum considerations. In the subsequent 18 years, the integrative nature of the model has been translated into exemplary units of study, beta-tested, and found to be statistically significant and important educationally for use with gifted populations of learners across multiple states, school districts, and grouping patterns (VanTassel-Baska, Bass, Ries, Poland, & Avery, 1998; VanTassel-Baska, Zuo, Avery, & Little, 2002). While the article presaged a new model for curriculum development, it represented primarily a research-based perspective on what was already working in separate curriculum being used at the time.

SPECIAL ISSUE ON CURRICULUM IN 1998

A more contemporary issue of *Gifted Child Quarterly* was also devoted to curriculum, this one conceived and commissioned by Ann Robinson as editor in

1998. This issue was dedicated to the curriculum wisdom and work of A. Harry Passow and contained two seminal pieces of note. The first was the publication of the William and Mary science curriculum study on using problem-based learning units in elementary classrooms (VanTassel-Baska et al., 1998). The study broke new ground in its use of a quasi-experimental study in 45 classrooms to demonstrate the significant level of scientific research skills attained by students using the units over their comparison counterparts. It also suggested that grouping patterns were not important in the delivery of the curriculum, with cluster, pull-out, and self-contained all being successful settings for use of the units of study. The study also revealed, however, that much more growth was possible for gifted students than attained, especially in the areas of higher level thinking in designing experiments. Implementation data suggested that both teachers and students found the units engaging and motivating. This study represented a major breakthrough in curriculum studies of the gifted by demonstrating empirically the value of differentiated curriculum.

The second piece included in this special issue was an interview with A. Harry Passow before he died in 1997 (Kirschenbaum, 1998). It chronicles his 40 years of work with curriculum issues and the realities of that work in special projects and his own teaching. A special part of the interview was his recollection of working with a future Westinghouse scholar, feeling his way with an extraordinary learner, yet always giving him his choice as he explored deeper project-based attainment. Passow's notion of "conversation" as the basis for facilitating independent study rings highly contemporary with current work on social-cognitive learning even though it took place 55 years ago. Passow's wisdom also comes through in his belief that curriculum for the gifted must be both excellent and equitably available lest we be unsuccessful in our work to upgrade all of education. He was heartened by the new emphasis in curriculum development, using different models to accomplish similar goals.

CURRICULUM AS CREATIVE PRODUCTION

Work in curriculum that threads throughout the 25-year period is well represented through three articles by Renzulli (1982, 1988, 1992), which share common themes. Each is concerned with qualitative differentiation. Each offers a different model for thinking about curriculum development. Finally, each article employs a set of commonplaces to explain and articulate what matters in curriculum for the gifted: the features of the learner, the teacher, and the dynamism of process-product curriculum operating within a goal of developing creative productivity in individuals.

In his 1982 article, Renzulli noted the elusiveness in defining qualitative differentiation for the gifted and decried the then common practice of teacher-developed curriculum on the grounds of its being questionable in quality and utility. Rather he posited the use of real problems as the central focus of designing curriculum for the gifted in an attempt to move away from prescribed curriculum as promoted by teachers and textbooks, presented to students, providing predetermined pathways of learning, and resulting in predetermined products. Knowledge in a real-problem approach to curriculum, according to Renzulli, becomes a variable of instruction rather than a predetermined outcome. While inquiry becomes the central process, the role of the teacher in such a schema is as facilitator or navigator of discipline-specific concepts and methodology as well as resource scout.

The 1988 article on his multiple menu model moved to a consideration of differentiation through planning guides that consider both problem-based knowledge and the instructional techniques that foster it. In the model, knowledge and techniques equate to curriculum, which leads to instructional products, the heart of differentiation, according to Renzulli. He provided a set of menus that correspond to knowledge and instructional objectives, instructional strategies and sequences, and artistic modifications. The idea of the menus highlighted the importance of each aspect of the curriculum and the flexibility that may be involved in designing in each feature.

In the 1992 article, Renzulli turned from the practical to the theoretical in his paper on the development of creative productivity through deliberate acts. He posited that characteristics of the gifted learner, the teacher, and curriculum contribute to providing "ideal acts of learning." One of the most interesting and insightful aspects of the paper was the special notion about the emerging func-tion of the optimal match between the personality of the learner and the nature of the tasks in respect to their "interestingness" that leads to task commitment. His insistence on paying equal attention to student ability, interest, and learn-ing style in the selection process was well-articulated in this paper. The central curriculum features emphasized were the structure of the discipline as an emphasis through key concepts and methodologies as well as its appeal to the imagination. The teacher was cited as needing to have strong disciplinary knowledge in at least one area, exhibit the personality characteristics of flexibility, openness to inquiry, energy and optimism, and a love for what she teaches. The article concluded with a plea for research on the process of learning how to become a creatively productive person and the critical nature of the talent development process.

CONTRIBUTIONS TO
CURRICULUM FROM OTHER SOURCES

Several articles published in other journals add to our appreciation of curriculum work over the past 25 years. In their review of 101 practices, Shore and Delcourt (1996) remind us of our limited research base on several areas within the field, including curriculum differentiated in ways beyond the accelerative mode.

Piirto (1999) presented a postmodern vision of curriculum for the gifted that transcends the pragmatic views held by many in our field, exhorting educators to consider issues of gender, class, and race biases for examining discourse and power principles in curriculum work. Ford and Harris (2000) provide an important way to think about multicultural curriculum for gifted programs, suggesting the need to tailor curriculum effectively for learners from different cultural backgrounds through merging the heuristic principles of Bloom and Banks.

A few studies examined content-specific issues in curriculum for the gifted. Sowell (1993) carefully reviewed mathematical programs for the gifted and concluded that effective programs employed strong acceleration and grouping approaches in delivering curriculum. Lynch (1992) found that a compressed fast-paced summer class in the sciences effectively prepared academically talented secondary students for early admission to high school science course-work, a major boon in keeping gifted students in advanced science learning. Ravaglia, Suppes, Stillinger, and Alper (1995) contributed a rare article on the impact of the on-line EPGY program on learning. The study suggested that for many of the selected students, the technology-based curriculum was efficacious in advancing their mathematics and science learning. VanTassel-Baska, Johnson, Hughes, and Boyce (1996) found gifted students excelled in a curriculum of higher level thinking in language arts through literary analysis and interpretation, persuasive writing, and language study in comparison to students not receiving such a curriculum. VanTassel-Baska, Avery, Little, and Hughes (2000) also found that schools and districts were positively impacted by a curriculum innovation implemented for gifted learners.

Some studies of curriculum intervention also focused on models of teaching and learning that facilitated academic growth. Gallagher and Stepien (1996) studied secondary students in social studies classrooms, finding that the students using a problem-based learning approach gained as much traditional content learning as did the group not engaged with the PBL model. An earlier study (Gallagher, Stepien, & Rosenthal, 1992) found significant improvement in prob-lem-solving schema for secondary students enrolled in a PBL-based course. Friedman and Lee (1996) tested three instructional models for the gifted and found the cognitive-affective model to be superior in enhancing group inter-action and level of discourse.

ISSUES AND TRENDS IN CURRICULUM FOR THE GIFTED

Quantitative and qualitative differentiation has been the bedrock issue in thinking about appropriate curriculum for the gifted over the entire span of time repre-sented by these articles. Understanding how much to accelerate a child's learn-ing, when, and in what area, remains a quantitative concern in differentiated practice. Yet more attention has been afforded to the qualitative side of curriculum. What constitutes qualitative differentiation has produced 11 models in the field, all aimed at describing these qualitative features. Regardless of the model presented, all have the common feature of generative learning of the gifted as the base of appropriate differentiation, with an emphasis on using higher level concepts and processes to promote it. This staple formula for thinking about differentiation, however, has yielded considerable confusion and difficulty in practice, creating a need for simplifying the process for teachers into instructional processes to be applied.

The future trend in this area may rest with using curriculum already differentiated for gifted learners as a group and tailoring it for special gifted learners in a given context. Work like the William and Mary units and others under development through other Javits projects may become the models for the field in trying to ensure differentiated practice rather than relying on individual teachers to make inferences about what it should be. Evidence currently suggests that in general both teachers of the gifted and regular classroom teachers are underutilizing differentiation practices for gifted students (VanTassel-Baska, in press). More well-designed and differentiated materials are clearly needed to provide ample exemplars of what appropriate differentiation looks like and how it may be taught and assessed in practice. The field also needs more, not fewer, quality packaged materials that are research-based, with proven effectiveness for gifted learners.

A second issue in curriculum for the gifted is the relative paucity of curriculum and program articulation across the years of schooling. One way to build such articulation is to plan for it. The majority of school districts do not have a curriculum framework or a scope and sequence that provide a central tool for communicating about curriculum to stakeholders in the district and serve as a touchstone for effective practice. A curriculum framework would provide a set of K-12 goals and outcomes for the gifted so that teachers, parents, and students could understand the structure of the program across years. A scope and sequence by content area provides further delineation of goals and outcomes within major strands of study. Minimally, districts should be able to demonstrate how students who are verbally and mathematically talented have differentiated outcomes at key levels of the schooling process. Ideally, such work would be available in all areas of the core curriculum and in selected noncore areas such as foreign language and the arts as well. Underlying this issue is a lack of program leadership and coordination from which the field is currently suffering. Very few people are assigned full-time responsibility for administering gifted programs, with little or no priority placed on curriculum development work that could move a program to a higher level of functioning on behalf of gifted learners.

The trend needed to stem the tide of idiosyncratic unit development is a full-scale effort to build models of curriculum practice at the district level that endures across teachers, grade levels, and years of the program. However, in order for such frameworks to be useful and viable, they must form a part of the professional development program for gifted education and be seen as critical partners in curriculum enhancement. Only strong curriculum leadership in school districts can ensure that such curriculum work is ongoing and practiced.

A third troubling issue in curriculum for the gifted is alignment with state standards and hallmark programs for the gifted. How do we ensure that the curriculum employed in schools is appropriately aligned with what all students are learning yet goes beyond it in important ways? Work on such alignment may very well be a state responsibility. A model now exists for such work in the state of Oregon where teams of state curriculum consultants worked alongside teachers of the gifted to create a state document on curriculum alignment, disseminated to all districts. Equally important is the task of aligning curriculum at elementary and middle schools to the hallmark secondary programs of Advanced Placement and International Baccalaureate. While both College Board and the IBO have organized vertical teaming and pre-IB, respectively, the field of gifted education also has a responsibility to ensure that connections exist in programs to prepare students for strong participation later in their schooling since both programs are seen as the best examples of rigor and quality that exist in K-12 schooling.

A trend to deal with this issue of alignment has already begun as seen in the state of Oregon. Individual school districts also have undertaken this challenge. Places as diverse as Greenwich, Connecticut, Montgomery County, Maryland, and Salt Lake City, Utah, have developed models of alignment work that have great merit for the field. This trend can only continue as gifted education becomes more integrated into the mainstream of general education. In the case of AP and IB, gifted educators must realize that all selective colleges are looking for students to have participated in these programs or to have taken dual enrollment courses as a proxy for high school course rigor. Without such options, these students will not gain admission. In several school districts, data suggest that identified gifted students are seriously underrepresented in Advanced Placement programs and performance levels are also below expectation. (VanTassel-Baska & Feng, in press). Thus the movement to create stronger alignment to these programs appears to be justified.

Finally, I must return to the issue voiced by Passow over the last 25 years, that of curriculum balance. Partially because we run programs that are part-time and partially because we have not clearly articulated our curriculum goals and outcomes for gifted learners, curriculum balance is deeply at risk. Little evidence suggests that the affective development of gifted students is occurring through special curricula for the gifted. Moreover, interdisciplinary efforts at curriculum frequently exclude the arts and foreign language. Only through acknowledging and applying curriculum balance in these areas are we likely to be producing the type of humane individual Passow envisioned. These areas of the curriculum are as vital if not more so than our obsession to demonstrate increased academic learning. Yet the issue is complicated by the fragmentation of programs at every level, the practice of inclusion which results in even less time being devoted to flexible grouping and differentiated practice, and teachers lacking a background in gifted student needs for social, emotional, and aesthetic development.

The trend toward balance will only come into being as we return to an understanding of serving gifted learners comprehensively, of ensuring that a full set of curriculum options across domains is available to them at an appropriate level. It also means recognizing that social-emotional nurturance and contact with the arts of expression are as necessary as food and water in a curricular structure. Professional developers must become more sensitive to incorporating this larger vision of curriculum emphases into work with teachers and parents. As more gifted learners bring disabling characteristics and habits into school, we must be prepared to provide for them through a balanced emphasis in our curriculum structures.

CONCLUSION

The trend for curriculum designed for the gifted in the future must embrace paradox. It must provide students a rigorous, high-quality experience that readies them to successfully traverse the next level of educational challenge in a selective university as well as ground them in self-learning and social learning of the moment. It must help them find true self in the midst of growing toward a professional career. It must inculcate a healthy sense of respect for civilization's past accomplishments as well as a desire to shape a new and better world in the future. Such a curriculum must first be envisioned, then developed, and then implemented. The real challenge for the future of curriculum in this field is the preparation of educators committed to the vision of curriculum as the core of what makes gifted education a worthwhile enterprise.

REFERENCES

Ford, D. Y., & Harris, J. J. (2000). A framework for infusing multicultural curriculum into gifted education. *Roeper Review, 23,* 4-10.

Friedman, R. C., & Lee, S. W. (1996). Differentiating instruction for high-achieving/gifted children in regular classrooms: A field test of three gifted-education models. *Journal for the Education of the Gifted, 19,* 405-436.

Gallagher, S. A., & Stepien, W. (1996). Content acquisition in problem-based learning: Depth versus breadth in American studies. *Journal for the Education of the Gifted, 19,* 257-275.

Gallagher, S. A., Stepien, W., & Rosenthal, H. (1992). The effects of problem-based learning on problem solving. *Gifted Child Quarterly, 36*(4), 195-200.

Jacobs, H. H. & Borland, J. H. (1986). The interdisciplinary concept model: Theory and practice. *Gifted Child Quarterly, 30*(4), 159-163. **[See Vol. 4, p. 93.]**

Johnson, D. T., Boyce, L. N., & VanTassel-Baska, J. (1995). Science curriculum review: Evaluating materials for high-ability learners. *Gifted Child Quarterly, 39*(1), 36-43.

Kaplan, S. N. (1982). Myth: There is a single curriculum for the gifted! *Gifted Child Quarterly, 26*(1), 32-33. **[See Vol. 4, p. 41.]**

Kirschenbaum, R. J. (1998). Interview with Dr. A. Harry Passow. *Gifted Child Quarterly, 42(4),* 194-199. **[See Vol. 4, p. 13.]**

Lynch, S. J. (1992). Fast paced high school science for the academically talented: A six-year perspective. *Gifted Child Quarterly, 36*(3), 147-154.

Maker, J. C. (1986). Developing a scope and sequence in curriculum. *Gifted Child Quarterly 30*(4), 151-158. **[See Vol. 4, p. 25.]**

Passow, A. H. (1986). Curriculum for the gifted and talented at the secondary level. *Gifted Child Quarterly, 30*, 186-191. **[See Vol. 4, p. 103.]**

Piirto, J. (1999). Implications of postmodern curriculum theory for the education of the talented. *Journal for the Education of the Gifted, 22*, 324-353.

Purcell, J. H., Burns, D. E., Tomlinson, C. A., Imbeau, M. B., & Martin, J. L. (2002). Bridging the gap: A tool and technique to analyze and evaluate gifted education curricular units. *Gifted Child Quarterly, 46*(4), 306-316.

Ravaglia, R., Suppes, P., Stillinger, C., & Alper, T. (1995). Computer-based mathematics and physics for gifted students. *Gifted Child Quarterly, 39*(1), 7-13.

Renzulli, J. S. (1982). What makes a problem real: Stalking the illusive meaning of qualitative differences in gifted education. *Gifted Child Quarterly, 26*(4), 147-156. **[See Vol. 4, p. 45.]**

Renzulli, J. S. (1988). The multiple menu model for developing differentiated curriculum for the gifted and talented. *Gifted Child Quarterly, 32*(3), 298-309. **[See Vol. 4, p. 115.]**

Renzulli, J. S. (1992). A general theory for the development of creative productivity through the pursuit of ideal acts of learning. *Gifted Child Quarterly, 36*(4), 170-182. **[See Vol. 4, p. 65.]**

Robinson, A. (1998). Curriculum and the development of talents. *Gifted Child Quarterly, 42*(4), *192-193.*

Shore, B. M., & Delcourt, M. A. B. (1996). Effective curricular and program practices in gifted education and the interface with general education. *Journal for the Education of the Gifted, 20*, 138-154.

Sowell, E. J. (1993). Programs for mathematically gifted students: A review of empirical research. *Gifted Child Quarterly, 37*(3), 124-132.

Tomlinson, C. A., Kaplan, S. N., Renzulli, J. S., Purcell, J., Leppien, J., & Burns, D. (2002). *The parallel curriculum: A design to develop high potential and challenge high-ability learners.* Thousand Oaks, CA: Corwin.

VanTassel-Baska, J. (1986). Effective curriculum and instructional models for talented students. *Gifted Child Quarterly, 30*(4), 164-169. **[See Vol. 4, p. 1.]**

VanTassel-Baska, J. (in press). Meta-evaluation findings: A call for gifted program quality. In J. VanTassel-Baska & A. X. Feng, (Eds.). *Designing and utilizing evaluation for gifted program improvement.* Waco, TX: Prufrock.

VanTassel-Baska, J., Avery, L. D., Little, C., & Hughes, C. (2000). An evaluation of the implementation of curriculum innovation: The impact of the William and Mary units on schools. *Journal for the Education of the Gifted, 23*, 244-270.

VanTassel-Baska, J., Bass, G., Ries, R., Poland, D., & Avery, L. D. (1998). A national study of science curriculum effectiveness with high ability students. *Gifted Child Quarterly, 42*(4), 200-211. **[See Vol. 4, p. 147.]**

VanTassel-Baska, J., & Feng, A. X. (in press). *Designing and utilizing evaluation for gifted program improvement.* Waco, TX: Prufrock.

VanTassel-Baska, J., Johnson, D. T., Hughes, C., & Boyce, L. N. (1996). A study of language arts curriculum effectiveness with gifted learners. *Journal for the Education of the Gifted, 19*, 461-480.

VanTassel-Baska, J., & Little, C. A. (2003). *Content-based curriculum for high-ability learners.* Waco, TX: Prufrock.

VanTassel-Baska, J., Zuo, L., Avery, L. D., & Little, C. A. (2002). A curriculum study of gifted-student learning in the language arts. *Gifted Child Quarterly, 46*(1), 30-44. **[See Vol. 5.]**

Wheatley, G. H. (1983). A mathematics curriculum for the gifted and talented. *Gifted Child Quarterly, 27*(2), 77-80. **[See Vol. 4, p. 137.]**

1

Effective Curriculum and Instructional Models for Talented Students

Joyce VanTassel-Baska

Northwestern University

This article presents an historical perspective on the evolution of three curriculum and instructional models that have been shown to be effective with gifted learners in various contexts and at various grade levels. It argues for consideration of all three models in a comprehensive program for gifted learners.

Editor's Note: From VanTassel-Baska, J. (1986). Effective curriculum and instructional models for talented students. *Gifted Child Quarterly*, *30*(4), 164–169. © 1986 National Association for Gifted Children.

M any people have been attracted to the issue of curriculum for the gifted because they feel it is new territory. While it is true that curriculum has not been a central focus in the field until recently, it would be inappropriate to conclude that we need new models and methods to provide appropriately differentiated learning experiences for gifted learners. The purpose of this paper is to present effective curriculum and instructional models that should form the basis of our curriculum efforts and to discuss their relevance to current school practices.

Over the last twenty years, general principles about appropriate curriculum for gifted children have been delineated. Ward (1961) developed a theory of differential education for the gifted that established specific principles around which an appropriate curriculum for the gifted would be developed. Meeker (1969) used the Guilford Structure of Intellect (SOI) to arrive at student profiles that highlighted areas of strength and weakness so that curriculum planners could build a gifted program to improve weak areas. Curriculum workbooks were structured specifically to address this need in the areas of memory, cognition, convergent thinking, divergent thinking, and evaluation. Renzulli (1977) focused on a differentiated curriculum model that moved the gifted child from enrichment exposure activities through training in thinking and research skills into a project-oriented program that dwelt on real problems to be solved. Gallagher (1975) stressed content modification in the core subject areas of language arts, social studies, mathematics and science. Stanley, Keating, and Fox (1974) concentrated on a content acceleration model to differentiate programs for the gifted. Recent writings, including Feldhusen and Kolloff (1978), Maker (1982), and VanTassel-Baska (1984) have stressed a confluent approach to differentiation of curriculum for the gifted that includes both acceleration and enrichment strategies. Passow (1982) formulated seven cardinal curriculum principles that reflect content, process, product, behavioral, and evaluative considerations.

In examining the state of the art of curriculum and instruction for the gifted, it is clear that there is a multiplicity of approaches that are adopted wholesale for classroom use without adequate testing in a research context and without consideration of their value in the overall educational context. In fact, the recipe approach seems the most popular at the present time. Throw together a special unit on the latest topic of interest in the larger socio-cultural context, add creative problem-solving, mix with higher level thinking skills, and stir in a special research project until done. In order to implement appropriate curriculum for gifted students, there must be concern for the faithful translation of sound models for curriculum and instruction into an action research arena where effectiveness can be continually tested. The curriculum and instructional models presented in this paper have all been tested and found effective with gifted learners. Furthermore, each model emerges from a clearly delineated theoretical and research context.

The three relatively distinct curriculum models that have proven effective with gifted populations at various stages of development and in various domain-specific areas may be termed: 1) the content mastery model; 2) the process/product research model; and 3) the epistemological concept model.

THE CONTENT MODEL

The content model tends to emphasize the importance of learning skills and concepts within a predetermined domain of inquiry. Gifted students are encouraged to move as rapidly through the content area as possible and thus content acceleration in some mode tends to dominate the application of this model in practice. When the diagnostic-prescriptive (D $\to$ P) instructional approach is utilized, students are pre-tested and then given appropriate materials to master the subject area segments prescribed.

The D $\to$ P instructional approach has proved effective in controlled settings, but has not been widely practiced in regular classrooms for the gifted. Several reasons appear to account for this: 1) like any individualized model, it requires a highly competent classroom manager to implement, for if used appropriately, each student may be working on a different problem, chapter, and even book at the same time. Regardless of the rhetoric surrounding individualization, very little of it is actively practiced in basic curriculum areas; 2) most pull-out gifted programs do not focus on core content areas and therefore avoid the model, even though such teachers are frequently highly skilled in individualized classroom management, and 3) the approach has not been particularly valued by many educators of the gifted because of its insistence on utilizing the same curriculum and merely altering rate. The lecture-discussion approach to the content model is more widely practiced at the secondary level, but its effectiveness is highly dependent on teachers being well versed in the structure as well as the content of their discipline. Too frequently the content model disintegrates into learning the exact same skills and concepts as all learners are expected to do in the school context, only doing more exercises and drill in a shorter period of time.

In the D $\to$ P approach, teachers and teaching assistants act as facilitators of instruction rather than as didactic lecturers; although many content-based programs for the gifted place a strong emphasis on lecture and discussion. The curriculum is organized by the intellectual content of the discipline and is highly sequential and cumulative in nature, making a proficiency-based model for achievement outcomes very feasible.

The D $\to$ P approach to the content model has been utilized effectively by the talent search programs across the country, particularly in mathematics (Keating, 1976; Benbow and Stanley, 1983). VanTassel-Baska (1984) has shown the effectiveness of the model in teaching Latin. And foreign language teachers have used the model for years to ensure English syntactic mastery in their students. Clearly it represents the most individualized instructional approach to basic curriculum for the gifted that might be undertaken, and embodies a continuous progress philosophy that schools can understand.

The more typical approach to content-based instruction, however, is one that presets the mastery level of expectation for students, frequently requiring more advanced skills and concepts to be mastered one year earlier. The content model employs existing school curriculum and textbooks, so it is not costly to implement. And it attempts to respond to the rate needs of individual students, allowing the very able to move more quickly through the traditional curriculum.

In successful implementations of the model, teachers have made important alterations in the organization of the subject matter being taught. For example, in the fast-paced Latin program, the concepts spread out incrementally over the first three chapters of the book are synthesized into a matrix study sheet, presenting students all five Latin cases, three genders, and two numbers in their various combinations all at once. Homework is assigned only from the third unit where all the interactions of gender, number and case may be practiced. Thus 30 hours of instructional time may be reduced to four or five at the most. And gifted students have mastered the important concepts governing beginning Latin syntax in economical fashion.

Thus what appears as a simple process of moving more quickly through the same basic material takes on a level of sophistication in actual practice. The effective D → P teacher reorganizes the content area under study according to higher level skills and concepts so that the focus of student prescriptive work is in larger increments that carry with them a holistic picture of the topic under study.

The content mastery model for curriculum and instruction also carries with it the capacity to reduce the regular skill-based curriculum for gifted learners in reading as well as mathematics to approximately one-third the time currently expended. This process occurs through two distinct approaches to modifying the curriculum: 1) allowing students to move through the skill development areas at a rate commensurate with their capacity, testing for proficiency and assigning work based on documented increased levels of development, and 2) reorganizing basic skill areas into higher level skill clusters in order to conserve mastery learning time and promote more efficient and challenging learning experiences for talented students.

The first approach might be accomplished through the following modifications:

Reading Curriculum: Topic: Word Attack Skills

Typical Learner Sequence:

Recognizing and Sounding out Consonants	→ Recognizes and Sounding out Vowels	→ Phonemes	→ Prefixes, Suffixes

D → P Gifted Learner Sequence:

Pretest on Reading	→ Analysis of skill gaps inhibiting reading	→ Prescription of work on phonemes, prefixes, and suffixes

The second approach would be accomplished through this additional modification, again in the reading curriculum:

Typical Learner Sequence:

Topic: Word Attack Skills

Subtopics: Recognizing and sounding out consonants, recognizing and sounding out vowels, phonemes, and prefixes and suffixes.

D → P

Gifted Learner Sequence:

Topic: Reading recognition (whole words)

Subtopics: Word attack skills

Prefixes and suffixes

Root words

Through these two modifications then, gifted students can master the typical skill-based curriculum in less time and at an appropriate level of complexity and challenge. For much of the elementary reading, mathematics, and language curriculum, this approach is feasible and efficacious for gifted learners.

The content mastery model, however, does have some limitations and drawbacks. It does not work well in learning tasks where speed and compression are not a relevant consideration. One could hardly imagine reading Shakespeare based on the tenets of content mastery, nor probing a significant world problem. In addition many teachers have interpreted the content mastery model to be merely "covering material" faster and assigning greater amounts of homework, so that many special classes using it deteriorate into a focus on the quantity of consumed material rather than the quality of the learning experience.

THE PROCESS-PRODUCT MODEL

The process/product model places heavy emphasis on learning investigatory skills, both scientific and social that allow students to develop a high quality product. It is a highly collaborative model that involves teacher-practitioner-student as an interactive team in exploring specific topics. Consultation and independent work dominate the instructional pattern, culminating in student understanding of the scientific process as it is reflected in selective exploration of key topics.

Discussed in the literature under the rubric of programs like enrichment triad and the Purdue model (Renzulli, 1977; Feldhusen and Kolloff, 1978), this approach to curriculum for the gifted can be viewed as successful. At the secondary level, special science programs for the gifted have used the model (VanTassel-Baska and Kulieke, 1986). And institutions like Walnut Hills

High School in Cincinnati, Bronx High School of Science, and the North Carolina School of Math and Science have practiced the model as a part of their high-powered science programs for a number of years.

The model seeks to engage the student in problem-finding and problem-solving and to put him in contact with adult practitioners. In the field of science, for example, scientists from Argonne National Laboratory work with academically talented junior high students during the summer to help them develop research proposals for project work during the following academic year. Students actively engage in the generation of a research topic, conduct a literature search, select an experimental design, and lay out their plan of work in a proposal. The proposal is then critiqued by their instructor and the scientist. In this way then, students focus on process skill development in scientific inquiry and strive to develop a high quality product. The following chart delineates the three stages of the inquiry process used in the Northwestern-Argonne program.

Pre-Inquiry (Level 1 skills)

____ 1. The student has acquired scientific knowledge relevant to the question being asked.

____ 2. The student has done a review of related background literature.

Methods of Inquiry (Level 2 skills)

____ 1. The student plans to:
  ____ a. use the techniques of identifying objects and object properties.
  ____ b. use the technique of making controlled observations.
  ____ c. examine changes in various physical systems.
  ____ d. order a series of observations.
  ____ e. classify various physical and biological systems by coding and tabulating data.
  ____ f. use the techniques of ordering, counting, adding, multiplying, dividing, finding averages, and using decimals.
  ____ g. demonstrate the rules of measurement as applicable to specific physical and biological systems (i.e., length, area, volume, weight, temperature, force, or speed).
  ____ h. conduct an experiment by identifying and controlling variables.

____ 2. The student has created operational definitions for the variables under study.

____ 3. The student has stated a testable research hypothesis.

____ 4. The student plans to manipulate some type of materials.

____ 5. The student has followed the specified proposal format.

Interpretive Inquiry Skills (Level 3 skills)

____ 1. The student transformed the observed results into graphs, tables, diagrams, and reports.

____ 2. The student drew relationships among things he or she had observed.

____ 3. The student generalized from his observations.

____ 4. The student interpreted tabular and graphical data.

____ 5. The student used the skills of interpolation and extrapolation to make predictions based on his data.

____ 6. The student made inferences based on his data.

____ 7. The student related data to statements of hypotheses.

____ 8. The student related previous work to his/her own.

____ 9. The student used the specified project format.

____ 10. The student developed some limitations of his study.

The process-product model for curriculum and instruction of the gifted differs from the content mastery model in that content is viewed as less important and rarely acts as the organizer for this type of curriculum. Student interest is a mainspring for what "curriculum" will be studied. The nature of the evaluation effort is product-based rather than proficiency-oriented, and the focus is on studying selected topics in-depth rather than moving through a given domain of inquiry in a fast-paced manner.

While the model has worked well in some pull-out programs for the gifted and as a part of a total science program at the secondary level, it does present organizational problems for many schools: critics contend that the focus of this model creates confusion around the curricular scope and sequence of learning at any given level of instruction and creates a need for articulating new process and product dimensions into an adopted scope and sequence continuum for the gifted. Furthermore, the model at the elementary level tends to devalue core content elements in the traditional curriculum, and to overvalue independent learning strategies at that stage of development.

Nevertheless, it is the curriculum and instructional model most closely allied with the recommendations of national teacher groups in both science and mathematics that tend to favor a student-directed, hands-on, inquiry-based process of problem-solving, where students are engaged in the act of constructing knowledge for themselves.

THE EPISTEMOLOGICAL MODEL

The epistemological concept model focuses on talented students' understanding and appreciation of systems of knowledge rather than the individual segments of those systems. It reflects a concern for exposing students to key ideas, themes, and principles within and across domains of knowledge so that schemata are internalized for amplification by new examples in the future. The role of the teacher in this model is as questioner, raising interpretive issues for discussion and debate. Students focus their energies on reading, reflecting, and writing. Aesthetic appreciation of powerful ideas in various representational forms is viewed as an important outcome of this model.

The model is very effective with gifted learners for several reasons. First of all, the intellectually gifted child has unusually keen powers to see and understand interrelationships; therefore, conceptual curriculum is useful, for its whole structure is based on constantly interrelating form and content. Concept curriculum is an enrichment tool in the highest sense, for it provides the gifted with an intellectual framework not available in studying only one content area, but rather exposes them to many not covered in traditional curricula. Furthermore, it provides a basis for students' understanding the creative as well as the intellectual process through critically analyzing creative products, and being actively engaged in the creative process itself. And lastly, it provides a context for integrating cognitive and affective objectives into the curriculum. A discussion of ideas evokes feelings; response to the arts involves aesthetic appreciation, and study of literary archetypes creates a structure for self identity.

Many writers in the field of gifted education have advocated the epistemological approach to curriculum for the gifted (Ward, 1961; Hayes-Jacob, 1981; Maker, 1982; Tannenbaum, 1983). And some extant curriculum has been organized around the model at both elementary and secondary levels. The College Board Advanced Placement Program in history (both American and European) as well as their literature and composition programs rely heavily on this curriculum and instructional model.

The Junior Great Books program, Philosophy for Children, and Man: A Course of Study (MACOS) are elementary programs using the approach. Each of these programs stresses the use of Socratic questions to stimulate an intellectual discussion among students on an issue or theme. Creating analogies across a field of inquiry is encouraged, and interdisciplinary thinking is highly valued. Recent curriculum development efforts for the gifted have attempted to utilize the epistemological framework (VanTassel-Baska and Feldhusen, 1981; Gallagher,

1982). And larger curriculum projects in the past, such as CEMREL's mathematics program at the secondary level and the Unified Mathematics program at the middle school level, have utilized a holistic approach to the organization of content.

At the Secondary level, humanities programs have often been the reservoir for the use of this model with talented learners. One approach to framing discussions with the humanities is to structure questions about a work of art (whether it be music, painting, or literature) that asks students to examine an "art" object from a variety of perspectives. For example, the following questions might be posed about a poem:

1) What is it? (What's the subject matter?)

2) What is it made of? (What is its form?)

3) What ideas does it convey? (What does it mean?)

4) What is its context? (How would you categorize it historically?)

5) How do you relate to it? (What is its personal value?)

6) How good is it? (What is your evaluation of its artistic merit?)

Through these several lenses, then, gifted learners can explore the humanities as a collection of creative products assembled by individuals over the centuries, and reflect on their relationship to each other in specified dimensions. Thus appreciation for the arts can be developed through "seeing" them from various points of view.

While the concept-based model of curriculum offers the advantages of a unified view of a field of inquiry often undertaken by scholars in individual disciplines, it requires well-trained teachers to implement it effectively. Teachers need to possess not only in-depth knowledge about one field of inquiry but also must have the capacity to make appropriate connections to other disciplines as well. And there is a need to keep in place a consistent vision around the exploration of concepts. Furthermore, schools have never really known how to treat such curriculum organizationally. At the secondary level, should students receive an English credit for a humanities course or a social studies credit? Should humanities be offered only at senior level as an elective or earlier as a mandatory course? The very strength of this curriculum and instructional model as an integrating force frequently breaks down in the organizational decision-making over "where it fits." As with the other two models discussed, developing a scope and sequence within the epistemological orientation would seem to be necessary to allow for appropriate student exposure and progressive development in the realm of ideas.

The concept model for curriculum and instruction differs considerably from the nature of the previous two models (see Figure 1). It is organized by ideas and themes, not subject matter or process skills. It is a highly interactive model in its instructional context, which contrasts with the more independent modes

Figure I   Contrasting Curriculum/Instructional Models for the Gifted

A (content) ↓	B (process/product) ↓	C (concept) ↓
fast-paced	in-depth on selected topics	epistemological
proficiency-based	product based	aesthetics-based
D → P approach	resource-oriented	discussion approach
organized by intellectual content	organized around scientific process	organized by themes and ideas
teacher as facilitator	collaborative model	Socratic method

of instruction used in the other two models. Concern for the nature and structure of knowledge itself is a major underlying tenet. And evaluation of students engaged in this model typically requires evidence of high level aesthetic perceptions and insights rather than content proficiency or a culminating product of high quality.

Implementation of Curriculum and Instructional Models

The explication of these three models may be useful in advancing our understanding of how the confluent approaches to curriculum that are currently advocated might be implemented in the context of school-based programs. Clearly, it is not advantageous to select one model over another when planning appropriate curriculum over a span of years, for each approach responds to different characteristics and needs of gifted learners. Acceleration and in-depth as well as broad-based enrichment opportunities are all valuable for the gifted.

There is a need, however, to consider the nature of separate curriculum areas which may lend themselves more readily to one model than another. And within a population of gifted learners, there may be important differences to consider in relationship to curriculum models. There is a motivational factor that must be considered for certain types of curriculum approaches that involve independent investigations or studying a content area at a fast rate. Learning preferences among talented learners should also be considered. Some gifted students prefer to learn rapidly and go on to more sophisticated work at a higher level; others prefer to examine a problem from all sides and deliberate over it in depth. As Renzulli (1978) has demonstrated, task commitment is a necessary student variable to perform well in the process-product curriculum model. And the concept model may work best with students evidencing high level verbal capacity and broad-based reading behaviors. Figure 2 presents a matrix that matches model type with content organizational issues and salient student characteristics.

The real issue is how best to conceptualize and operationalize the functional utility of these models at different stages of development and in different program organizational models. Figure 3 presents a confluent model of the three curriculum and instructional approaches as they might be viewed within

Figure 2

Model Type	Preferred Content Match	Salient Student Characteristics
A Content	Mathematics (traditional) Foreign Language English Grammar Reading	Independent learner High achievement motivation
B Process/ Product	Science Mathematics (problem-solving orientation) Writing	High interest in single topic Task commitment

C Concept	Humanities
	Social studies (e.g. history,
	  economics)
	Literature
		High level verbal reasoning skills
		Broad-based interests and
		  reading behavior

Figure 3   School-Based Curriculum Model Linkages on an Academic Year Cycle

Modifications of Core Curriculum	Extended Core Curriculum	Curriculum Integration

D → P Content Approach	Process/Product
	  Research Approach
		Epistemological Concept
		  Approach

A	B	C

Allows for speeded,
  compressed, economized
  version of regular
  curriculum
	Allows for development of
	  generic problem
	  finding/problem solving
	  skills in selected
	  curriculum contexts
		Allows for idea
		  discussion/generation within
		  and across disciplines

an academic year program at the local school district level. Each model is allotted equal amounts of instructional time and equal focus in a student's program.

While a full-time grouping model would be the most feasible to operationalize this confluent model, it could be considered under other grouping patterns as well, notably resource room and pull-out where regular classroom teachers or other specialists would facilitate models A and B. Model C work then would be reserved for gifted program time.

As with the adaptation of any curriculum model, partial or selective implementation may also be appropriate for individual students at a given stage of development. Students may elect to participate in a special humanities seminar but not elect to engage in accelerated study, for example. However, adaptations in the integrative pattern should be viewed as student-selected alternatives rather than limitations in the school-based program options.

Effective curriculum and instruction for the gifted has reached a stage of evolution where existing theoretical and research-based models need to be systematically translated into practice at the local level. Competition among these models has dissipated the effect of building a strong differentiated program for the gifted that addresses all of their intellectual needs within the core curriculum and beyond it to all levels of instruction. The synthesis of the content, process-product, and concept models provides a clear direction for meaningful curriculum work.

REFERENCES

Benbow, C., and Stanley, J. (1983). *Academic precocity: Aspects of its development.* Baltimore, MD: Johns Hopkins University Press.

Feldhusen, J., and Kolloff, M. (1978). A three stage model for gifted education. *G/C/T, 1,* 53–58.

Gallagher, J. (1975). *Teaching the gifted child* (2nd Ed.). Boston: Allyn & Bacon.

Gallagher, J. (1982). *Leadership.* New York: Trillium Press.

Hayes-Jacob, H. (1981). *A model for curriculum and instruction: Discipline fields, interdisciplinarity, and cognitive processes.* Unpublished doctoral dissertation, Columbia University, New York.

Keating, D. (1976). *Intellectual talent.* Baltimore: The Johns Hopkins Press.

Maker, C. J. (1982). *Curriculum development for the gifted.* Rockville, MD: Aspen Systems Publication.

Meeker, M. (1969). *The structure of intellect: Its interpretation and uses.* Columbus, OH: Charles E. Merrill Publishing Co.

Passow, H. (1982). *Differentiated curricula for the gifted/talented* in Kaplan, Sady et al., *Curricula for the Gifted,* Committee Report to the National/State Leadership Training Institute on the Gifted and the Talented, Ventura County, California: Office of the Superintendent of Schools.

Renzulli, J. (1977). *The enrichment triad.* Wethersfield, CT: Creative Learning Press.

Renzulli, J. (1978). What makes giftedness? Re-examining a definition. *Phi Delta Kappan, 60,* 180–184, 261.

Stanley, J., Keating, D., and Fox, L. (1974). *Mathematical talent.* Baltimore: The Johns Hopkins Press.

Tannenbaum, A. (1983). *Gifted children.* New York: Macmillan.

VanTassel-Baska, J. (1984). Appropriate curriculum for the gifted. In J. Feldhusen (Ed.), *Toward excellence in gifted education* (pp. 45–83). Denver: Love Publishing Co.

VanTassel-Baska, J., and Feldhusen, J. (Eds.). (1981). *Concept curriculum for the gifted K-8.* Matteson, IL: Matteson School District #162.

VanTassel-Baska, J., and Kulieke, M. (in press). *The role of community-based resources in developing scientific talents: A case study, Gifted Child Quarterly.*

Ward, V. (1961). *Educating the gifted: An axiomatic approach.* Columbus, OH: Charles Merrill Company.

2

Interview with Dr. A. Harry Passow

Robert J. Kirschenbaum, Ph.D.

This interview with Dr. A. Harry Passow was conducted at the annual meeting of the American Educational Research Association in Chicago, Illinois in April 1991. At the time of the interview, Dr. Passow was the Jacob H. Schiff Professor Emeritus of Education at Teachers College, Columbia University. Where possible, bibliography entries have been added for the publications on which Dr. Passow comments in the interview.

RJK: How did you first become interested in the education of gifted and talented students?

Editor's Note: From Kirschenbaum, R. (1998). Interview with Dr. A. Harry Passow. *Gifted Child Quarterly*, 42(4), 194–199. © 1998 National Association for Gifted Children. Reprinted with permission.

HP: I was on the staff of an organization at Teachers College called The Horace Mann-Lincoln Institute of School Experimentation, doing work on leadership training in curriculum development in the early '50s. It was the only endowed educational research institute in the country, and so we could choose our own research agenda, as long as it was oriented toward the improvement of the public schools in cooperation with the school systems. Dr. Hollis Caswell, then the dean of Teachers College and my mentor, commented that anything published by the Institute under the present research agenda would always list the names of the other, more senior colleagues first, so he encouraged me to strike out into my own field of study. At that time, the high schools were under attack with books such as Bestor's Educational Wastelands and Admiral Rickover's Education and Freedom bemoaning the condition of American education. So, after further conversation with Dr. Caswell, we decided that it was important to determine what impact America's high schools were having on bright students. Were they as bored, neglected, and miseducated as the critics claimed?

In February 1954, I started the Talented Youth Project. One of my first papers, which I presented that summer, was called "What of the Talented in America's High Schools?" My first research assistant was Dr. Abraham Tannenbaum. Dr. Miriam Goldberg joined us a year or two later as a research associate. For the next 12 years we studied ability grouping, underachievement, mathematics programs for able students in junior high school, counseling, and programs for bright students in rural areas. By 1964–5, I had become interested in the "disadvantaged," realizing that that population, then and now, contained the largest reservoir of underdeveloped talent.

RJK: Anyone who opens up a journal in gifted education today can find articles on the same topics you investigated through the Talented Youth Project. After the Soviet Union launched Sputnik in October 1957, there was a great concern that America's schools were no longer up to the challenge of educating our youth to maintain our lead in science and technology. How does the situation today compare to what was happening in the late '50s?

HP: During the '50s, Dr. James Conant, then president of Harvard University, conducted a study of the American high school. He discussed his study with a number of us at Teachers College and told us that, while he was focusing on the general high school population, he was especially interested in the academically talented.

RJK: Weren't those the students he saw at Harvard?

HP: Right, in part. Perhaps the reason he sought me out was because of my espoused belief that one could effectively educate the brightest students in a comprehensive high school open to all students. At the time, people like Rickover disagreed with this belief; he wanted to have highly selective schools like the Bronx High School of Science all over the country. When Sputnik went up, Dr. Conant was asked by the National Educational Association (NEA) to chair a conference on the academically talented. Following the conference, the NEA initiated a project called "The Academically Talented Student" that produced 10 booklets (called the "green books"). They discussed the education of the gifted student in science, math, and all other subjects areas.

The National Defense Education Act (NDEA) was passed in 1958 and it provided the impetus for curriculum reform in science, math, and foreign languages, later expanded to other subjects, that lasted into the '60s. The NDEA (1958) was originally designed to improve the math and science curriculum for bright students, as well as the teaching of math and science in general. The programs that emerged were available to all levels of students, but were most appropriate for the brighter students. It was acknowledged that bright students needed a differentiated curriculum in the content areas in order to maximize their educational development. Consequently, there was more recognition of the specific curricular needs of the gifted and talented than there is today.

In 1983, a report on science and math for the year 2000 said that, while we know there are bright students and they need a different program, we shouldn't worry about them very much. There is a philosophical difference behind making a decision to try and improve education for everyone across the board or rather we adopt that goal while also recognizing that gifted and talented youngsters need special attention for the sake of our country's future. That's a fundamental difference. Dr. Paul Brandwein and I have just edited a book called *Gifted Young in Science* in which we have contributors discuss how to provide special programs for the gifted while also upgrading education in general.

RJK: Could you speak more directly on the equity vs. excellence issue? Is the goal of raising the standards of all students in general education compatible with the goal of identifying high achieving students and providing them with special programs to help them pursue the highest standards of excellence?

HP: I have always thought the equality vs. excellence debate poses a false dichotomy. I believe the real question is how to do both because otherwise you can't do either. In gifted education, we've had to face the issue of elitism all along and have made the mistake of trying to convince general educators and the public that gifted education isn't elitist. Equity means equal educational opportunities. Students should have equal access to excellent educational programs. One does not educate minority students at the expense of non-minority students or vice versa. If we do that, we're not providing equity or excellence for either group. In a democracy, we must be committed to making appropriate provisions for all students regardless of their differences or similarities. Everyone deserves an excellent program, but not all excellent programs are identical. The gifted and talented student should not receive services at the expense of the general student population, but neither should the gifted and talented student be shortchanged because there are students in the general population who are being underserved.

RJK: In these days of limited resources . . .

HP: That's precisely the point I am trying to make. We can't take from one to give to the other. Education of the gifted must be an integral part of our effort to provide adequate and appropriate programs for all children. Whether we have limited or unlimited resources, we need to strive to achieve both equity and excellence, or we have failed. We're talking about quality education for everyone. We need to use our limited resources in an intelligent and creative fashion. Moreover, a good gifted program shouldn't cost a lot of money.

RJK: However, to have a good gifted program, we need a teacher of the gifted who requires one more salary.

HP: True, for some programs additional teachers are needed, but for others it is a matter of reassigning or deploying teachers differently. I have argued that every teacher is a teacher of the gifted, but we don't usually perceive teachers in this way. We assign one person to teach the gifted and talented and that lets the rest of the teachers "off the hook," and only that teacher is viewed as being responsible for gifted education. There is no doubt that it's difficult for the regular teacher with 35 students to provide appropriate curriculum activities for a few gifted students, but it's not impossible, especially if we help the teachers with staff development and supplementary services. Yes, a teacher for the gifted is needed, but that person should not be the only teacher responsible.

RJK: Studies repeatedly show that most do not provide differentiated activities for gifted and talented students. In fact, most teachers provide very little in the way of activities that encourage students to practice and develop their higher level thinking skills and creative abilities. It doesn't matter if we blame poor pre-service training, inadequate in-service activities, bureaucratic constraints that force teachers to stick slavishly to a textbook-based curriculum, or administrators that are only concerned with the attainment of minimal competencies. The majority of teachers are mainly intent on helping students reach and maintain grade level skills.

HP: I'll accept that as partly true. I do not accept the portrait of an inept teaching staff working under impossible restrictions. But do we solve this problem by accepting as a fact that all teachers do not differentiate and hire a teacher of the gifted to do so? Often the program for the gifted is in direct conflict with the regular program. By this, I mean that when gifted children leave the regular class, the classroom teacher is left in a situation that does not necessarily stimulate creativity and productive activity. The alternative is to attack the problem of training teachers to provide services for gifted and talented students in the regular classroom so that the special provisions for the gifted and the program are complementary. I think that it is the responsibility of educational leaders to help teachers create a quality educational program for all students in appropriate settings and situations.

RJK: Isn't it a prime responsibility of the teacher of the gifted to try to establish a gifted program that is integrated into the regular program?

HP: Absolutely. One of the primary responsibilities of the teacher of the gifted is to communicate with the rest of the teaching staff as to what is going on in the gifted program in a way that will inform others of activities they can do with gifted and talented students in their classes. This was brought home to me when we were implementing a Talented Youth Project in seven small high schools in Lewis County in upstate New York. Each of the high schools nominated the three "most gifted students" in the 11th and 12th grades. The students came to Lyons Falls in the center of the county every Tuesday afternoon for a three-hour seminar. Since each week they were missing 20% of their class time in three subjects, the teachers gave them a lot of "busywork" to catch up on. The students resented it and wanted to drop out of the program. We realized that we had to do a better job of informing the teachers of what we were doing, so we invited them to participate in the seminars to both educate them about gifted education and also to provide them with ideas they could take back to their schools to upgrade the quality of education for the rest of their students, including the gifted students. Teachers of the gifted who perceive their role as only working with a small group of students are isolating themselves and their students from the rest of the school and providing an incomplete experience.

RJK: On a different note, what have we learned in the last 40 years?

HP: There are a number of things worth considering. We are studying the nature of giftedness and talents to a greater extent and in different ways. Different conceptions of giftedness have led us to believe that gifted and talented students are a very heterogeneous group and therefore need different kinds of educational experiences. Consider, for example, that we have 17 conceptions of giftedness described in Sternberg and Davidson's book, *Conceptions of Giftedness*. These conceptions are not totally different, of course, but they reflect the fact that we are thinking differently about the nature of giftedness and what is needed to develop or nurture it. No longer do we simply consider a gifted child to be a good student in school with a high IQ. "Rapid learner" was the term originally used to label the gifted.

I wrote a chapter in the *57th Yearbook of the National Society for Studies in Education* (NSSE), published in 1958, called "Enrichment in the Education of the Gifted," in which I stated that there are three ways of educating the gifted: enrichment in the regular classroom, ability grouping, and acceleration. Then, the focus was on administrative ways of taking care of gifted children. Now, we are giving much more attention to curriculum differentiation and instructional strategies. Now there are numerous gifted program models and that's a major difference from our earlier approach. Grouping is rearing its "ugly head" again.

RJK: Don't people point to gifted education as a form of grouping and criticize it for that reason?

HP: Some programs do represent a form of grouping. I believe that there is a need to have gifted and talented students in special groups at least part of the time. My colleagues and I published a study in 1966 on the effects of ability grouping and stated that grouping doesn't make any difference by itself; it's what one does in the groups. Some researchers of grouping say that grouping is detrimental to slow learners and average students and it really doesn't make much difference with gifted students. The problem with research is that it looks at the outcomes being studied as the consequence of grouping—classroom climate that is associated or created with the grouping. Usually, such studies do not assess the differentiated goals, but only the goal set for all students. In many instances, the grouping of gifted and talented students is perceived as creating an elite. In a 1955 publication, we stated that the problem occurs when the creation of programs for the gifted is perceived to be at the expense of other students or to give these students an unfair advantage. Of course, we have no justification for doing that. If the regular program is inadequate for all, it needs improvement. It will not be improved by moving the gifted to a special program unless serious efforts are made to do so. If the gifted program is simply a way of avoiding responsibility for all children, it is elitist.

RJK: Researchers feel that lowered expectations are a byproduct of grouping low achievement students together, and that's why grouping hurts these students.

HP: It's not a byproduct, but it is an attitude that exists, particularly when minority students are the ones in the lower group and prejudice leads to lowered expectations. If those students are black and poor, there's a tendency for some people to feel that they can't learn under any circumstances. Another factor is that in most inner city schools, most students are from disadvantaged, minority backgrounds, and many are not doing well in school. The lowest readers who aren't eligible for special education are put into Chapter 1 programs. I argue that the problems stem from our attitudes and lack of knowledge of what instructional strategies are necessary for reaching these children. When I went to New York State College for Teachers at Albany, we aspired to teach in New York City because that school system was considered to be one of the best in the world. Then, after the war, teachers found that, with the growth of the suburbs and the change in population, they were no longer effective in reaching the children of the new minorities.

RJK: What do you have to say to the doomsayers who decry our public education system and point to declining test scores and other problems as proof? Critics say we're falling behind the Japanese in productivity, and that our children are just plain lazy. Many of these same people say that we did such a better job in the "good old days" when we worked harder and led the world in productivity and creativity. Have we gone so far downhill?

HP: I have been concerned with school reform for many years. Schools are more problematic today because society is more problematic. Yes, some things are worse now, but our children know more and learn more than ever before. Some test scores have declined, but other scores have gone up. The new norms on recently revised intelligence tests have been adjusted upwards, which means that the average student knows more.

RJK: But the international comparisons . . .

HP: In 1959, I was a member of the original group to design studies of international educational achievement. I sat with the late Dr. Robert Thorndike, one of the pioneers in measurement theory, and others at the UNESCO Institute in Hamburg, Germany. We literally cut out questions from tests to come up with the first test to be used to measure international levels of science achievement. At that time, we all agreed that we didn't want a "horse race" among nations because no test can take into account the differences among cultures and societies. Simplistic comparisons of test scores across countries wouldn't make any sense. That isn't what has happened, though, and scores have been compared ever since. On the other hand, we must not forget that our universities are the envy of the world and our children attend those colleges and universities.

The comparisons are invariably made with Japan. They have a longer school year (i.e., 250 days), go to school six days a week, and have more active support from their families, particularly their mothers. Some of what Japanese students do in school, our students do as part of extracurricular activities. The students work incredibly hard to get into one of the few available prestigious schools, and then they relax and have a good time until it's time to go to work for one of the large corporations. Theirs is an entirely different culture that cannot be compared easily to our own.

RJK: What do you think about the idea of a national curriculum in science?

HP: I'm against it. The problem with the national curriculum is that it becomes a Procrustean bed. Reports like *A Nation at Risk* and others that came out in the early '80s expressed very little faith in our teachers' ability to provide an adequate curriculum to our students. The reports reflected a "buckle down, Winsockie" mentality. ("Buckle down, Winsockie" was a song popular in the '40s, whose lyrics said that we only had to try hard enough or "buckle down," get to work, and we could win at anything.) The solution drawn from this perspective is to raise "standards" in order to raise achievement. How do we raise standards? By increasing the number of courses in the main subject areas that students need to pass to graduate from high school—four years of math, four years of English, three years of science, etc.—and they have to pass competency tests as well. School reform takes more than structural changes—more academic courses, more tests, more homework, more requirements for promotion and graduation.

RJK: Would you agree that every high school should have Advanced Placement classes in calculus?

HP: Sure, but that's not what a national curriculum is. If you want to say that every high school should have a calculus class, or we should increase the number of students taking physics, that's quite different from having a national curriculum that mandates calculus be required for all students. A national curriculum can be a rigid framework. Also the problem with competency testing is that the minimum competencies become the expected outcomes. I don't support national testing if it relies on multiple choice questions because they are very limited in the scope of what they can assess. In the '80s, in a number of states, the school year was lengthened to 180 days in an effort to raise standards. Lengthening the school day or school year without curricular and instructional changes is meaningless.

RJK: Should the school year be lengthened further?

HP: I don't care about the length as much as what is being done to use those 180 days effectively. When *A Nation at Risk* came out, I felt the report was full of contradictions. For example, it said that teachers come from the lowest quartile of the college student population, and then recommended that the school day be lengthened—we should make our children stay in the classrooms with these incompetent teachers for a longer period of time? It's a question of how to use the time that's allocated effectively and creatively.

RJK: On a more positive note, what have been some of your greatest satisfactions in your career?

HP: I have a great deal of satisfaction from having participated in some of the major events in education over the last 40 years. It's nice to have been working in the field of gifted education long before it was fashionable. It was nice to work in the area of disadvantaged students before that was recognized as a major problem. It's nice to have been involved in the International Studies of Educational Achievement from the start. I'm glad I had the opportunity to have studied school reform and made comments about the direction we're going.

RJK: Are there any particular events or people in gifted education that you are proud to have influenced?

HP: Many, many, but I will cite one from my high school teaching days. I had a Westinghouse talent winner in 1947 who I'll always remember. His name was William Renegal. I was a science teacher who taught biology, chemistry, and physics in a small rural school near Buffalo, N.Y. William was a real "pain in the neck" because he knew so much more than the other 30 students in the class. Instead of having him in class all the time, I let him work in the stock room on independent study projects, and during lunchtime, he and I would meet to discuss his work. He was interested in the rare earth metals. I suggested he submit his project to the Westinghouse competition, and he turned out to be one of the 40 finalists. The fact of the matter is that I wanted him out of the class, but I did what a good teacher of the gifted does by guiding him to use his ability to explore his interests as deeply as possible.

RJK: How do you define giftedness and talent?

HP: In 1955, when we were making plans for the Talented Youth Project, Miriam Goldberg, Abe Tannenbaum, and I argued extensively over the definition of giftedness. We finally defined the gifted person as an individual with potential for outstanding achievement in a socially valuable area. That's still not a bad definition.

RJK: Dr. Paul Witty is given credit for that definition, isn't he?

HP: I could claim that Paul Witty got it from us, since I worked with him on several projects. We both arrived at this conception about the same time. But seriously, it doesn't matter as long as children are being helped.

I like our definition because it has plenty of leeway to include individuals who haven't had opportunities to demonstrate their abilities. It touches on the identification, nurturance, and utilization of giftedness. We're concerned in most programs with identification and nurturance, but equally important is the utilization of that potential.

RJK: Your definition places giftedness in a social context and highlights the fact that giftedness exists only so far as the existence of high ability is valued, but I have problems with the term "potential," especially as it is commonly used in the field to mean high test performance. Many people do not see any evidence of gifted potential in individual students who do not do well on standardized tests. How can students demonstrate their potential for giftedness? How can we ensure full participation of ethnic minority students and girls and women in fields in which they are under-represented?

HP: In *Gifted Young in Science: Potential Through Performance*, edited by Dr. Paul Brandwein and myself, we argue that educators need to provide an environment in which a youngster can demonstrate his or her potential or aptitude to learn and to perform.

RJK: Should we be concerned that women don't enter the hard sciences in equal numbers to males? While we should try to ensure that women who want to enter those fields are not discouraged through prejudicial treatment and obstacles, is it a value judgment that they should be represented in equal numbers in every field?

HP: It would seem that males and females have an equal potential to excel in science. Therefore, women should at least have an equal opportunity to enter the science and math fields. We ought to find out why they do less well in the SAT-Math compared to their performance on the SAT-Verbal. I don't think they are genetically inferior to males in math, which means that there are social and cultural factors that we need to understand. We ought to open up doors of opportunity. We should not insist that since women make up 51% of the population, they should comprise 51% of scientists, but we can do a much better job of helping females recognize and develop their talents in these areas. We need to nurture their potential for success in science.

RJK: I can't argue with your use of potential in this sense. How do you characterize the role of personality and dispositional factors in giftedness and talent?

HP: They are very important. I will be giving a paper at the International Conference on Giftedness at the Hague this summer entitled "A Neglected Area of Giftedness: The Affective Domain." We tend to focus so much energy on developing academic achievement and higher order thinking skills that we ignore the importance of the affective factors in the development of thinking skills and high achievement.

RJK: What do you think about the phrase "emotional giftedness" that is now being used?

HP: I don't think of "emotional giftedness" as a separate characteristic or kind of giftedness but rather in terms of the emotions of gifted and talented children. I don't want to create a new area of giftedness, but we have to be concerned about feelings, attitudes, motivations, self-concept, values, and the personalities of individuals. Instructionally, we have to provide guidance and create an environment that stimulates and supports learning. We also need to understand the relationship of gifted and talented children to their parents and families.

RJK: Are people in the field doing a better job of helping parents of gifted and talented students raise their children than years ago?

HP: I doubt it. We didn't do a particularly good job back in the '50s. We had meetings for parents of the gifted, but we didn't do very much in the way of supporting parents. There were a few books by people like Dr. Ruth Strang who wrote *Helping Your Gifted Child*. The problem now is that parenting is different in many ways from what was happening 30 or 40 years ago. There are more single parents, and society poses more problems for families and vice versa.

RJK: What do you think Drs. Leta Hollingworth and Lewis Terman would say about the state of gifted education if they were alive today?

HP: They're two different people. Terman studied over 1,500 students with high IQ scores but he didn't intervene. On the other hand, Hollingworth was a curriculum developer and started a school for the gifted (through Teachers College). Neither one of them would be unhappy, but she would be more of an advocate and activist.

RJK: If you were starting out today, what area of gifted education would you focus on?

HP: I would focus on curriculum. That's what I have done in my career. I don't think we understand what a differentiated curriculum is, even today. We have a lot of pieces, but we have not been able to put them together. I don't have a "model" or any great theory.

RJK: It seems to me that you have had a social conscience that transcends individual projects and research. You have been awarded positions of leadership because your agenda has not been a personal one, but a socially committed one. You have inspired others to become advocates for the gifted and talented student.

HP: I would hope so. One of the things I have done in my classes and presentations is to take what I said in the '50s and repeat it as if I had just formulated those views. It is disheartening that no one sees through my chicanery because it suggests that we haven't made much progress. On the other hand, maybe what we said then is as relevant today as ever before.

BIBLIOGRAPHY

Bestor, A. E. (1953). *Educational wastelands: The retreat from learning in our public schools.* Urbana, IL: University of Illinois Press.

Brandwein, P. F. & Passow, A. H. (1989). *Gifted young in science: Potential through performance.* Washington, DC: National Science and Teachers Association.

Goldberg, M. L., Passow, A. H., Cam, D. S., & Neill, R. D. (1966). *A comparison of mathematics programs for able junior high school students: Volume 1.* Final report. Washington, DC: U.S. Office of Education, Bureau of Research. (Project No. 3-0381).

Goldberg, M. L., Passow, A. H., Justman, J., & Hogue, G. (1965). *The effects of ability grouping.* New York: Teacher College Press.

Passow, A. H. (Ed.). (1963). *Education in depressed areas.* New York: Bureau of Publications, Teachers College, Columbia University.

Passow, A. H. (1958). Enrichment for the gifted. In N. B. Henry (Ed.), *Education for the gifted. Fifty-seventh yearbook of the National Society for the Study of Education: Part II* (pp. 193–221). Chicago: University of Chicago Press.

Rickover, H. G. (1959). *Education and freedom.* New York: Dutton.

Sternberg, R. J. & Davidson, J. E. (Eds.). (1986). *Conceptions of giftedness.* Cambridge: Cambridge University Press.

Strang, R. M. (1960). *Helping your gifted child.* New York: Dutton.

U.S. Department of Education (1983). *A nation at risk: The imperative for educational reform.* Washington, DC: Author.

3

Developing Scope and Sequence in Curriculum

C. June Maker

University of Arizona, Tucson

Three of the major questions educators of the gifted must address now and in the future can be answered by the development of a curriculum scope and sequence: (1) How do the understandings, skills, and values we expect children to develop fit together? (2) How do we assure that a student develops or is provided the opportunity to learn the understandings, skills, and values that will be important in future personal or career development? (3) How does the student's learning in one setting or at one grade level mesh with his or her learning in a different setting or at a different grade level? In other words, how do educators avoid gaps and repetition in both activities and learning?

Answers to these queries are not easily developed, and the questions are often not addressed. In the past, when programs for the gifted existed in one or two schools, or at one or two grade levels within a school district, such questions

Editor's Note: From Maker, C.J. (1986). Developing scope and sequence in curriculum. *Gifted Child Quarterly*, *30*(4), 151-158. © 1986 National Association for Gifted Children. Reprinted with permission.

were not even asked! However, the field has advanced in the past few years, and to continue this progress, effective and defensible answers must be found for these and other similar questions. Educators of the gifted must respond to the criticisms of other educators regarding our lack of articulation, clear goal-setting, and coordination with other programs in the educational setting.

One important way to respond to some of our critics and to answer the questions outlined above is through the development of scope and sequence for the curriculum. The purposes of this article are to (a) describe the elements needed in a scope and sequence for a program for gifted students, (b) suggest a general process for developing a scope and sequence, and (c) present some examples of different scope and sequence projects.

A thorough and in-depth discussion of all the issues and processes involved in the development of a scope and sequence is not possible in a short article such as this, so only some of the most important ideas can be presented and a few examples provided. The processes described are based on the author's personal experiences in assisting individual teachers, school districts, and one state department of education in the development of a scope and sequence for curriculum. Initially, the ideas and processes were used with individual teachers working within a school district's program and curriculum framework. The processes and four examples of products were presented in *Curriculum Development fot the Gifted* (Maker, 1982a). After publication of the book, the author modified the process described for use with individuals based on attempts to follow it with larger groups in different settings. This article presents an introduction to and summary of the basic ideas and processes.

NECESSARY ELEMENTS OF A SCOPE AND SEQUENCE

For the purposes of this article, *scope* is very simply defined as the extent of what is taught or the understandings, skills, and values that are goals of the program. The *sequence* is the order in which the understandings, skills, and values are addressed. A scope and sequence for a program for the gifted must differ in some important ways from the scope and sequence often developed in other educational programs. Some of these differences follow:

1. It must be flexible, to permit both students and teachers to pursue their individual interests.

2. It should focus on abstract principles and concepts rather than specific facts.

3. It should include process skills such as higher levels of thinking and problem-solving as a separate scope and sequence that is integrated with the development of content understanding.

4. It should include an emphasis on development of types of sophisticated products integrated with the content and process.

5. It must not restrict the students' opportunities to pursue accelerated content, processes, or products.

6. It must include input from scholars and researchers in academic areas regarding the importance of principles, concepts, skills, and values.

7. It should provide opportunities for exposure to a variety of content areas, skills, values and types of content.

8. It should focus on concepts that are important in several academic areas, with the goal of integrating rather than separating what is learned.

9. It must build upon and extend the regular curriculum for efficiency and articulation in learning, but must not duplicate the regular curriculum.

10. It must include the input of a variety of professionals experienced in curriculum development and those experienced in education of the gifted.

A GENERAL PROCESS

To develop a curriculum scope and sequence that meets the criteria outlined above, the following general process is suggested. At each step, ideas for implementation of the process are presented along with examples of possible products.

Choose Key Individuals and Define their Roles and Tasks

Teachers and educators directly involved in the program for gifted students should be primarily responsible for the development of curriculum scope and sequence. However, other educators, parents and concerned individuals should be involved in some way. For example, in one school district, the teachers selected a content area of interest and worked with representatives from other grade levels to develop student outcome objectives. Parents (of gifted students) who possessed expertise in academic areas were helpful in the writing process. Curriculum specialists were helpful in reviewing the products and identifying ways the program for the gifted could extend the regular curriculum and suggesting ways to prevent overlap or redundancy with this curriculum. If regular classroom teachers are also responsible for provisions for gifted students, representatives from this group should also participate in the process.

Develop Curriculum Goals that Address Content, Process, and Product Expectations that Are Differentiated from Gifted Students

Curriculum goals should reflect both the connections with overall educational goals of the district and the differences in expectations for gifted students. As goals, they can be stated in general terms, but must be clear enough to guide the development of student outcome objectives in the next phase. In the Tucson

Unified School District (Maker and High, 1983), goals were written in the areas of content, process, product, and affective development. Following is an example of goals in each area:

1. Present content that is related to broadbased issues, themes, or problems in an interdisciplinary format. (content)

2. Develop critical and higher level thinking skills in both cognitive and affective areas. (process)

3. Develop products that redefine or challenge existing ideas, incorporate new and innovative ideas, and utilize techniques, materials, forms, and a body of knowledge in an innovative way. (product)

4. Encourage the development of sound relationships, including tolerance of human differences, respect for the needs and rights of others, and recognition of the contributions of others. (affective)

Educators involved in the program for gifted students should assume the major responsibility for writing curriculum goals, but should arrange for extensive input from others, especially parents. One way to gather ideas from others is to develop tentative statements of goals and to send these to parents, classroom teachers, administrators, other concerned educators, and gifted students, asking them to indicate the extent of their agreement or disagreement with each. They should also be asked to list additional goals they believe are important, but are not included in the list. Revisions, additions, and deletions can be made on the basis of the ideas gathered. Another way to solicit input from others is to hold meetings of parents, classroom teachers, administrators, other concerned educators, and gifted students. Groups are then asked to assign a priority to these goals. The writing team, consisting mainly of educators of the gifted, must then take these ideas and formulate them into clear goal statements that can guide the development of student outcome objectives.

Analyze Teaching-Learning Models to Determine their Appropriateness in Meeting Curriculum Goals

Too often, in programs for gifted students, the chosen model or models determine the goals rather than the goals determining the models used! Only after goals are developed and clarified is it appropriate to make decisions about the models to be used. One should not minimize the importance of models, however. They provide a thoughtful framework, along with guidelines for development of objectives and teaching activities, that have been tested in educational settings. Many models have been based on extensive research and development activities, and others have an extensive research base showing their effectiveness in reaching certain goals (Maker, 1982a, 1982b).

Many practical and theoretical aspects of models should be considered before their adoption (Maker, 1982b). The examples presented here pertain only to the model's usefulness in meeting curriculum goals and in providing guidelines for the development of student outcome objectives.

In the Tucson Unified School District, teachers familiar with the various teaching-learning models often used in programs for the gifted first listed the models that could be useful in meeting each goal (Maker and High, 1983). For example, for the content goal outlined above (Present content that is related to broadbased issues, themes, or problems . . .), the teachers listed Jerome Bruner's approach to teaching the Structure of a Discipline and Hilda Taba's Teaching Strategies Program. They identified several models useful in meeting the process goal (Develop critical and higher level thinking skills . . .): Guilford's Structure of Intellect, Kohlberg's Discussions of Moral Dilemmas, Osborn-Parnes' Creative Problem Solving Process, Williams' Strategies for Thinking and Feeling, Bloom's Taxonomy of Cognitive Objectives, Taba's Teaching Strategies Program, Taylor's Multiple Talent Approach, Krathwohl's Affective Taxonomy, and Ennis' Critical Thinking Behaviors. For the product goal, they recommended Guilford's Structure of Intellect, Osborn-Parnes' Creative Problem Solving Process, Renzulli's Enrichment Triad, Treffinger's Self-Directed Learning Approach, and Taylor's Multiple Talent Approach. The models listed as useful in meeting the affective goal (Encourage the development of sound relationships, including tolerance of human differences, respect for the needs and rights of others . . .) were Kohlberg's Discussions of Moral Dilemmas, Hilda Taba's Teaching Strategies, and Krathwohl's Taxonomy of Affective Objectives.

Next, the teachers analyzed the models to determine their usefulness in providing guidelines for developing student outcome objectives that were clear, specific, and observable. Criteria for selecting the models for this task included (a) the clarity of the model's objectives, (b) the extent of the model's orientation to observable student outcomes, (c) the comprehensiveness of the model in meeting a goal, and (d) the ease with which the model could be combined with others to provide a comprehensive listing of student outcomes related to a particular objective. With respect to the above goals, Taba's model, with influences from Bruner, was used for development of content objectives while Taba's model also formed the basis for the process objectives related to higher levels of thinking. Ennis' list of critical thinking skills was used to define student outcome objectives for the critical thinking aspect of the process goal stated above. For the product goal identified above, Renzulli's Enrichment Triad was the primary model used in developing objectives, with ideas integrated from three other sources: Torrance's writings, Guilford's Structure of Intellect and Treffinger's Self-Directed Learning Approach. For the affective goal identified above, a synthesis of several models was used. After useful models have been identified for each goal, student outcome objectives should be written for each goal.

Develop Specific Objectives (Stated as Student Outcomes) for Every Program Goal

Content. Content goals are most appropriately stated as generalizations/ principles to be discovered, key concepts to be learned, or themes. Abstract ideas and principles provide direction in the selection of specific information to be taught while also allowing flexibility to both the teacher and student in the selection of specific examples or areas of study. Stating content goals in one of the three ways listed above also provides a framework for supplementing without duplicating the content taught in regular classrooms.

Teachers in the Tucson Unified School District wrote generalizations in each content area, such as the following:

1. People develop individual cultures. However, all cultures share common characteristics as they evolve toward increasing complexity and refinement.

2. Living things are interdependent with one another and with their environment.

3. Effective oral communication relies on active listening and active speaking skills such as prediction, review, organization, and recall.

4. Understanding of place value is crucial to the use of number systems. Specific number systems have a variety of uses.

These generalizations will serve as the content objectives of the total program, K-12. Certain aspects of these generalizations are taught at each grade level, using a "spiral curriculum" approach as suggested by Bruner.

All the generalizations from each content area were then given to at least three scholars and experts in the appropriate areas, who were asked to review these statements to determine whether (a) the list included all the principles necessary for future study in the identified discipline, (b) all the principles were important for students to learn, and (c) the list was biased in any way. When comments were received, the generalizations were revised.

Next, teachers analyzed the generalizations to identify concepts important to developing an understanding of each of the principles and the information necessary for teaching these concepts. After identifying what needed to be taught, they examined the regular curriculum to determine if and at what grade level the necessary concepts and information were being taught. This process was extensive, but resulted in documents indicating clearly how the curriculum in the gifted program builds upon, extends, and is different from the regular curriculum. Table 1 provides an example of the format used by this group to list the concepts and information involved in the development of a generalization.

In the State of Hawaii, teachers identified an overall theme and three general statements that would guide the selection of content in the entire program. They then developed themes related to this overall theme, that would form the basis for content selection at each of four grade levels: K-3, 4-6, 7-8, 9-12.

Table I   Sample Generalization, Concepts, and Data from a Curriculum Scope and Sequence

GENERALIZATION: Numeration: Understanding of place value is crucial to the use of number systems. Specific number systems have a variety of uses.

Concept Development Data	Regular Program						GATE Program					
Concept: Use of number systems												
How to recognize and write numerals.	I	D	M	M	M	M	D	M	M	M	M	M
How to count and label sets.	I	D	M	M	M	M	D	M	M	M	M	M
How to use ordinal numbers.	I	D	M	M	M	M	D	M	M	M	M	M
How to compare sets.	I	D	M	M	M	M	D	M	M	M	M	M
Study of positive and negative integers.				I		D		I	I	M	M	D
Concept: Various number systems												
Study of Roman numerals.		I	D	M				I	D	D	M	M
Study of various other numeration systems, i.e., Arabic Roman, Egyptian, depending on units of study.	I							D	D	D	D	D
Study of hexadecimal system as relating to computers.											I	D
Study of binary system as relating to computers.											I	D

Source: From "Tucson Unified School District Curriculum Development Project" by C. J. Maker and M. H. High, 1983.

Note: I—Introduce, D—develop, M—maintain

Generalizations were then written for each grade level. The overall theme was selected because of the potential for (a) integrating many of the ideas being taught in programs for the gifted, and (b) providing a vehicle for connecting the curriculum for the gifted with the regular curriculum. Themes for each grade level were chosen because they were closely related to the content taught in the regular curriculum at those grade levels, but also offered possibilities for broadening and extending the students' learning in a coordinated manner. Table 2 provides a sample of the format used by this group to list themes.

In Tucson and Hawaii, the content scope and sequence permits flexibility while providing direction and coordination for the curriculum. For instance, with regard to the first example of a generalization written by the Tucson teachers (People develop individual cultures . . .), a number of different cultures could be studied, depending upon the background of the teacher and/or the interests of the students. A common emphasis, however, would be the identification of elements common to these varied cultures and an examination of how these characteristics change and how they relate to the evolution or refinement of a culture. The same flexibility and direction is inherent in the thematic approach used by the Hawaii teachers. Since the Hawaii schools use a resource room model as their only service delivery method, the thematic approach was most appropriate. Tucson, however, has self-contained classes for gifted students at the elementary level, so more detail was needed in their content scope and sequence than in the document developed for Hawaii.

Process. Statements of student outcomes for process skills are very similar to statements of student outcomes written for regular education. However, an important difference that causes difficulties in writing specific, observable objectives is that the goals for gifted students often involve long-term use and refinement of skills rather than simple acquisition of skills. Usually, this results in more complex goals for which it is difficult to develop clear student outcomes that can be measured or observed. In other words, there is often no end when one can say, for example, that "problem-solving skills" have been developed, but rather, there is continual improvement and refinement. Thus, success in meeting objectives often must be measured by degree of improvement in the skills.

The objectives for processes are more appropriately stated separately from content because most can and should be developed in all content areas. However, stating these objectives separately should not lead to separation of the teaching of processes from the teaching of content and the development of products. Integration of the three areas should come in the development of units of study and teaching activities.

Some examples of process objectives developed in Tucson for the goal of critical and higher levels of thinking are the following:

1. Higher levels of thinking
   a. Students will make supportable inferences about causes and effects.
   b. Students will support inferences with authoritative sources, accurate information, specific examples, other evidence and/or logic.

Table 2   Sample Themes, Concepts, and Generalizations from a Curriculum Scope and Sequence

Overarching Theme: Man and the Universe
Overarching Concepts
The Universe and all things in it are in a constant state of flux.
Man continually searches for meaning and knowledge.
Man affects and is affected by his environment.
All people, past and present, have adapted their beliefs and behavior in the face of universal needs and problems.

Grade Level Themes and Generalizations

K-3 *Interaction/Reaction*	4-6 *Laws of Nature vs.*	7-8 *Conflict/Harmony*	9-12 *Independence/Interdependence*
1. Man is a product of his beliefs and environment.	1. Interaction of people has made it necessary to set up rules and form governments.	1. Man deals with conflict and harmony as he searches for meaning.	1. All knowledge is interrelated.
2. Different people and cultures have different environmental concerns.	2. Man's control and modification of nature results in changes in environment.	2. Conflict can be a positive force.	2. People search for meaning and knowledge by discovering patterns in what they know, and then using, transforming, extending, breaking, or relating these patterns in new ways.

Source: From "Curriculum Recommendations for Gifted Programs in the State of Hawaii" by C. J. Maker and the State of Hawaii, 1985.

33

    c. Students will formulate conclusions that are accurate and applicable, and which integrate information and ideas from many different sources.

    d. Students will formulate generalizations that are accurate, applicable to a variety of situations, abstract, tentative, and inclusive.

2. Critical thinking

    a. Students will accurately judge whether a statement follows from the premises.

    b. Students will accurately judge whether a statement is an assumption.

    c. Students will accurately judge whether an observation statement is reliable.

The Hawaii teachers made more connections with the regular curriculum in the process area than they did in content, and more connections with the regular curriculum in processes than did the Tucson teachers. One reason for this difference in connectedness is that the regular curriculum in the State of Hawaii is mainly process-oriented, while the regular curriculum in the Tucson Unified School District is mainly content-oriented. A difference in orientation of the regular curriculum necessitates a more detailed analysis of what is taught in the regular curriculum and a closer connection with it to avoid repetition and provide a differentiated program.

Process goals for the gifted students in Hawaii schools are the same as those identified for all students, so the regular curriculum was analyzed according to these goals. Then, the process objectives and skills were examined to determine which ones needed to be developed in gifted students earlier than they are taught to other students (acceleration) and which skills gifted students needed to develop that are not taught to other students (enrichment). Examples of the process goals, objectives, and skills (as well as the format for the scope and sequence) are presented in Table 3.

Product. Product objectives can be developed in several ways, depending on the needs and orientation of the program. First, the objectives can be written as criteria that will be used to judge all student products regardless of their format or purpose. For example, the Tucson teachers developed objectives such as the following:

1. Student products will reflect an unusual or different perspective of the subject (e.g., visual, philosophical, historical, logical, emotional, or scientific).

2. Student products will demonstrate an application of basic information and methodology appropriate to the problem or question being investigated.

3. Student products will be designed for effective communication to an appropriate audience (e.g., be organized, interesting, utilize acceptable standards).

Table 3 Sample Process Goals, Objectives, and Skills for a Curriculum Scope and Sequence

Regular Program					Area	Performance Expectation	Gifted Program				
3	6	8	10	12			3	6	8	10	12
					Analyzes available information to study issues						
X						• Seeks assistance from a variety of people and considers suggestions offered by others.	I	D	D	D	D
						• Investigates and utilizes a variety of school and community resources.	I	D	D	D	D
						• States/summarizes/lists what is known about the situation.	I	D	D	A	A
					Identifies a problem/problems/hypothesis based on the issues						
						• Asks appropriate questions to identify and clarify a problem.	I	D	D	A	A
						• Raises questions related to a problem.	–	–	D	A	A
						• States or writes the problem using the necessary information in a concise manner.	–	–	D	A	A
X						• Formulates hypotheses about a problem based on available information.	I	I	D	A	A
						• Selects appropriate research methodology for research questions: – historical study – case study – descriptive study – correlational study – experimental study			–	D	D

(Continued)

35

Table 3 Continued

Regular Program					Area	Performance Expectation	Gifted Program				
3	6	8	10	12			3	6	8	10	12
					Draws conclusions or generalizations based on the alternative or hypothesis and related information						
		X				• Arrives at a conclusion and checks its reliability.	I	D	D	D	D
		X				• Interprets the organized information and draws generalizations.	I	D	A	D	A
		X				• Uses relevant relationships to draw conclusions in a problem-solving situation.		I	D	A	A
		X				• Checks correctness of conjectures and conclusions by organizing, analyzing, and evaluating information.		I	D	A	A

Source: From "Curriculum Recommendations for Gifted Programs in the State of Hawaii" by C. J. Maker and the State of Hawaii.
Note: I—introduce, D—develop, A—apply independently

A sequence of skill development that will achieve these objectives would include, for example (to meet objective number two above), the teaching of a variety of research methods, increasing in complexity and sophistication as the students progress through the program. Skills related to the third objective would include assessment of audience needs, mastery of a variety of formats for product presentation, methods for organizing information to be presented, and many others.

A different approach to development of a product scope and sequence is to state goals in terms of the expectations for products, and then to design objectives that address *types* of products students will be expected to master. For example, the Hawaii teachers developed goals such as the following:

1. Student products will synthesize new and existing information in a way unique to the student.

2. Student product development will include an evaluation based on self-developed criteria.

Some examples of objectives and the sequence of skills to achieve objectives are presented in Table 4. Criteria to be used in assessing student products of each type would be based directly on the goal statements listed above.

The goals, objectives and sequence of skills for achieving these objectives in the three areas of content, process, and product constitute the major part of the scope and sequence. However, to facilitate the use of goals, objectives, and sequences of skills in an appropriate and individualized manner, two additional activities should be a part of the process of developing scope and sequence.

Select or Develop Instruments or Procedures that Should Be Used for Needs Assessment in Areas Addressed by Program Goals and Objectives

It is crucial that a scope and sequence for gifted students not be used in a lock-step manner. The scope and sequence should facilitate, rather than inhibit learning. Thus, teachers should not assume that just because a student is in the fourth grade, he or she has mastered certain skills. Conversely, one also should not assume that the student has not mastered certain skills. If used appropriately, the scope and sequence will provide checkpoints for skill and content development rather than dictating exactly when these can be learned.

Both informal and formal procedures should be developed (or selected) to evaluate student needs with respect to the curriculum goals and objectives. These procedures must yield specific information that can be used in instructional planning for individual students, and must be directly tied to the student outcome objectives. Needs assessment procedures can also be used (as post-tests) to evaluate student progress and the success of the curriculum.

Unfortunately, there are few published and widely-available tests that measure objectives common to programs for gifted students that provide information

Table 4 Sample Product Scope and Sequence

		Essential or Optional	K-3	4-6	7-8	9-12
2.0	**Written**					
2.1	Book with illustration	O	I	D	D	D
2.2	Essay	E			D	A
2.3	Journal—Scientific, literary, historical	E	I	D	D	D
2.4	Narration—First person/second person	E			D	D
3.0	**Media**					
3.1	Cassette tape	E	I	D	A	A
3.2	Transparency	E			D	A
3.3	Computer programming	E			D	A
3.4	Slide-Tape	O			D	D
3.5	Film-making	O				
3.5.1	Silent				D	D
3.5.2	Sound				D	D
3.5.3	Animation				D	D
3.5.4	Feature film				–	D
3.5.5	Documentary				–	D
4.0	**Fine Arts**					
4.1	Visual Arts					
4.1.1	Drawing	E	I			
4.1.2	Painting	E	I			
4.1.3	Graphics (lettering)—printing, posters, silkscreening, textile	E		I	D	
4.1.4	Sculpture (3 dimensional products)	E	I			

Source: The material was adapted by a team of teachers in the State of Hawaii from a publication from "Scope and Sequence for High Potential Program," by Barbara Christensen, Independent School District #622, North St. Paul, Maplewood, and Oakdale Schools, Minnesota.

Note: I—introduce, D—apply independently

useful in instructional planning. Thus, it is necessary to develop informal checklists and tests, and to use selected parts of existing instruments.

Many people indicate that they have difficulty selecting instruments for assessment of process, but that finding instruments for content assessment is much easier because of the availability of achievement tests. I would caution that there are very few achievement tests that measure conceptual understanding of the kind usually viewed as important in a program for the gifted. Standardized achievement tests rarely yield data useful in instructional planning because only general scores are reported to teachers, without an analysis of these scores related to learning objectives.

Develop Sample Units and Lesson Plans

Sample units and lesson plans should accompany the scope and sequence to show how the objectives and skills in the three areas of content, process, and product should be integrated. Too often, the teaching of process is separated from the teaching of content, and the existence of a separate scope and sequence for these areas could create the impression that they should be taught separately.

Development of supplementary materials can be a way to recognize the creativity of certain teachers. Units and lesson plans can be developed by individuals working alone, and existing units or plans can simply be included. It is very important, however, that these materials follow a standard format, and that they all include certain types of information. The format and exact information to be included in units or lesson plans should be provided to those interested in writing them. Meetings to explain the format and answer questions would be necessary. Sample units and lesson plans using the required format would also be useful as models. Finally, each unit or lesson plan should have a cover sheet summarizing what is contained within it, especially listing which content, process, and product objectives are addressed.

Implementation

The final task of the team involved in development of a scope and sequence is to hold meetings and workshops in which the product is presented and explained. Simply sending it to administrators, teachers, or curriculum specialists is not enough. Those involved in the writing should be available to answer questions and to provide assistance in implementation. Depending upon the experience and sophistication of the teachers involved in the program, workshops and other inservice training may need to be planned.

SUMMARY

The development of a curriculum scope and sequence can provide effective answers to the three major questions presented at the beginning of this article.

We can show how the learning of a variety of understandings, skills, and values fits together; we can assure that students are given opportunities to learn what will be useful to them in the future; and we can avoid gaps and repetition in learning. The process described in this article has been useful in a variety of settings, and has resulted in the development of scope and sequence documents that meet the requirements outlined. Although there will need to be variations and modifications because of the differences and needs in different settings, the examples are provided because of their potential to be helpful in designing a scope and sequence useful in each reader's situation.

REFERENCES

Christensen, B. (undated). *Scope and sequence for High Potential Program*. Available from Barbara Christensen, Independent School District #622, North St. Paul, Maplewood and Oakdale Schools, Minnesota.

Maker, C. J., & High, M. H. (1983). *Tucson Unified School District curriculum development project*. Available from C. June Maker, Department of Special Education, University of Arizona.

Maker, C. J. (1982a). *Curriculum development for the gifted*. Rockville, MD: Aspen Systems Corporation.

Maker, C. J. (1982b). *Teaching models in education of the gifted*. Rockville, MD: Aspen Systems Corporation.

Maker, C. J., & State of Hawaii (1985). *Curriculum recommendations for gifted programs in the State of Hawaii*. Available from Margaret Donovan, Consultant, State of Hawaii Department of Education, OIS, General Education Branch, 189 Lunalilo Home Road, Rm. A-20, Honolulu, HI 96825.

4

Myth: There Is a Single Curriculum for the Gifted!

Response by Sandra N. Kaplan

P resent day myths are often a consequence of lack, misinterpretation, or fear of knowledge. A lack of understanding about the purposes for developing curriculum, a misinterpretation of the elements for and uses of curriculum, and a fear of the expectations placed on teachers and students once it is developed and disseminated are factors that need to be addressed in order to disprove the myth that there could or should be a single curriculum for all gifted students.

DEVELOPING CURRICULUM

Sometimes a belief in a single curriculum for the gifted is perceived to be synonymous with the concept of developing curriculum for these students.

Editor's Note: From Kaplan, S. (1982). Myth: There is a single curriculum for the gifted! *Gifted Child Quarterly*, 26(1), 32–33. © 1982 National Association For Gifted Children. Reprinted with permission

Proponents arguing against the formalized construction of curriculum for the gifted envision developed curriculum as means of regimenting and inhibiting the teacher and ignoring the individuality of learners. The intent of predetermined, designed or developed curriculum is confused with the implementation of such curriculum once it is constructed.

The need to develop curriculum is analogous to the need to use a map to explore a given environment. Just as a map provides the traveler with the possible and alternative routes to select in order to arrive at a given destination, a predetermined, designed, or developed curriculum provides the teacher and the learner with clearly expressed goals and objectives that can be individually experienced and attained. The purpose of a developed curriculum is not to confine the teacher or learner; it is to define the expectations of the teaching/learning process.

Absence of a developed curriculum for the gifted assumes that:

1. every teacher is able to or interested in being a curriculum writer or developer;

2. there are no common experiences that underscore appropriately differentiated curriculum for the gifted;

3. if a general curriculum is developed, all learners will have to experience it in the same way.

These assumptions are faulty and can be negated by anwers to these questions. Why aren't teachers asked to write their own textbooks or courses of study? Why aren't individuals who desire to be credentialed as teachers allowed to take *any* course offering at the university rather than the required courses with options within defined areas of study?

The need and major purpose for developing curriculum for the gifted is predicated on knowledge that there is a set of common and required learning experiences for all gifted students and that teachers are responsible and accountable to provide these for the gifted. An understanding that a predetermined or developed curriculum must be *modified* to meet the needs, interests, and abilities of individual gifted learners is essential. In addition, it is important to recognize that effective teaching and learning are best affected by design and not by happenstance. The issue may not be whether or not curriculum for the gifted should be developed; the issue may be how developed curriculum should be used.

A SINGLE CURRICULUM

Support for the concept of a single curriculum for the gifted would not be difficult to comprehend. A single curriculum would certainly make the teaching task easier, eradicate the ambiguity that exists among educators of the gifted as to the definition and principles governing appropriately differentiated curriculum, settle the debate among researchers and theorists concerning the selection and application of curricular models, stimulate the sales of commercially produced curriculum for the gifted, and support the belief that gifted students represent a homogeneous population. However, the concept that a single curriculum could be developed to accommodate the gifted is as fallacious as the idea that a developed curriculum is all that is necessary to adequately provide for these learners.

An analysis of the possible reasons for the emergence of the myth that a single curriculum is appropriate for the gifted could, in fact, be the best means to dispel this myth. As researchers and theoreticians advocate the use of particular models for the construction of curriculum, confusion reigns between the purpose of a model for curriculum and a model curriculum. Allegiance to a given model can trap more than enhance the curriculum. While a model can provide directionality, it is often noted that adherence to a given model can force all learners into the same curricular experiences without regard for individual differences in prerequisite learnings, needs, and interests.

Another reason that the single curriculum is viewed as the answer to educating the gifted is the unequal balance between the demand that teachers attend to the gifted and the attention given to teacher training systems to prepare them for this demand. Confronted with the expectations to differentiate curricular experiences for the gifted, teachers seek the single, best, or right way to fulfill these expectations. Vulnerability to one's own concept of a successful professional, to one's class or group of gifted learners, and to the parents of these children, teachers look for a single curriculum to solve their dilemma.

In many cases, identification and evaluative issues lead teachers to believe that a single curriculum will satisfy the needs of all the gifted. An identification process that emphasizes the differences between the gifted and the nongifted without also stressing the differences among the gifted justifies the concept of a single curriculum. It encourages teachers to respond to the uniqueness of the group of gifted learners rather than to the individual learners that comprise the group. Lack of evaluative data describing the impact of differentiated curricula on the education of the gifted has caused many teachers to look for the single proven curriculum. If a particular curriculum is thought "to work," this criterion becomes the basis for selecting and using a particular single curriculum.

Still another reason for believing that there could be a single curriculum for the gifted is the proliferation of commercially prepared curriculum currently available. While all publishers profess to have "the" answer to how to educate the gifted, such curriculum is usually presented without being field tested and without data to validate the worth and appropriateness of the curriculum for the gifted. Too often, the need for curriculum outweighs concerns for the selection procedures for and uses of this curriculum. Even though commercially prepared curriculum facilitates the teaching/learning process, it should be used as an adjunct to, rather than the curriculum for the gifted.

SUMMARY

Curriculum means the cumulative and comprehensive set of learning experiences related to the attainment of cognitive and affective personal, societal, and institutional goals. These goals are responsive to the characteristics that define the nature of giftedness. There are common elements that underscore curriculum for all gifted learners. Although the gifted share common characteristics, they also differ from each other in needs, abilities, and interests. Therefore, any curriculum must be modified to accommodate the individual gifted learner while still responding to the general nature and needs of all gifted learners. There cannot be a single curriculum for the gifted since there is not a single prototype of a gifted learner.

5

What Makes a Problem Real: Stalking the Illusive Meaning of Qualitative Differences in Gifted Education

Joseph S. Renzulli

The whole process of education should thus be conceived as the process of learning to think through the solution of real problems.

(John Dewey, 1938)

Editor's Note: From Renzulli, J. (1982). What makes a problem real: Stalking the elusive meaning of qualitative differences in gifted education. *Gifted Child Quarterly, 26*(4), 147–156. © 1982 National Association for Gifted Children. Reprinted with permission.

Is there a pot of gold at the end of the rainbow?

During the course of my involvement in the gifted child movement, I have observed a never-ending quest to define those things uniquely or qualitatively different about the types of curricular experiences which should be recommended for gifted and talented students. Indeed, the term "qualitative differentiation" has emerged as one of the field's major contemporary cliches. More attention has been given to this search for our identity than any other issue in theoretical literature concerning giftedness, with the possible exception of the age-old concern of who are the gifted and talented. Like searches for the fountain of youth and the pot of gold at the end of the rainbow, this quest for the meaning of qualitative differentiation has largely eluded us. This has resulted in a great deal of controversy and confusion about one of the major issues that could very well determine whether our field survives as an entity in special education. As I stated in an earlier article appearing in a previous issue of this journal (Renzulli, 1980), if we are going to survive and prosper as a specialized field of knowledge, we must become as adept at defining those things for which we stand as we have been in dealing with the educational practices we oppose.

My own attempt to deal with the issue of qualitative differences in learning was largely put forth in *The Enrichment Triad Model* (Renzulli, 1977). In the intervening years I have given a considerable amount of thought as to whether or not Triad had the "power" to stand up to the very criticisms described in the early chapters of that book. A good deal of that thought was stimulated by two main influences. First and foremost have been the experiences I have gained as a result of the many Triad-based programs which have developed over the years. It has been my good fortune to have become directly or indirectly involved in many of these programs. Through them I have learned a great deal about "what works," and also what we are capable of delivering in view of our own abilities and resources. These experiences have enabled me to reflect further upon the Triad Model, as well as other models that have been proposed to guide programming for gifted students.

Because I am a pragmatist in the tradition of John Dewey, I believe that theories or models[1] aren't worth a plug nickel unless they can give specific and practical direction to the day-by-day operations of a program for the gifted. The words *specific* and *practical* are emphasized because it is always easy for us ivory tower types to make suggestions to teachers of the gifted that are easily acceptable. However, they are almost impossible to achieve in view of our own abilities, interests, and the amounts of time we can reasonably devote to the task of programming for gifted youngsters. With a flick of my pen, for example, I could easily recommend that teachers of the gifted write an advanced level curriculum on mythology, futuristics, computer programming, or any other esoteric or traditional topic for that matter. In the best tradition of the idealist, I could also go on to suggest that this curriculum be based on the most important concepts and recent knowledge developed in these content areas, and that it should make use of the best learning techniques and latest left brain/right brain jargon. We should, of course, mix in a heavy dose of Bloom's *Taxonomy* for good measure.

I might even go so far as to recommend that we involve a few academic scholars in the development of our curricular units, just to make sure that the content is "truly advanced." Now who can argue with this seemingly infallible folk wisdom? My experience with lots of programs and teachers of the gifted allows me to say without hesitation—I can!

There are several reasons why I am not in favor of a gifted program that requires teachers to assume major responsibility for developing a curriculum. One of the main purposes of this article is to put forth an argument that defends this point of view and also deals with some additional concerns about what is or should be the right and proper curriculum for the gifted and talented. My argument will be based on both theoretical and practical concerns, but at this point I would like to mention briefly one issue that might be classified as a political concern. When people from the ivory tower sagely expound wisdom about developing their own curriculum, most experienced teachers of the gifted tend to ignore it completely or say it is a good idea, hoping that someone else will do it! When this advice falls into the hands of administrators or supervisors, however, it may result in unrealistic requirements being placed on teachers who are less than wildly enthusiastic about developing their own curriculum. The by-products of such pressure are usually a large amount of frustration, tension between teachers and their supervisors, a relatively small yield in terms of curriculum actually produced, and an always unsettling feeling about the quality of our efforts.

Lest the reader accuse me at this point of being a complete heretic about curriculum development, allow me to offer two reservations to the above statements. First, I believe that teachers who have a strong desire to be the authors of curricular materials in self-selected areas of study should be given every encouragement to do so; the teacher-as-author represents one of the highest levels of creative productivity in our profession. Nevertheless, one should only assume this role if she or he is highly motivated to do so. High motivation alone will not, of course, guarantee quality products. However, it is a much better starting point than forcing teachers to develop curricula because someone thought it would be a good idea. Once a person has made a commitment to be an author of curricular materials, he or she must also be willing to approach the task with the same professionalism and concern for quality as an author who is under contract with a commercial publisher. (If this last requirement sounds somewhat harsh, keep in mind that our self-stated goal is to produce high quality, advanced level curricula, reaching "above and beyond" that which is offered in the regular school program.)

A second reservation is that I am not against accelerated, prepackaged, or advanced curricular units. Indeed, I wish that more high quality material was available, especially in the areas of research and methodological skills. At the same time, general education, from diapers through doctorate, has largely emerged as a prepackaged supermarket of curricular units. I don't think that we can solve the problem of qualitative differences in learning by simply adding more "canned" units to the shelves. I will try to elaborate on this argument in more detail in one of the sections that follow.

A second factor that has stimulated additional thought on my part about qualitative differences in learning has been interaction with other theorists and model builders in gifted education. For better or for worse, Triad has been "out there," in print and in action, for others to examine, to criticize, and to raise the kinds of questions that have caused me to rethink my position. There is nothing so powerful in the growth of knowledge as a point-of-view on which others can take aim. When I originally wrote Triad, I stated in the preface that it was my hope to create "a great in-house dialogue" about the meaning of qualitative differentiation. This dialogue has indeed taken place and will undoubtedly continue to take place in the years ahead. I am indebted to my colleagues for this opportunity to debate the issues because I believe that the emergence of quality will only come about when persons are open and honest enough to confront the issues in which we all have a personal interest and professional stake. Through private conversations, occasional public forums, and personal correspondence, I have exchanged thoughts and ideas with many of the leaders in gifted education and these exchanges have helped me to prepare the analysis that is presented in this article.

John Dewey, won't you please come home. In many ways, the ideas put forth in *The Enrichment Triad Model* are based on both an interpretation of the educational philosophy of John Dewey and my desire to translate this philosophy into a practical plan for program development. For this reason I am a little embarrassed to begin this section by disagreeing, however slightly, with the quotation by Dewey that appears at the beginning of this article. I would like to believe that all educational experiences should be built around the pursuit of real problems. However, I have long since come to realize that efficiency in the learning process is more easily achieved if we make some use of contrived problems or exercises and if we employ certain methods of teaching that are not necessarily associated with the discovery of a solution to real problems. Simply stated, there is nothing wrong with teaching children the times tables or vocabulary words using methods that may involve memorization, repetition, and other contrived exercises such as using words in a sentence, looking up their meanings in a dictionary, and alphabetizing this week's spelling list. Ultraliberal educators may disagree with this traditional stance, but the fact remains that these methods have served us well for hundreds of years in providing mass education for the general population.

My concern in this article is not with general education, but rather with qualitative differences in the education of gifted youngsters. In this regard I would like to suggest that one of the major ways we can guarantee such differences is to make real problems the central focus of any plan for gifted education. Before attempting to develop a definition of "real problems" let us examine the rationale for giving these problems such a prominent role in our plan to educate gifted youth.

If there are any two overriding factors that have brought the field of gifted and talented into existence they are:

  1. nature has not made every human being a carbon copy of every other, and

  2. civilization has continuously produced men and women who have done more than merely learn about or replicate existing knowledge.

If such were not the case, the growth of civilization would be totally dependent upon the *accidental* discovery of new knowledge. Our field does not glorify the copyists or the high level replicators of knowledge and art, and only rarely does history remember people who have made accidental discoveries. Rather, our focus has been on men and women who have purposefully made it their business to attack the *un*solved problems of mankind. It is for this reason that educators of the gifted constantly invoke such names as Einstein, Edison, Curie, Beethoven, Duncan, and a host of others who have made creative contributions to their chosen fields of endeavor. If mankind's creative producers and solvers of real problems are constantly held up before us as idealized prototypes of the "gifted person," then it seems nothing short of common sense to use their *modus operandi* to construct a model for educating our most promising young people. This is not to say that we should minimize the importance of providing gifted youngsters with the most advanced courses or experiences involving existing knowledge. Good old-fashioned book learning of the accumulated, organized wisdom of the ages helps to provide the stuff out of which new ideas and breakthroughs in knowledge will occur, but a major focus within such courses (or independent from any course) should be on the production of new knowledge. Such production is a function of both mastery of the concepts and principles of a given field, and the creation of a learning environment that purposefully and unequivocally tells youngsters that they can be creative producers. People sometimes seem skeptical when my colleagues and I describe case after case involving outstanding examples of creative and productive work emanating from students participating in Triad-based programs. There is a very simple reason for the quantity and quality of this productivity. From their earliest years in the program, our students are constantly stimulated to explore new and interesting topics and ideas. They are encouraged to develop creative problem-solving techniques and research skills. They understand that they are in this gifted program because we expect them to develop not only the techniques, but also the attitude and task commitment for going beyond existing knowledge. Attitudinal development, a strong belief in one's ability to be a creative producer, is as important as the learning of content. For example, there were probably a thousand people who knew as much about the theory of flight as the Wright Brothers, but Wilbur and Orville made it fly.

Let us now turn our attention to the definition of a real problem. The word "real," like so many other concepts in education, gets tossed around so freely that after a while it becomes little more than another piece of useless jargon. My research on the meaning of a real problem did not produce a neat and trim definition, but I was able to come up with the following list of characteristics which will serve as a set of parameters for analyzing this important concept. Please review the following list with an eye toward determining whether or not you are in agreement with each statement.

CHARACTERISTICS OF A REAL PROBLEM

1. A real problem must have a personal frame of reference, since it involves an emotional or affective commitment as well as an intellectual or cognitive one.

2. A real problem does not have an existing or unique solution.

3. Calling something a problem does not necessarily make it a real problem for a given person or group.

4. The purpose of pursuing a real problem is to bring about some form of change and/or to contribute something new to the sciences, the arts, or the humanities.

To help us clarify the meaning of what makes a problem real, I have selected a few sample activities from a number of gifted programs. Please review each of the following examples and classify them according to the following five types of learning activity:

A. The Pursuit of a Real Problem.
B. The Study of Societal Issues
C. A Simulation Activity
D. A Training Exercise
E. A Puzzle

Example 1: Train A left the station at 9:00 a.m. and is traveling south at 50 mph. Train B left the same station at 10:00 a.m. and is traveling south at 75 mph. How long will it take Train B to catch up with Train A?

Example 2: High school students discuss and debate several topics in an Advanced Seminar in Social Studies. The topics include Urban Migration, Energy Depletion, Rising Crime Rates, Drug Abuse, and World Food Shortages. They read a wide variety of advanced level background material and prepare position papers on selected topics.

Example 3: Please fill in the letters that should appear in the blank spaces. O T T F F S _ _ _

Example 4: A primary program for gifted students is organized to resemble a model community. To increase their knowledge of government, the children elect their own officials and learn about various occupations and community helpers by means of roles and responsibilities assigned to them. They design a city flag and compose a song to develop artistic abilities, and learn math by printing their own "money" for use in a play store.

Example 5: Sandy, a high school junior, became interested in problems of teenage drinking after hearing a lecture by a cultural anthropologist who spoke at a seminar sponsored by the gifted program. She decided to conduct a comparative study of the differences in attitude between teenagers and adults with regard to various issues raised by drinking and dating practices. She reviewed similar studies in professional journals and obtained books on appropriate research methodology. After designing and field testing a survey instrument and interview schedule, she gathered and analyzed data obtained from a random sample of young people and adults. A research report was prepared and serialized in a local newspaper. Presentations describing her research and recommendations were made to student groups, service clubs, and other adult groups in the community.

A general concensus among various groups of educators has resulted in the following classifications for these examples:

Example 1. . . . D (also could be E)

Example 2. . . . B

Example 3. . . . E

Example 4. . . . C

Example 5. . . . A

Each example is a worthwhile educational activity, and I believe that under the right circumstances, all of them could become stepping stones to one or more types of real problems. As they presently exist, however, only Example 5 has been designated a real problem. In a later section we will return to this example and see if we can use it to develop a list of questions which will help us force out the important characteristics of a qualitatively different learning experience.

Viva la Difference. I would like to approach our search for qualitative differences in learning by asking you to join me in a comparison between two models of learning and instruction. Neither model has a name (we will simply refer to them as A and B) and at the beginning of our analysis we will avoid any conclusions about their appropriateness for helping us to define qualitatively different experiences for the gifted.

We will examine the two models in terms of four major variables, these variables being the role of the student, the role of knowledge, the role of creativity (and other processes), and the role of the teacher. This comparison is depicted in Table 1.

Table 1   A Comparison of Two General Models of Learning and Instruction

Variables	Learning/Instructional Model A	Learning/Instructional Model B
I. The Role of the Student		
II. The Role of Knowledge (or Content)		
III. The Role of Creativity (and Other Processes)		
IV. The Role of the Teacher		

MODEL A

Initially, we will make only one assumption about the two models. Let us assume that Learning/Instructional Model A consists of the major principles and practices that have guided the regular curriculum. This assumption is necessary to help us put the problem into proper perspective. Many regular curricular methods and materials are appropriate for gifted students. However, if every variable that we analyze ends up in the same column as the regular curriculum (i.e., Learning/Instructional Model A), then we may be forced to conclude that there really are no basic differences between regular and gifted education. At this point I want to emphasize that I am not belittling or mini-mizing the importance of any practices that might end up in the Model A column. Indeed, I will begin by placing Types I and II Enrichment from my own Triad Model in that column. I will also take the liberty of placing Type III Enrichment in column B. (In a certain sense, we might entitle this section of our analysis, "In Defense of Type III Enrichment.") We will examine each variable by presenting a chart comparing the two models in accordance with the most important features of each variable.

The Role of the Student

I consider this variable to be the most important part of the argument because I believe the central focus of all educational endeavors should be the student. In the regular curriculum, the student is generally cast in the role of a learner of lessons and a doer of exercises, and in most cases, these lessons follow what I have termed the Four-P Approach (see Table 2). Most lessons are *prescribed* by the teacher or textbook and are *presented* to students without affording them much opportunity to decide whether or not they want to par-ticipate. In the majority of cases, the lessons we use in the regular curriculum

Table 2   The Role of the Student

Learning/Instructional Model A	Learning/Instructional Model B
The Four-P Approach: Prescribed, Presented, Predetermined Pathways, Predetermined Products	Student Selection of Topic(s) Guaranteed
Didactic or Instructive in Design	Inductive or Investigative in Design
Student's Role Is That of Learner of Lessons and Doer of Exercises	Student's Role Is That of First-Hand Inquirer
Student Is Consumer of Content and Process	Student Is Producer of Knowledge and Art

have *predetermined pathways* to the solution of problems. There is a correct way to derive the formula of a triangle, diagram a sentence, or determine the imports and exports of a Latin American country. Even in areas such as creativity training, we have managed to spell out the five basic steps of creative problem solving. Finally, most prescribed exercises have *predetermined products* as their ultimate goals—that is, students are expected to come up with a correct answer which is usually agreed upon beforehand. Some variation of products is encouraged in creativity training, yet, the first three Ps have been plainly evident in most of the creativity training activities I have observed.

Model A is also very didactic in nature—it is generally aimed toward instructing students *about* something or teaching them to use a particular process skill that we have prescribed as being good for them. Whenever I think about Model A, I am reminded of a statement made by Mortimer Adler in a speech delivered at the University of Connecticut. He said, "For the gifted person, the person who really wants to learn something, too much instruction is insulting." An unfortunate reality about most of the regular curriculum is that we *instruct* students almost all of the time. We must now raise the same questions about the types of things we typically do in gifted programs. How much time do we spend instructing *these* students? How much of that instruction is Four-P oriented? It is in this regard that we must analyze not only the individual activities we use, but also the models that are proposed to guide the total gifted program. Whenever someone tells me that their program is based on Guilford's (1967) Structure-of-Intellect model or Bloom's (1956) *Taxonomy of Educational Objectives*, the Four-Ps immediately come to mind. These psychological models of human ability were never intended to be program planning models, especially for gifted programs which are trying desperately to break the shackles of too much structure and too many predetermined objectives.

On the Model B side of the ledger, I would like to summarize the major features by referring to Figure 1. This diagram should be "read" beginning with the lightbulb at the center and moving toward the outer rings. We will deal with most of the concepts in Figure 1 under The Role of the Teacher, but it is presented at this time to point out the *central* role students play in selecting topics

Figure 1   Targeting on Type III

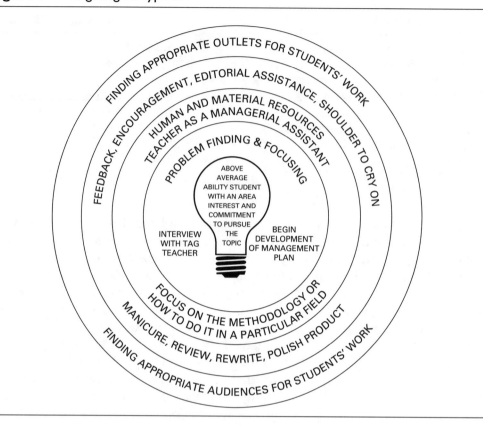

for individual or small group study. The student's role in Model B is also mainly investigative in nature. Sandy, the student mentioned in Example 5, used investigative methodology to obtain observational evidence about the existence of certain attitudes in her community. In this case, her primary role was transformed from that of lesson learner to one which made her into a first-hand inquirer.

We cannot leave this discussion about the role of the learner without coming face-to-face with the age-old issue of Acceleration versus Enrichment. I believe that acceleration should be an important part of any program for the gifted. However, a model that relies primarily on the use of accelerated curriculum is undoubtedly based on quantitative rather than qualitative differences in learning. I have attempted to depict these two types of differences in Figure 2, and will clarify them through the use of an example.

When I was in school, subjects such as algebra and French were the uncontested province of the high school. When a new spirit of educational reform started to take place, some wise persons suggested that younger people might be able to master these traditionally secondary school subjects. Subsequently, it was not uncommon to find algebra offered to students in the seventh and eighth grades and French offered to students as early as the third or fourth grade. In the early years of gifted programming in America, one of the first "innovations"

Figure 2   The "Course Shifting" Approach to Differentiation: Is It Quantitative or Qualitative?

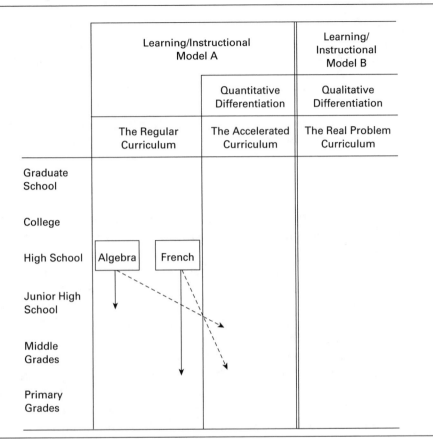

was simply affording bright young students an opportunity to take courses that were ordinarily scheduled for later grade levels. The currently popular radical acceleration model recommends that high scorers on mathematics aptitude tests be encouraged to take college level courses in math. Predictably, these high scorers have earned good grades in their advanced math courses and this undisputed fact is certainly justification for making opportunities to make advanced work available to younger students. My concern with this approach, however, is that the learning model and the role of the learner have not changed. To paraphrase Gertrude Stein, " . . . course, is a course, is a course." The student is still cast mainly in the role of a lesson learner and the instruction is still mainly of the Four-P variety.

The Role of Knowledge

It would probably take nothing short of an entire book to do justice to the role knowledge should play in curriculum for the gifted, but any discussion

Table 3   The Role of Knowledge

Learning/Instructional Model A	Learning/Instructional Model B
Linear Sequential Processing of Information	Cyclical and Frequently Simultaneous Processing of Information
Knowledge Is Accumulated and Stored for (Possible) Future Use	Knowledge Is Only Sought When Needed for Present Use
Students Use Knowledge to Study About Problems	Students Use Knowledge to Act Upon Problems
Teacher/Textbook Predetermines What Information Will Be Used	Needed Information Is Determined by the Problem as it Unfolds

about this important topic should begin with at least two basic assumptions. First, *knowledge is important*! This statement may sound obvious, if not trivial, but a great deal of the recent rhetoric in gifted education has denigrated knowledge or content in favor of process training and a largely unsubstantiated belief that the gifted person is "process oriented." Knowledge is grist for the mill of the mind and we cannot escalate our processes of mind unless we are feeding this mill with ever-increasing amounts of relevant information. *Relevant* is the key word here, and the secret of doing this without turning student into encyclopedia-heads will be discussed shortly.

A second assumption is that when we are purposefully attempting to develop qualitatively different materials, materials that go above and beyond the regular curriculum, we ordinarily are not interested in dealing with mundane or trivial knowledge. Our party line talks about *advanced* concepts and *higher* levels of thinking; and therefore, we must avoid focusing our efforts on unimportant knowledge. But who, you might ask, can judge what knowledge is important as opposed to mundane or trivial? That is the key question and the focal point around which we will compare the role of knowledge in Models A and B.

Perhaps the best way to highlight the importance of this question is with an example. I know of one youngster named Paul who spent several months digging out the factual details of everyday weather reports for a time period spanning *fifty* years. The temperatures and amount of snowfall in Hartford, Connecticut, on December 11, 1936 (or any other day), may seem trivial indeed, but it became a very important piece of information in helping to explain why the roof of our multimillion dollar civic center collapsed under a heavy burden of ice and snow. In this case, more detailed knowledge led to more accuracy in the analysis, which in turn resulted in Paul's placing more confidence in the conclusions of his research.

In most prepared materials comprising the regular curriculum, knowledge is treated in a linear and sequential fashion. Even the best textbooks and curriculum guides present students with important facts, major concepts, and underlying principles. After students have ingested the required information, they are usually asked to "do something" with it to demonstrate their comprehension, answer questions, discuss critical issues, prepare a paper or project, etc. They might also be expected to store the information for possible future use.[2] Although I am not necessarily criticizing this almost universal approach to the manner in which knowledge is utilized in the engineered curriculum, I believe we should judiciously avoid recreating the same mode for gifted education.

With the advent of Bloom's *Taxonomy* (1956), persons within the field of the gifted and talented who support the curriculum development approach to differentiation felt they had at last found the magic formula for constructing qualitatively different materials. Lessons and units were prepared that typically began with presented content and "knowledge questions," and proceeded in a step-by-step fashion through analysis, synthesis, and evaluation. In analyzing these materials, there are certain obvious conclusions we must reach. First, they are almost always based on the Four-P approach. Secondly, the important processes listed in Bloom's *Taxonomy* are a part of the right and proper education for all students, not just the gifted. Third, the learning process is still being treated in a linear and sequential fashion. This is my main concern at this juncture in our analysis. There is nothing wrong with the linear and sequential treatment of content and process, but, once again, isn't that the approach that characterizes most of the regular curriculum? Furthermore, when one is pursuing a real problem, neither the content nor the processes can be laid out in a predetermined order. If such were the case, we would undoubtedly be dealing with yet another training exercise.

Let us now turn our attention to how knowledge is used in Model B. When students begin work on problems that hopefully will emerge as bona finde examples of Type III Enrichment, they are steered in their initial contact with knowledge toward exploring the ways in which knowledge is organized within a particular discipline. The investigative methodology is directed toward adding new knowledge to that discipline. In Paul's case, for example, this structure of knowledge (or knowledge about knowledge) approach required him to find out where and how information in meteorology was stored, how he could retrieve it, and the analytic methods necessary for utilizing existing knowledge to create new knowledge. Philosophers and persons who have written extensively about the subject of knowledge (see, for example, Machlup, 1980), refer to this approach as knowledge of . . . , knowledge about . . . , and knowledge how. . . . And, I might add, they always consider knowledge how—how one adds new knowledge to a field—to be the highest level of involvement within our discipline.

In Triad-based programs, we rely heavily on "how-to-books" for this early experience with knowledge about a field and especially with the "knowledge how" dimension of a field. Once students begin to shape up their problems and focus in a manner that reflects the accumulated wisdom of a field, they usually have a better perspective on the specific types of additional information they need to seek out. This pattern of information gathering and processing repeats itself many times, thus resulting in "back-and-forth" movement among the

Figure 3   Input/Process/Product Model

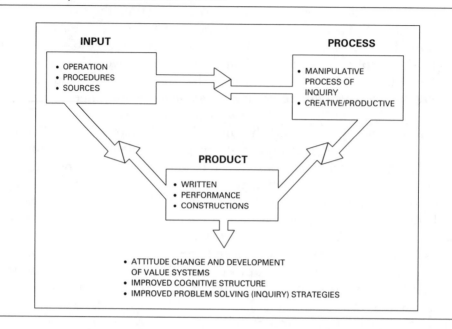

three major components depicted in Figure 3. Knowledge is thereby dealt with in a cyclical manner, and there is usually a simultaneous, rather than linear, processing of information. The importance or relevance of any given piece of knowledge is determined by the nature of the problem, which, along with the structure of the discipline, steers us toward appropriate input operations, procedures, and sources. I have also found that a frequent by-product of this process is the generation of creative ideas and new topics for investigation.

Returning now to the key questions. What knowledge is relevant? What knowledge is important? What knowledge is of greatest worth? The answer is that all knowledge is important, but it is only important to certain persons, at certain times, and in certain situations. Knowledge becomes real to the individual when he or she needs the information. If a real problem does anything for the learning process, it is to set up situations in which certain kinds of knowledge become relevant through necessity. Just as purpose creates real involvement on the parts of individuals, so also does it create a real need for knowledge.

The Role of Creativity (and Other Processes)

Emphasis on the thinking and feeling processes has been an important part of programming for the gifted and talented, and I believe this focus has been a generally favorable part of the overall movement. Since I have dealt with the role of process training in other publications (see especially Renzulli, 1977, pp. 5–1; 1980, pp. 5–6), only a brief rationale will be given here for placing

Table 4   The Role of Creativity and Discovery Learning

Learning/Instructional Model A	Learning/Instructional Model B
Situational Creativity	Real Creativity
Predetermined Discovery	Real Discovery

creativity, discovery learning, and other processes in the Model A column. First, process training activities are good for all students. This fact alone prevents them from being offered as the major rationale for qualitative differentiation. Secondly, because these activities are almost always based on the Four-P approach, the role of the student does not change. If we criticized the content-centered curriculum because it was supposedly guilty of "killing kids heads" with names, dates, formulas, and other facts, we must be equally cautious about an approach that simply and repeatedly triple-dips students in one process after another.

My main concern about creativity training is that it is situationally specific, i.e., based on presented situations or problems, and therefore, the responses of students are almost always products which have been "discovered" before. In other words, the products are new or creative for the individual but not new in the sense of coming up with a response that never existed before. Let me quickly add two reservations to the above statement. First, there is nothing wrong with this kind of training—all students should learn the process and how to apply it to problems they encounter in both the presented curriculum and real problems faced in their daily lives. Secondly, if a student comes up with a truly unique and practical suggestion for solving a problem, and develops a personal commitment to follow through on her or his suggestion, then we have the makings of a real problem situation. It is exactly for this reason that a direct connection is portrayed between Type II Enrichment, i.e., process training, and Type III Enrichment in the Triad Model.

In Learning/Instructional Model B, the focus upon real problems helps us to provide students with opportunities for developing products that are genuinely creative and/or truly unique contributions to knowledge. The study by Sandy is an example. To be certain, other persons have undoubtedly conducted studies using similar variables, instruments, and techniques, but her particular study and data base resulted in research findings about her community that never before existed. Therefore, her product is unique. She also made a "real discovery" rather than the discovery of a fact or principle we predetermined she should discover by neatly laying out tidbits of information which would lead to an existing conclusion. (A colleague of mine refers to the so-called guided discovery method as "sneaky telling.") Guided discovery is a good technique for helping all youngsters better understand existing knowledge, but let us not confuse it with the real thing and the creation of new knowledge.

Before leaving the process issue, I would like to clarify my position on the product/process controversy because I have been characterized as being overly concerned with students' products. I believe that products growing out of real problem situations are indeed important, but only insofar as such products serve as vehicles whereby the processes can be applied in authentic fashion. The processes we focus upon in structured training have no value in and of themselves unless we can put them to work in applied situations, and, as can be seen from the bottom of Figure 3, the ultimate outcome of the total model is not a product but rather three general sets of processes. Even these processes are of no value, however, without opportunities for additional, and hopefully more challenging, application.

The Role of the Teacher

The ways in which teachers' roles vary from Model A to Model B have been touched upon or implied in the foregoing discussion about the first three variables used in this analysis. Table 5 summarizes the main roles played in each model, and I want to emphasize at the outset that I am not minimizing the importance of teacher activities in Model A. In view of the requirements placed upon classroom teachers who work within a system almost totally dominated by the Four-P approach, it is nothing short of amazing that many teachers have been able to transform large parts of the regular curriculum into challenging and exciting endeavors. My concern here, however, is that we don't end up asking teachers of the gifted to play the same role traditionally assigned to classroom teachers.

The teacher's major responsibilities in Model B are summarized in the concentric circles surrounding the lightbulb in Figure 1 and have been elaborated upon in greater detail in the section of *Triad* dealing with Type III Enrichment. Our discussion here will focus upon what it means to be an expert in these Model B responsibilities and why this role is important in helping students pursue learning experiences that truly go beyond those ordinarily pursued in the regular curriculum.

Let us begin our discussion of the teacher's role by posing a dilemma with which we are all familiar. Teachers of the gifted cannot possibly be (or become) subject matter experts in the many topic areas in which their students are and should develop high levels of interest and task commitment. This is especially true at the elementary level where teachers are usually expected to provide services encompassing a variety of areas. A popular old educational myth is that "the teacher should learn along with the child," but this questionable ideal is hardly possible when you have several students working on a wide variety of topics. If the teacher's expertise is perhaps limited to a certain subject matter area, or if he or she is unwilling to allow youngsters to venture into certain topic areas lest the teacher's subject matter of competency be quickly outdistanced, there is a danger of imposing the same kind of control on the differentiated curriculum as we have placed on the regular school program.

Table 5   The Role of the Teacher

Learning/Instructional Model A	Learning/Instructional Model B
Administers Curriculum	Methodological Assistant
Orchestrates Exercises	Managerial Assistant
"Pseudo Expert" in Most Curricular Areas	"Expert" in the Above Two Activities
Provides "School House" Evaluation	Helps Student Seek Real Audience Evaluation

At the secondary level, teachers generally are more specialized in one or two subject matter areas, but in most cases they are far from being true experts in these subjects. For example, the teacher of history is usually not a historian, the physics teacher is not a physicist, and the music teacher ordinarily is not a composer. Keeping in mind our goal of truly advanced learning opportunities for the gifted, it is easy to see how students, even at the secondary level, can quickly outdistance their teachers in subject matter competency, especially if this competency relates to highly specialized topics within any given course or subject. Nevertheless, this is how it should be, because the alternative is to put reins on students whenever they challenge the upper limit of any teacher's expertise. We cannot promote the development of our next generation of leaders and creative producers if we are constantly reining in our most able students.

The way out of this dilemma is for teachers of the gifted to become true experts in certain basic skills that relate to the management of advanced level work. An important part of these managerial techniques is knowing the concepts underlying the structure of knowledge and investigative methodology discussed in *The Role of Knowledge*. I emphasize the word concepts because it is equally unrealistic for teachers to become proficient in the structure/methodology of several disciplines. They should, however, know that all areas of knowledge are characterized by certain organizational patterns, human and material resources, research methods and techniques, and vehicles for communicating findings with others who share a mutual interest. Another important role is demonstrating a willingness to help students locate resources, to open doors, and knock down barriers as they occur. In Sandy's case, the teacher helped her identify and obtain books on questionnaire design and interview technique, even though these books were located in a college library many miles from Sandy's community. In Paul's case, the weather bureau was at first unwilling to allow him access to the data he needed, necessitating intervention on the part of Paul's teacher to help open the door.

I have known many teachers of the gifted who are indeed real experts in the aforementioned techniques and have the energy to reach out beyond the always limited resources of their own buildings, libraries, and facilities. Their expertise is plainly evident in the accomplishments of their students and in the excitement and commitment these students always display in the pursuit of their individual goals.

THE Q-DEG QUIZ

Before we wrap up this analysis of our search for the illusive meaning of qualitative differences in gifted education, I want to reiterate my position on one or two items discussed in connection with Learning/Instructional Model A. I am not "against" prepared curriculum, curriculum development, or the inclusion of accelerated courses in our overall programming efforts for the gifted and talented. Neither am I "against" the Structure-of-Intellect model or Bloom's *Taxonomy*. All of these approaches should be included in a comprehensive plan for meeting the diversified needs of highly able youngsters. My main concern is that we look within these or any other approaches for opportunities to bring about honest changes in the four variables previously analyzed—the roles of students and teachers and the impact of knowledge and process. When we make these kinds of changes, I believe we will also then be taking a giant step forward, toward defining qualitative differences in learning. I have no doubt whatsoever that with appropriate modification some of the factors we have placed in the Model A column could very well end up differing enough from the regular curriculum to be transferred to Model B.

At the beginning of this article an argument was introduced that equated real problems with qualitative differences in learning. I would like to close by proposing a series of questions I call the Qualitative Differential Education for the Gifted (Q-DEG) Quiz. The questions were designed to be somewhat of an "acid test" for qualitative differences in learning and can be raised in connection with any particular piece of work a youngster does in a special program. If you agree that Sandy's study of teenage drinking and dating is representative of a real problem, you might want to keep her in mind as you review the questions.

In Sandy's case, the answers to the first four questions are NO; the remaining three are YES. These answers represent for me the characteristics of a qualitatively different learning experience and the makings of a real problem.

The Q-DEG Quiz

	YES	NO
1. Did every student do it?	—	—
2. Should every student do it?	—	—
3. Would every student want do to it?	—	—
4. Could every student do it?	—	—
5. Did the student do it willingly and with zest?	—	—
6. Did the student use appropriate resources and methodology?	—	—
7. Was the work directed toward having an impact upon an audience?	—	—

The teacher must keep alive
The spark of wonder
To prevent it from becoming
Blase from over-excitement,
Wooden from routine,
Fossilized through dogmatic
Instruction, or dissipated
Through random exercise
Upon trivial things.

(John Dewey, 1938)

NOTES

1. I must admit that I have not been able to differentiate in my own mind the differences between a theory and a model and will therefore take the liberty of using the terms interchangeably. I will also use the term, gifted education, to avoid the more cumbersome but proper education of the gifted.

2. I'm certain everyone reading this article remembers, for example, the Eleventh Amendment to the Constitution and the Articles of Confederation!

REFERENCES

Bloom, B. S. (Ed.). (1956). *Taxonomy of educational objectives, handbook I: The cognitive domain*. NY: McKay.

Dewey, J. (1933). *How we think: A restatement of the relation of reflective thinking to the educational process*. NY: Health.

Dewey, J. (1938). *Experience and education*. NY: MacMillan.

Guilford, J. P. (1967). *The nature of human intelligence*. NY: McGraw-Hill.

Machlup, F. (1980). *Knowledge and knowledge production*. Princeton, NJ: Princeton University Press.

Renzulli, J. S. (1977). *The enrichment triad model: A guide for developing defensible programs for the gifted and talented*. Mansfield Center, CT: Creative Learning Press.

Renzulli, J. S. (1980). Will the gifted child movement be alive and well in 1990? *Gifted Child Quarterly*, 24 (1), 3–9.

6

A General Theory for the Development of Creative Productivity Through the Pursuit of Ideal Acts of Learning[1]

Joseph S. Renzulli

The University of Connecticut

The great thing in this world is not so much where we stand as in what direction we are moving.

—Oliver Wendell Holmes

Editor's Note: From Renzulli, J. (1992). A general theory for the development of creative productivity through the pursuit of ideal acts of learning. *Gifted Child Quarterly*, *36*(4), 170-182. © 1992 National Association For Gifted Children. Reprinted with permission.

This article presents a general theory for developing creative productivity in young learners by examining the interactions between and among the learner, the curriculum, and the teacher. Further interactions within the learner dimension of the theory are examined by analyzing the relationships between and among learners' abilities, interests, and learning styles. Teacher interactions are examined by analyzing teachers' knowledge of the discipline that they are teaching, instructional techniques, and the teachers' "romance" with the discipline. The curriculum is examined by analyzing the structure of disciplines, the content and methodology of disciplines, and the discipline's appeal to the imagination of students. Also proposed is a three-dimensional research paradigm for examining creative productivity: (a) the types of creativity we are attempting to develop, (b) the domains in which creative pursuits are carried out, and (c) the contextual variables that influence the creative process.

INTRODUCTION

The history and culture of mankind can be charted to a large extent by the creative contributions of the world's most gifted and talented men and women. What causes some people to use their intellectual, motivational, and creative assets to achieve outstanding manifestations of creative productivity, while others with similar or perhaps even more considerable assets fail to attain high levels of accomplishment? The folk wisdom, research literature, and biographical and anecdotal accounts about creativity and giftedness are nothing short of mind-boggling: yet we are still unable to answer this fundamental question. Although it would be tempting to present yet another "combination-of-ingredients theory" to explain why some people achieve and others do not. I will forgo this temptation for two reasons. First, several writers (Tannenbaum, 1986; Mönks, van Boxtel, Roleofs, & Sanders, 1985; Sternberg & Davidson, 1986; Renzulli, 1978a, 1986) have already speculated about the necessary ingredients for creative productivity. These theories have called attention to important components of and conditions for creative accomplishment, but they fail to explain how the confluence of desirable traits ignites that inexplicable spark that gives rise to what Briggs (1990) has called "the fire in the crucible." That certain ingredients are necessary for creative productivity is not debatable; however, the specific traits, the extent to which they exist, and the ways they interact with one another will continue to be the basis for future theorizing, research, and controversy. For the present, we can assume that there are indeed minimum levels or thresholds of desirable combinations of assets that can be collectively summarized under the general headings of cognition, personality, and environment. Major contributions to these general areas of theory and research have been summarized in collected works on the topic such as *Conceptions of Giftedness* (Sternberg & Davidson, 1986), although most theorists agree that there is considerable overlap between and among the general categories.

Putting the Research to Use

The value of any theory in an applied discipline resides mainly in the power of that theory to generate research. Many of the ideas put forth in this article are derived from observations of outstanding learning experiences that have been characterized by the several interactions between and among teachers, learners, and the curriculum that form the organizational components of the theory. Practical applications would include additional methods of analyzing learner dimensions, more effective ways of selecting and training teachers, and greater attention to the development of curriculum that respects the subcomponents that form the three dimensions of the curriculum component of the theory. Although an emphasis in our field has been on teacher training, the advanced levels of knowledge, requirements for curriculum development, and especially the need for teachers with a "romantic" relationship with a discipline may require that future practice focus on teacher selection as much as teacher training.

Most theorists would agree that excess amounts of certain traits (e.g., intelligence) do not necessarily compensate for limited assets in other areas; and that some characteristics in extreme forms (e.g., perfectionism) may even be detrimental to creative productivity (Sternberg & Lubart, 1991, pp. 17–18). We need to learn more about all aspects of trait theory, but I also believe that new research in the 1990s and in the century ahead must begin to focus on that elusive "thing" that is left over when everything explainable has been explained. This "thing" is the true mystery of our common interest in creative productivity and the area that might represent a new frontier for research in the 21st century. I am not so bold as to think I can specify an agenda for this research; however, the suggestions offered here are certainly logical next steps that build upon what we already know and that hopefully will point the way toward future breakthroughs in understanding the manifestation of human potential.

The second reason that I will not revisit trait theory is that my own orientation is both psychological and educational; therefore, my work over the years has focused on the application of theory and research to practical situations in schools and classrooms. My major concern, from the perspective of an educational psychologist, is that my work be grounded in theory and research that allows for hypothesis testing but at the same time have practical applications that show promise for teaching and guiding the development of our most potentially able young people. Thus, when reference is made to the overall goal of my work—increasing creative productivity in young people—I am most concerned about this phenomenon in a developmental perspective. What we know about world-famous creative producers, the Edisons and the Curies, certainly guides us on our journey toward understanding this mysterious phenomenon, but my concern is with how we can promote a disposition toward creative productivity in today's classrooms. This kind of creative productivity, in most cases, will never be recorded in the annals of eminence, but if we can create a *modus operandi* for such productivity in larger and larger numbers of young people, then we may actually be contributing to the encouragement and development of Nobel Prize winners in the 21st century.

If we have learned anything over the past several years about human abilities, it is that knowledge about theories and research dealing with creative productivity are only an entry point for the pragmatist and the educational practitioner. Unless we can find ways of putting knowledge to work in practical real-life situations (schools and classrooms), our knowledge may lead us to more and better theories and to higher and higher degrees of sophisticated research, but it will not help us to increase the number and quality of creative persons on this earth. What also intrigues me in this regard is the distinct advantages that may result from practical applications, even if such applications fall short of rigorous theoretical underpinnings. One of my favorite sayings is, "If you truly want to understand something . . . try changing it!" I believe that our understanding of creative productivity will increase if we expand the rate of change through practical applications in an experimental context, even if such experimentation deals with some admittedly unconventional, obscure, ambiguous, and even downright nonsensical concepts. All of the knowledge in the world about the learner will come to naught unless we also examine the two other components that affect the act of learning: the teacher and the curriculum. Finally, if we are to advance our understanding of creative productivity, we must have a sense of the ideal, the way that things should be under optimal conditions. But we also must be cognizant of the realities that prevent us from achieving the ideal, and most of all we must learn to devote our resources to those conditions which we have the highest probability of changing. We cannot tell young people when and into which families they should be born or what their parents should be like, nor can we influence to a large extent their nutrition, home life, financial support, or a broad range of chance factors that will affect their lives. But we can influence a number of school-related factors, and it is these factors that I will focus on in pointing out how we can promote creative productivity by devoting our resources to the development of ideal acts of learning.

The purpose of this paper, therefore, is to present a general theory for the development of creative productivity by providing students with opportunities to engage in what I will refer to as ideal acts of learning. The three major components of the theory are *the learner, the teacher, and the curriculum.* The relationship between and among these components and their respective subcomponents are presented in Figure 1. The Venn diagram has been selected to portray these

Figure 1   An Ideal Act of Learning

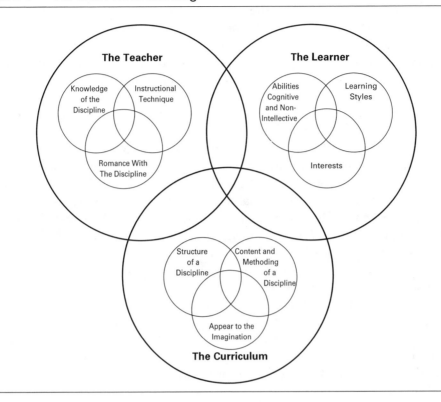

relationships because this type of diagram emphasizes dynamic *interactions* rather than linear relations. I would like to say at the outset that I am not proposing equity among the components and subcomponents. The circles undoubtedly vary in size from one learning situation to another, and even within a single learning situation. I am proposing, however, that all components must be present to some degree for ideal acts of learning to occur, an assertion, like any other theoretical proposition, which must ultimately be tested through research. Before proceeding, I would also like to say that this paper will not attempt to summarize the vast number of studies dealing with the learner, the teacher, and the curriculum. Rather, some pertinent examples will be cited within each component and subcomponent of the theory, and I will point out what I believe to be promising areas of future research and development.

THE LEARNER

Abilities

The vast majority of theory and research on human potential has focused on the cognitive and personality traits of the learner. One need only look at the almost endless list of tests for measuring intelligence, achievement, aptitude, and personality traits to realize the amount of research and development that has been devoted to this aspect of the learner. Although a good deal of this research has dealt with single traits (e.g., intelligence, risk taking, tolerance for ambiguity, perseverance, etc.), the confluence-of-trait theories have clearly emerged as the most promising vehicles for characterizing what we know about human abilities. In spite of all that has been done within trait and confluence theories, we still need more research that deals with the study of human abilities within the context of how these abilities are applied in the everyday world. We also need to examine why some persons who have the necessary components for creative productivity do not automatically manifest their potential in rigorous problem-finding and problem-solving situations. This recommendation is not a criticism of laboratory research or multivariate studies; however, a closer examination of *how* creative people do their work in real life situations will, I believe, add new insights beyond those that have focused on why they pursue complex tasks and which abilities they bring to their respective endeavors. The evolving-systems approach developed by Gruber and Davis (1988) uses a case-study methodology that allows researchers to focus on the interactions and relationships between and among a large number of issues. This approach seeks to understand how one organizes and reconstructs a life to form a system of knowledge, purpose, and affect that can lead to creative work. Gruber and Davis recommend the following three propositions for understanding the events related to creative problem solving:

1. Each creative person is a unique configuration.

2. The most challenging task of creativity research is to invent means of describing and explaining each unique configuration.

3. A theory of creativity that chooses to look only at common features of creative people probably is missing the main point of each life and evading the main responsibility of research on creativity. (p. 245)

Although past and present paradigms have served us well in advancing our understanding of creative productivity, the above propositions suggest that we need to go beyond the person, process, product paradigm that has guided research on creativity for the past several decades. And we also need to go beyond case studies of eminent persons, however valuable these studies have been in helping us to gain insights into the creative process. Because of my own interest in examining creative productivity in young people, I would like to recommend that the methodology suggested by Gruber and Davis (i.e., intensive studies of eminent persons) be applied to intensive studies of young people *at work* on problems that focus on authentic applications of cognitive, affective, and motivational processes. A figural representation of such a research paradigm is presented in Figure 2. In addition to the personological variables that have dominated research for so many years, these studies should also examine the

Figure 2   Paradigm for Case Study Research on the Development of Creative
Productivity in Young People

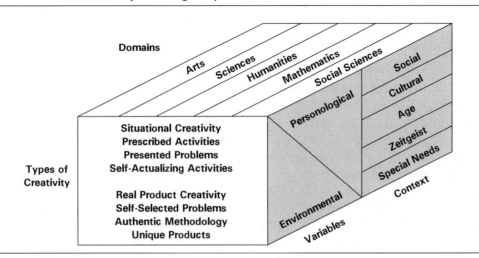

influence of environmental variables, the contexts in which young people
pursue their work, and the domains within which they are working. As Feldman
(1988) has pointed out, creative work requires mastery of a domain but does not
necessarily require mastery as an end point. Rather, the significant extension and
examination of the domain are the goals of the creative work. The personological variables studied should also be extended to include new and exciting ideas
such as Feldman's perspectives on the role of insight and transformations
(Feldman, 1988). And although major new research initiatives should be made
in the segment of Figure 2 dealing with real problem creativity, there is still much
to be learned about the types of situational creativity that are popular training
activities in programs for the gifted and talented.

It would be difficult to leave the abilities dimension of the learner without
speculating about some of the areas in which future research might be considered. Some of these recommendations overlap with the interest and learning
styles subcomponents of the learner; however, interrelationships rather than
discrete categories are the junctures that are emphasized in the Venn diagrams of
the general model. The suggestions that follow are not necessarily drawn from
the research literature. History, biography, autobiography, folklore, drama,
journalism, and fiction form the nonscientific rationale for these suggestions, some
of which undoubtedly fall into the unconventional and ambiguous categories
mentioned earlier.

One or a combination of these factors is usually present in persons who are the
object of our common concern; and indeed, it is usually these factors that have
brought such persons to our attention in the first place. My rationale for a list such
as this is that a better understanding of these factors might hold the key to finding
that elusive thing that is left over when everything explainable has been explained.

Interests

If there is a favored component in this overall model, and indeed in all of the work that I have done over the years, that component is interests. But what amazes and perplexes me the most about interests is that in spite of all that we know about the absolutely crucial role they play in learning and high levels of creative productivity, we know remarkably little about how and why interests originate in young people. I believe that all cognitive behavior is enhanced as a function of the degree of interest that is present in an act of learning, wherever that cognitive behavior may be on the continuum from basic skill learning to higher levels of creative productivity. The relationship between interest and learning was undoubtedly recognized by the first humans on earth, and it became a topic of scientific inquiry in the 19th century when philosophers recognized the close relationship between interest and learning (Herbart, 1806/1965, 1841/1965; James, 1890). Dewey (1913) and Thorndike (1935) called attention to the important role that interests play in all forms and levels of learning. They also recognized the importance of the *interestingness* of tasks and objects[2] as well as the personal characteristics of the learner. Piaget (1981) argued that all intellectual functioning depends on the energizing role that is played by affective processes such as interests, and he used the term *energetic* to describe this dimension of human information processing. Numerous empirical studies have also demonstrated that individual interests have profound influences on learning (Krapp, 1989; Renninger, 1989, 1990; Schiefele, 1988), and developmental theorists have acknowledged the importance of interests. Albert and Runco (1986) state that "it is primarily in those areas in which one takes a deep personal interest and has staked a salient aspect of one's identity that the more individualized and 'creative' components of one's personality are energized" (p. 343). Gruber (1986) argued that the main force in the self-construction of the extraordinary is the person's own activities and interests. Gruber also maintained that the shaping of a creative life may not necessarily involve precocity, early achievement, and single-mindedness, qualities that many scholars have attributed to the gifted.

Research studies that have examined the long-range effects of participation in programs based on the Enrichment Triad Model (Renzulli, 1977b) have indicated that the single best indicator of college majors and expressions of career choice on the part of young adults have been intensive involvement in projects (i.e., Type III Enrichment) based on early interests (Hébert, in preparation). We also have learned that high-ability students who participated in a gifted program for 5 years or longer in which they displayed higher levels of creative productivity than their equally able peers were remarkably similar to their peers, with one notable exception. The more creatively productive group displayed early, consistent, and more intense interests (Reis & Renzulli, in preparation).

Although this research does not unravel the mystery of why interests are formed, the procedures used in Triad-based programs may provide some clues about how we can promote interest development. First, general interest assessment information is gathered through an informal instrument called the *Interest-A-Lyzer*

Figure 3   The Energizing Function

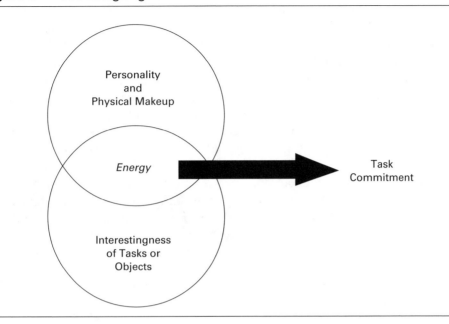

(Renzulli, 1977a) or a parallel form of the instrument specifically designed for primary age students entitled *My Book of Things and Stuff* (McGreevy, 1982). Next, a variety of interest development activities (Type I Enrichment) based on the general categories of interests for a given group are provided. An effort is made to select activities (e.g., speakers, demonstrations, visitations, etc.) within any given category that are likely to promote excitement and motivation. Subsequent discussions and debriefings are designed to explore potential follow-up investigations, but the follow-up must adhere to guidelines that define Type III Enrichment (i.e., based on the *modus operandi* of the practicing professional rather than the lesson learner). Student choice is the key ingredient in determining whether or not follow-up will be pursued. At this point, every effort must be made to promote interestingness of tasks or objects at each progressively complex level of involvement with the topic.

Interestingness of tasks and task commitment are interdependent constructs. One of the most frequently asked questions about my own work in connection with the three-ring conception of giftedness (Renzulli, 1978a, 1986) is: Where does task commitment come from? Although the answer to this question is undoubtedly a complex one, a major contribution to what may be called the energizing function is unquestionably the interaction between the amount of energy that is part of the individual's personality and physical make-up on one hand, and the interestingness of the task or object on the other. This relationship is represented in Figure 3.

Not all tasks and objects within a given domain are created equal so far as interestingness is concerned, and unfortunately there has been very little if any research that deals directly with ways of evaluating interestingness. Amabile (1989) reviewed several studies dealing with the ways in which work environments influence creativity, and Ward (1969) found that children who pursue creativity tasks in an environmentally rich room show higher levels of ideational fluency than children who performed in a bare room. Feldhusen, Hobson, and Treffinger (1975) found that subjects engaged in a divergent thinking task produced more original responses when provided with verbal stimuli associated with remote responses. If we are to capitalize on what we know about the crucial roles played by interest and task commitment in creative productivity, this type of research, which examines factors outside the individual, might help us to identify those topics that have the highest degrees of interestingness. This research might begin by recruiting persons with experience in a domain to identify those aspects of a topic that hold the greatest potential for stimulating interest and excitement on the parts of students. Although investigations of the energizing function will certainly add to our understanding of interest development and task commitment, this function is undoubtedly buried deep within the physical and psychological make-up of the individual. It is for this reason that a careful analysis of interestingness of tasks or objects is recommended as a potentially valuable area of inquiry within this general model.

Learning Styles

Several investigators have suggested that an area of major importance in which students differ is their style of learning. Learning styles have been variously defined according to psychological types such as introversion versus extroversion (Myers, 1980) and preference for varying degrees of structure in the learning process (Hunt, 1975). Kolb, Rubin, and McIntyre (1971) and Gregorc (1985) have proposed that styles vary according to preferences that can be plotted on axes ranging from concrete to abstract and from sequential to random. Dunn, Dunn, and Price (1975) proposed a definition and instrument based on student preferences for various physical characteristics of the learning environment (e.g., auditory and mobility preferences, comfort requirements, and preference for individual versus group work), and Barbe and Swassing (1979) have examined learning styles in terms of sensory modality preference (visual, auditory, tactile, and kinesthetic). Renzulli and Smith (1978) developed an instrument that assesses styles in correspondence with the following instructional techniques: Projects, Drill and Recitation, Peer Teaching, Discussion, Simulation and Teaching Games, Independent Study, Programmed Instruction, and Lecture (Smith, 1976). Sternberg's (1988) recent work on intellectual styles proposes that we examine this dimension of the learner according to preferences for function, which he describes in terms of legislative (creation, formulation, and planning), executive (the execution of plans and ideas), and judicial (monitoring, judging, and evaluating).

Most of the persons who have contributed to the literature on learning styles are in agreement about certain issues. First, there may be "natural" preferences for a particular style that are a function of personality variables; however, styles are also a function of socialization, and therefore several styles can be developed. Second, there is a complexity of interactions between and among styles, and styles further interact with abilities and interests. Third, certain curricular or environmental situations favor the applicability of some styles over others. In other words, there is a style-by-task interaction that is dictated by the nature of the material to be learned. Thus, for example, learning traditional mathematical concepts may favor structured, sequential styles and corresponding modes of instruction, whereas brainstorming possible approaches to addressing a societal problem will undoubtedly favor persons who are more extroverted, have greater preference for unstructured situations, and derive satisfaction from interacting with their peers. Finally, the reward structure of learning situations influences the development of style. Teachers who place a premium on order, control, and conformity are likely to promote more structured and less innovative styles in malleable learners. It is conceivable that long-term exposure to highly structured teaching may eventually result in a rigidity of style that minimizes adaptability to situations requiring the skills necessary for creative productivity. If personality factors or supportive family or peer intervention do not override school-created styles, persons with extremely high degrees of ability and interest in a particular area may fail to achieve their potential for creatively productive contributions.

Since it is the intent of this paper to focus on school-related recommendations, I will first offer an ideal (and perhaps obvious) suggestion, but I will also add a more realistic and systematic approach that we should consider in the majority of cases where the ideal cannot be accomplished. Ideally, we should attempt to match students with teachers and learning environments that capitalize upon their preferred style. Several studies have indicated that more effective learning results from this type of matching, especially in areas where the matching is based on preference for instructional methods rather than personality variables (James, 1962: Yando & Kagen, 1968; Pascal, 1971; Hunt, 1971; Smith & Renzulli, 1984). We should, therefore, devote considerable effort to analyzing the preferred learning styles of students and look for opportunities to place students with teachers who have compatible styles. But the style-by-task interaction mentioned above, and the fact that most teaching situations are group rather than individually oriented, ordinarily prevents us from achieving this ideal. To a large extent, the teacher and the nature of the subject matter structure the ways in which certain tasks will be pursued. Even in cases in which a single mentor can be arranged for an individual student, the match may be more in harmony with mutual interest in the topic rather than with a compatible learning or intellectual style.

A more realistic approach to capitalizing upon differences in learning style is to begin in the early years of schooling to provide young students with a broad range of experiences that expose them to various styles. In much the same ways that we provide systematic coverage and documentation of content, so also should we be exposing students to carefully planned ways of using various instructional styles. Thus, for example, a teacher might announce at the beginning of an instructional unit, "We are going to study the economic law of supply and demand by engaging in a simulation in which each of you will have control over the buying and selling of major food product groups." The teacher should explain what a simulation is, why it has been selected for use in connection with this topic, and how it compares with other instructional styles through which the topic might be taught. These advanced organizers should call attention to the pedagogy on the learning situation as well as the content and processes to be learned.

Following exposure to a particular style, a careful postlearning analysis should be conducted that focuses on the unique properties of the purposefully selected instructional technique. Students should be encouraged to discuss and record in their journals their reactions to the instructional technique in terms of both efficiency in learning and the amount of pleasure they derive from the technique. The goal of the postlearning analysis is to help students understand more about themselves by understanding more about their preferences in a particular situation. The collective experiences in learning styles should provide: (a) exposure to many styles, (b) an understanding of which styles are the most personally applicable to particular subjects, and (c) experience in how to blend styles in order to maximize both the effectiveness and satisfaction of learning. The ultimate goal of teaching students about learning styles should be to develop in each student both a repertoire of styles and the strategies that are necessary to assist students in modifying their styles better to fit future learning or career tasks. In much the same way that a golf player examines distance, wind conditions, and obstacles before selecting the appropriate golf club, so also should we teach students to examine learning situations with an eye toward selecting and applying the most appropriate styles.

In a certain sense, the type of training and analysis of styles suggested here might be viewed as a specific form of flexibility training typically associated with the pedagogy used in creative thinking. Although there are undoubtedly a variety of ways in which such training might be organized, the approach recommended here would focus on instructional methods that vary by degree of structure and how structure interacts with the nature of the material to be learned.

The Curriculum

Although much has been written about curriculum development for the gifted, a good deal of this material might best be described as ordinary lists of curricular principles or "should lists" that focus on thinking skills, abstract concepts, advanced level content, interdisciplinary studies, thematic approaches, and a blending of content, process, and product. A careful examination of these principles leads to the conclusion that they are applicable to most, if not all, of the general curriculum. The fact that there have been very few "small wars" between general and special curricular advocates or among persons writing about curriculum for the gifted is testimony to the acceptance of these lists of principles by both general and special educators. But the lack of controversy may also be indicative of a shortage of truly differentiated curriculum theory.

In an effort to identify what might be relatively unique aspects of curriculum for the gifted, a rationale was developed that combines a theory of knowledge (James, 1885: Whitehead, 1929) with contemporary conceptions of giftedness and the anticipated professional roles that we expect persons of high potential to fulfill in their future lives. This rationale also draws upon selected concepts from curricular and instructional theory, and it has been configured into a practical guide for curriculum writers entitled *The Multiple Menu Model for Developing Differentiated Curriculum for the Gifted* (Renzulli, 1988). A graphic representation of this model is presented in Figure 4: three of the major components of the model will be discussed in the sections that follow.

Structure of a Discipline

The predominant value of a discipline lies not so much in its accumulated facts and principles as in its systematic way of thinking about a body of knowledge—its forms and connections, its unsolved problems, its methods of inquiry, its aspirations for improving mankind, and the special way it looks at phenomena. A concern for structure even includes the folklore, humor, personalities, gossip, and insiders' knowledge that causes a person to be a member of the discipline rather than merely a student studying about the discipline. Curricular emphasis on the structure or "psychology" of a discipline is recommended because *advanced* involvement in any area of study requires that the interested novitiate learn how to think in the discipline. Perhaps an analogy will clarify what thinking in a discipline means. Some people can communicate in a non-native language, but they don't know how to think in that language. They communicate by simply translating words they hear or read into their native language, formulating a mental response in their native language, and then translating that response into written or spoken words in the non-native language. Similarly, in mathematics, some people can solve standard problems, even very complex ones, by using replicative thinking—simply "plugging" information into a formula and performing customary calculations. But without being able to think *mathematically*, it is unlikely that this person will be able to deal with nonstandard problems, let alone make contributions that will lead to the advancement of the discipline.

One of the most debated issues in curriculum is, Shouldn't all students be taught to think in the discipline? My answer to this question will obviously be controversial because it has implications about the grouping of students and, indeed, the very justification for having special programs for the gifted. I believe that all students should have the opportunity for experiences that lead to within-discipline thinking, but I also believe that *all curriculum should be arranged so that whatever paths students travel and whatever distances they travel on these paths must be appropriate to their unique abilities, interests, and learning styles.*

Figure 4 The Multiple Menu Model for Developing Differentiated Curriculum (JSR: 1987)

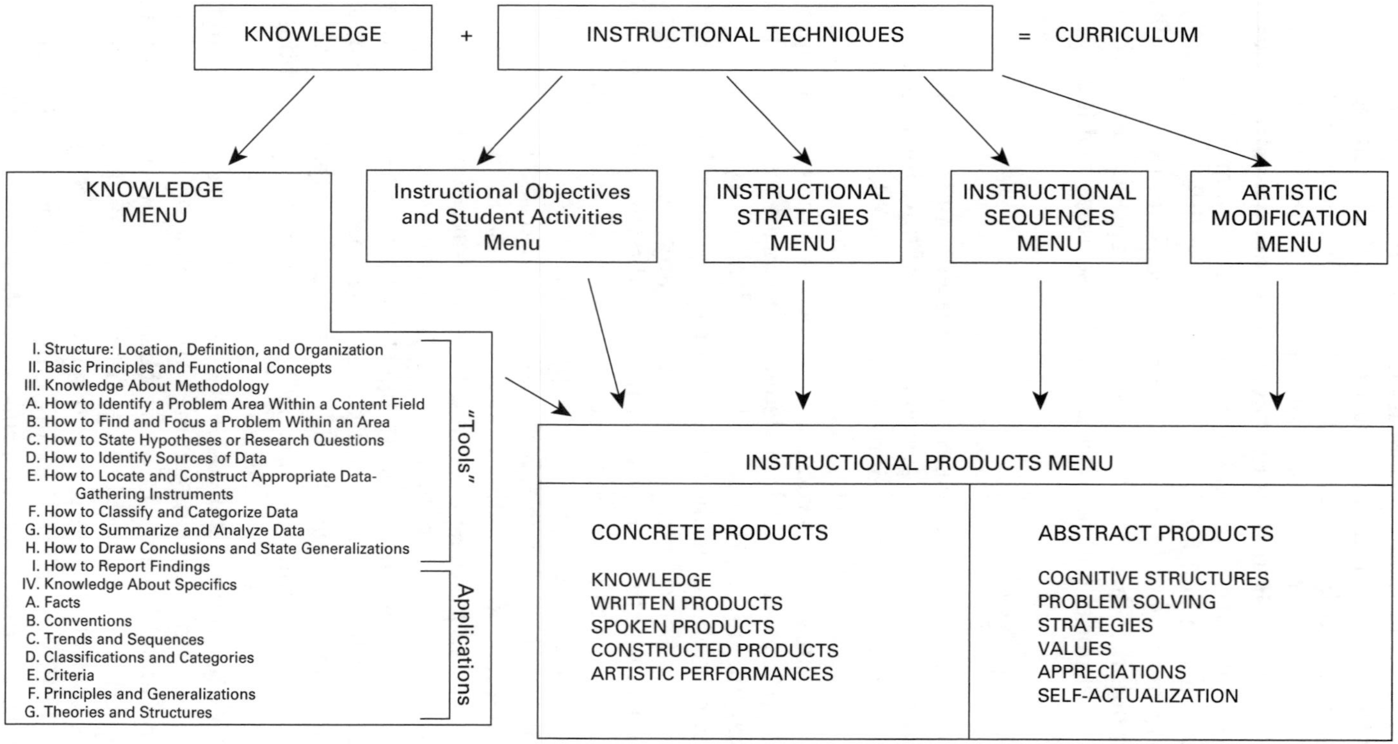

KNOWLEDGE + INSTRUCTIONAL TECHNIQUES = CURRICULUM

KNOWLEDGE MENU

"Tools"

I. Structure: Location, Definition, and Organization
II. Basic Principles and Functional Concepts
III. Knowledge About Methodology
A. How to Identify a Problem Area Within a Content Field
B. How to Find and Focus a Problem Within an Area
C. How to State Hypotheses or Research Questions
D. How to Identify Sources of Data
E. How to Locate and Construct Appropriate Data-Gathering Instruments
F. How to Classify and Categorize Data
G. How to Summarize and Analyze Data
H. How to Draw Conclusions and State Generalizations
I. How to Report Findings

Applications

IV. Knowledge About Specifics
A. Facts
B. Conventions
C. Trends and Sequences
D. Classifications and Categories
E. Criteria
F. Principles and Generalizations
G. Theories and Structures

Instructional Objectives and Student Activities Menu

INSTRUCTIONAL STRATEGIES MENU

INSTRUCTIONAL SEQUENCES MENU

ARTISTIC MODIFICATION MENU

INSTRUCTIONAL PRODUCTS MENU

CONCRETE PRODUCTS

KNOWLEDGE
WRITTEN PRODUCTS
SPOKEN PRODUCTS
CONSTRUCTED PRODUCTS
ARTISTIC PERFORMANCES

ABSTRACT PRODUCTS

COGNITIVE STRUCTURES
PROBLEM SOLVING
STRATEGIES
VALUES
APPRECIATIONS
SELF-ACTUALIZATION

An attempt has been made in the Multiple Menu Model to promote within-discipline thinking by recommending a series of curricular experiences based on the following questions:

1. What is the overall purpose or mission of this field of study?

2. What are the major areas of concentration of the field and its subdivisions?

3. What kinds of questions are asked in the subdivisions?

4. What are the major sources of data in each subdivision?

5. How is knowledge organized and classified in this field or subdivision?

6. What are the basic reference books in the field or subdivision?

7. What are the major professional journals?

8. What are the major data bases? How can we gain access to them?

9. Is there a history or chronology of events that will lead to a better understanding of the field or subdivision?

10. Are there any major events, persons, places, or beliefs that are predominant concerns of the field or best-case examples of what the field is all about?

11. What are some selected examples of "insiders' knowledge" such as field-specific humor, trivia, abbreviations and acronyms, "meccas," scandals, hidden realities, or unspoken beliefs?

Activities based on these questions should be developed in a way that places the learner in the role of a professional or first-hand inquirer in a field rather than that of a mere assimilator of information, however advanced that information may be. This can be done by creating a mind set in students that all knowledge should be viewed as temporary, imperfect, and imprecise. Every experience should be viewed as a confrontation with knowledge, and students should be empowered to believe that they have the license to question, criticize, and, most importantly, add their own interpretations and contributions to existing knowledge. The concept of validation of knowledge and the direct teaching of epistemology (i.e., different ways of knowing such as authoritarianism, empiricism, revelation, etc.) is another kind of confrontation that teaches students the metacognitive procedures for examining critically their own interpretations and creative contributions. A confrontation with knowledge means that everything that is already known, or that we hope students will acquire, is secondary to the development of mind in general and within-discipline thinking in particular.

Content and Methodology of a Discipline

Content selection is undoubtedly one of the most difficult problems curriculum developers face, and within this problem two overriding issues must be addressed. The first issue deals with which topics should be included in a course or curricular unit, and the second is the level of advancement or complexity with which the topics should be covered. With regard to the first issue, the approach suggested here is based on the work of Phenix (1964), who recommends that a focus on representative concepts and ideas is the best way to capture the essence of a discipline. Representative ideas or concepts consist of themes, patterns, main features, sequences, organizing principles and structures, and the logic that defines a discipline and distinguishes it from other disciplines. Representative ideas and concepts can also be used as the bases for interdisciplinary or multidisciplinary studies; however, issues related to structure that were discussed above should be considered when drawing on two or more domains of knowledge.

Building a curriculum on representative concepts also allows us to introduce an element of economy into content selection. The vast amount of material within any given discipline prevents unlimited coverage of content; therefore, material must be selected so that it is both representative and maximally transferable. A three-phase approach is recommended that takes into consideration the interaction between intensive versus extensive coverage and group versus individual learning situations. Thus, in Phase I (Intensive/Group), a representative concept in literature such as tragic heroes might be dealt with through intensive examination of two or three prototypical examples (e.g., *King Lear and The Autobiography of Malcolm X*). Selections of more than a single exemplar of the concept allow for both in-depth analysis and opportunities to compare and contrast authors' styles, historical perspectives, cultural differences, and a host of other comparative factors that single selections would prohibit. The payoff so far as transfer is concerned is to follow the in-depth coverage with a meta-analysis or debriefing of factors (i.e., characteristic themes, patterns, etc.) that define the representative concept. The goal of the meta-analysis is to help consolidate cognitive structures and patterns of analysis developed through in-depth study of a small number of literary selections so that they are readily available for use in future situations.

Phase II (Extensive/Group) consists of the perusal of large numbers of literary contributions dealing with tragic heroes to which similar cognitive structures and patterns of analysis can be applied. Although perusal of large numbers is recommended, coverage should be *purposefully* superficial but geared toward stimulating follow-up by interested individuals. This follow-up which might take place immediately or in later life, represents Phase III of the process, an Intensive/Individual examination of material dealing with the concept of tragic heroes. Phase III might be formal study or simply the more sophisticated appreciation that one derives from reading for pleasure or viewing a play.

The second issue in content selection, the level of advancement or complexity of material, must first and foremost take into consideration age and ability, maturity, previous study, and experiential background. Beyond these considerations, three principles of content selection are recommended. First, curricular material for high-ability students should escalate along a hierarchy of the following dimensions of knowledge: facts, conventions, trends and sequences, classifications and categories, criteria, principles and generalizations, and theories and structures. Second, movement toward the highest level, theories and structures, should involve continuous recycling to lower levels so that facts, trends and sequences, and so forth can be understood in relation to a more integrated whole rather than isolated bits of irrelevant information. Third, the cluster of diverse procedures that surround the acquisition of knowledge—that dimension of learning commonly referred to as "process" or thinking skills—should themselves be viewed as a form of content. It is these more enduring skills that form the cognitive structures and problem-solving strategies that have the greatest transfer value. When we view process as content, we avoid the artificial dichotomy and the endless arguments about whether content or process should be the primary goal of learning. Combining content and process leads to a goal that is larger than the sum of the respective parts. Simply stated, this goal is the acquisition of a scheme for acquiring, managing, and producing information in an organized and systematic fashion.

The best example of process as content can be found in teaching the methodology of a discipline. In my own work, and especially the Type III dimension of the Enrichment Triad Model (Renzulli, 1977b), the focus on methodology is mainly directed toward providing young people with first-hand experiences in the production of knowledge and helping them to confront the all-important issue of "what makes a problem real" (Renzulli, 1978b). This focus is based on what I believe to be the most powerful rationale for special education for the gifted and talented. Justification for special services for the gifted rests, in part, on the anticipated social roles that we expect young people of high potential to play in their future lives, both in terms of their own self-fulfillment and in the advancement of the human condition. Supplementary investments in their education are justified because we assert that these young people will be the leaders and contributors to their respective fields of professional involvement. If we accept this assertion, then it follows logically that a focus on methods of inquiry is the most direct way to prepare high-potential youth for these roles. A focus on methodology means more than just teaching students methods of inquiry as content. Rather, it is designed to promote an understanding of and appreciation for the application of methods to the kinds of problems that are the essence of particular fields of knowledge. The goal of a focus on methodology is to cast the young person in the role of a first-hand inquirer rather than a mere learner-of-lessons, even if this role is carried out at a more junior level than the adult professional. This role encourages young learners to engage in the kinds of thinking, feeling, and doing that characterize the work of the practicing professional because it automatically creates the kind of confrontation with knowledge described above.

Appeal to the Imagination

Within the context of curricular decision making, there is one additional consideration that should be addressed. Phenix (1964) has termed this concept the appeal to the imagination, and he argues very persuasively for the selection of curricular material that will lift students to new planes of experience and meaning. Material drawn from the extraordinary should allow students to "see more deeply, feel more intensely, and comprehend more fully" (p. 346). Phenix sets forth three conditions that should guide our thinking with regard to this concept and the role that teachers play in the pursuit of imaginative teaching. First, he points out that the means for stimulating the imagination differ according to the individual, his or her level of maturity, and the cultural context in which the individual is located. Second, the teacher must exemplify the imaginative qualities of mind we are trying to develop in students and be able to enter sympathetically into the lives of students. Finally, imaginative teaching requires faith in the possibility of awakening imagination in any and every student, regardless of the kinds of constraints that may be placed on the learning process.

There are, undoubtedly, different perspectives about how to select content that will appeal to the imagination. A curriculum with such a focus could easily fall prey to material that deals with seductive details or esoteric and sensational topics. I do not believe that seductive details and so forth are inherently inappropriate as curriculum material. Indeed, they often serve the important function of stimulating initial interest and creating what Whitehead (1929) called the romance stage with a topic or field of study. But if seductive details and sensational topics become ends rather than means for promoting advanced understanding, then we have traded appeal to the imagination for romanticism and showmanship.

How then should we go about selecting curriculum material that appeals to the imagination but is not based purely on sensationalism? I believe the answer rests, in part, on selecting content that represents powerful and controversial manifestations of basic ideas and concepts. Thus, for example, the concepts of loyalty versus betrayal might be examined and compared in political, literary, military, or family perspectives, but always in ways that bring intensity, debate, and personal involvement to the concepts. An adversarial approach to ideas and concepts (i.e., loyalty versus betrayal) also guarantees that the essential element of confrontation with knowledge will be present in selected curricular topics. In a certain sense, it would be feasible to write the history of creative productivity as a chronicle of men and women who confronted existing ideas and concepts in an adversarial fashion and who used existing information only as counterpoints to what eventually became their own unique contributions to the growth of knowledge. It was these confrontations that sparked their imaginations, and it is for this reason, I believe, that an appeal to the imagination should be a major curricular focus for the gifted.

THE TEACHER

The role of the teacher in almost any formal learning situation is well-recognized and may indeed be the most important single ingredient in this or any other model of learning. And when we view teachers in expanded roles as mentors and models, their significance in the lives of young people with high potential becomes more prominent. When Walberg, Rasher, and Parkerson (1980) examined the biographical antecedents of persons of accomplishment, they found that almost two thirds of their subjects were exposed to creatively productive persons at very early ages. Bloom (1985) reported that demanding teachers and mentors played an important role in the development of high-achieving youth, and Goertzel, Goertzel, and Goertzel (1978) concluded in their biographical study of eminent persons that mentors were especially important in evoking motivation. And a compendious biographical and autobiographical literature also points to the significant roles that dedicated teachers-as-mentors have played in the development of persons who have made important contributions to their respective areas of study.

Extensive studies on various aspects of teacher effectiveness have been summarized in publications such as the *Handbook of Educational Research on Teaching* (Gage, 1963, 1973; Wittrock, 1986), and a number of studies have been reported that deal with the general characteristics of teachers of the gifted (Bishop, 1981; Feldhusen & Hansen, 1988; Gear. 1979; Gowan & Brunch, 1967; Lindsey, 1980; McNary, 1967; Maker, 1975; Mulhern & Ward. 1983; Pierson, 1985; Whitlock & Ducette, 1989). Only a small number of studies have focused on the kinds of teachers that promote high levels of creative productivity in their students. One large sample study ($N = 671$) dealing with this topic (Chambers, 1973) found that teachers who fostered creativity tended to allow students greater choice in the selection of topics, welcomed unorthodox views, rewarded divergent thinking, expressed enthusiasm for teaching, interacted with their students outside of class, and generally conducted classes in an informal manner. In a study by Torrance (1981) that examined follow-up data of adolescent and adult creative behavior, 220 subjects provided anecdotal reflections about "teachers that made a difference." The findings support Chambers' conclusions and also point out teacher attitudes and techniques that helped young learners "fall in love" with a topic or subject to such an extent that it became the center of their future career image.

In a qualitative study by Story (1985) that focused on six teachers who were guiding students through Type III investigations, teachers of the gifted displayed several common characteristics. First, they established positive relationships with their students by always working in close proximity with them. The frequent verbal interaction between teacher and student was of high quality, including verbal motivation, higher level questioning skills, and a reciprocal sense of humor. The teachers were flexible about their use of time and scheduling, spending more time with students as it became necessary. Finally, the teachers recognized that their students' creative productivity was an ultimate goal, and thus, the teachers provided human and physical resources to help students realize this goal.

An attempt will not be made here to draw conclusions from the voluminous literature on teachers and teaching, nor will an attempt be made to point out the controversies that currently exist with regard to the selection and preparation of teachers. Rather, the focus will be on three major components that constitute the ideal teacher of the gifted and the ways in which these components interact with one another and with the learner and curriculum dimensions of the model. Finally, recommendations will be made for some suggested areas of research dealing with this crucial component of ideal acts of learning.

Knowledge of the Discipline

Arguments go back and forth about the degree to which teachers should be masters of the content area(s) in which they teach. For a number of years, a major emphasis in gifted education was placed on "process," and although no one ever stated directly that knowledge of a discipline was *un*important, an unspoken reality was that the majority of teacher training within the field dealt almost exclusively with instructional technique rather than advanced mastery of an academic or artistic discipline.

Many problems are inherent in the content versus process controversy in preparing teachers of the gifted, not the least of which is the age or grade level of one's students. It is reasonable to argue that primary and elementary grade teachers, those who are responsible for teaching several subjects rather than specializing in one area, cannot be expected to be expert in all areas. But it can also be argued that advanced coverage of any topic requires advanced knowledge and understanding on the part of persons who are directing the work of bright young people. The position taken here is that advanced competency in at least one discipline is important because it is through such content mastery and personal involvement that teachers, even if they are dealing with topics outside of their major area, develop the kind of appreciation for within-discipline thinking that improves the guidance of learning in other areas. Equally important for teachers of high-potential young children is an understanding of general research methodologies[3] and a repertoire of managerial skills that allows them to guide students through investigative activities (Renzulli & Reis, 1985).

Teachers at upper grade levels must, of course, develop advanced competency in their field of specialization, and I do not think that anyone would argue against advanced study in one's academic discipline as a minimum requirement for teachers of upper grade gifted youth. But advanced competency, in and of itself, is no guarantee that high-quality teaching will take place. We only need look at typical university teaching to realize that highly competent specialists often teach in uninspiring ways that are characterized by what Schwab and Brandwein (1962) described disparagingly as "memorizing a rhetoric of conclusions" (p. 24) and what Dewey (1929) critically called "the spectator theory of knowledge" (p. 23). Knowledge of the discipline means far more than merely knowing the facts, principles, and theories that define an area of knowledge. It also means knowing and understanding the role of methodology and being able to guide students through the application of methodology in real problem situations. It is this level of involvement—the application of authentic investigative methods to self-selected and personally meaningful problems—that I believe represents true differentiation in learning. In the sections that follow, two additional characteristics of teachers that transcend advanced knowledge and that are modeled on the teacher-as-mentor literature mentioned above will be discussed.

Instructional Technique

The essential issue regarding instructional technique, and especially technique that fosters creative productivity, is best phrased as a question. To what extent is effective technique a "natural" characteristic of the individual teacher, and to what extent can it be taught? Both personality and training contribute to the development of teachers who encourage and facilitate creativity. Years of training teachers of the gifted have led me to believe that certain personality characteristics are necessary for highly effective teaching of the gifted. These characteristics, which are generally found in confident but nonauthoritative persons, include flexibility, openness to experience and new ideas, a high energy level, optimism, commitment to excellence, and enthusiasm for living. These characteristics are viewed as "starting material," and they are important enough for me to recommend that *teacher selection should be a consideration that precedes teacher training*.

But training in pedagogy also plays an important role, and I have attempted to describe the areas upon which teacher training should focus in the four menus subsumed under Instructional Technique in Figure 4. The Instructional Objectives and Student Activities Menu addresses the following hierarchy of thinking processes: Information Pick-up (assimilation and retention), Information Analysis (higher order processing), Information Output (synthesis and application), and Evaluation (review and critique). The Instructional Strategies Menu identifies 14 teaching strategies that range along a continuum from structured to unstructured patterns for organizing learning. The Instructional Sequence Menu deals mainly with organizational and management techniques, and the Artistic Modification Menu focuses on techniques that personalize the teaching process and encourage teachers to put themselves *into* the material rather than merely teaching about it. Although teachers undoubtedly have "natural" preferences for specific techniques within the several categories that constitute each instructional menu, the broad range of differences that will be encountered in working with gifted students requires that a repertoire of techniques be developed. Ideal acts of learning will obviously be enhanced if there is a perfect match between teacher and learner styles. Perfect matches, however, are the exception rather than the rule: therefore, teacher training should be geared toward developing a range of teaching styles and encouraging a flexible use of styles to accommodate individual abilities, interests, and learning styles.

Romance With the Discipline

One of the characteristics that distinguishes truly inspiring teachers is their love for the material they are teaching. Most of what we know about teachers who have this romance with their discipline comes from biographical and auto-biographical accounts of well-known persons who were inspired and guided by an outstanding teacher. A recent book edited by John C. Board, *A Special Relationship: Our Teachers and How We Learned* (1991), consists of the memoirs of eminent persons from all walks of life who describe the important roles that outstanding teachers played in their early development. In analyzing the common themes that existed between teachers and learners, Board comments:

> These teachers, almost without exception, displayed masterful com-mand of their subject matter. All were caring. All were possessed of an uncanny ability to unleash youthful potential. All were demanding, all relentless in their determination to ignite in every student the will to excel. And all were, to borrow Louis Nizer's words, "alike in their boundless energy." (p. 19)

Board goes on to describe what he calls "an uncommon characteristic that great teachers hold in common," and that characteristic is their own passion for knowledge and learning. They view themselves as a part of the discipline rather than as a person who merely studies about it or teaches it to others. This characteristic may have more important consequences for the identification and development of high-level talent than is immediately obvious.

Although it is only speculation on my part, I believe that it is this romantic relationship with a discipline that causes certain teachers to seek out and nurture students of remarkable potential. In much the same way that the owner of a successful business or *objet d'art* wants to insure that a prized possession is passed on to someone who is a trustworthy recipient, teachers who have a romantic relationship with a discipline will be similarly concerned about the intellectual heirs of their beloved field of study. Our most obvious paradigm for master/apprentice relations is that the apprentice seeks out the master because of his or her reputation in a particular area of study. This scenario may very well be the case in most instances and at the earliest points of contact. But in cases where teachers are responsible for many students, and especially if the group is a highly select one to begin with, it may be the passionate teacher who identifies the *most* promising student and who provides this student with extraordinary opportunities, resources, and encouragement.

Although the teacher's technique and romance with a discipline may not be as objectively verifiable as the extent of knowledge and methodology that the teacher possesses, the importance of these characteristics in the development of creative productivity in young people should cause us to examine them more carefully. The careful study of talented teachers *at work* with high-potential students in learning situations that place a premium on creative productivity should be documented so that we can learn more about the special relationships that have been described in the literature. A good starting point for such studies might be to compile lists of teachers whose students have consistently performed well in situations where high-quality products (rather than test scores or grades) were the criteria for success: and the best procedure for this type of research is the qualitative, case study method. Studies of this type will undoubtedly be more time-consuming and less precise than multivariate or retrospective studies because we are seeking to examine a process rather than "measure traits," and we are also looking at a large number of contextual variables at the same time. But case studies that focus on painstaking examinations of the interactions between teachers and students in various age groups, cultures, disciplines, and learning environments may lead to some conclusions and generalizations that are replicable, even within these areas of teaching that many view as an art rather than a science.

Toward the Year 2000 and Beyond

Educational and psychological research has made remarkable progress during the past two centuries in helping us to understand the complex nature of giftedness. And the wide variety of programming options that have emerged during the latter part of the present century have helped us learn a great deal about practical ways better to serve young people of exceptional promise. But the continued growth of our field requires that we extend our research and development efforts into areas that have only been touched upon or largely ignored. It is time to go beyond the multitude of studies that deal with the same cluster of traits that have been the repeated focus of so much of our research. We still have not found "that elusive 'thing' that is left over when everything explainable has been explained." Therefore, we need to strike out on a path of bold new investigations that consider some of the admittedly vague but intriguingly enigmatic characteristics about which I speculated earlier in this article. We need to explore new research paradigms that focus on the intensive study of young people at work in practical and realistic learning situations that place a premium on creative productivity rather than structured lesson learning, regardless of how advanced that learning may be. In this regard, we must learn to view special programs as places that make giftedness rather than as places that merely find and nurture it. If we have learned anything during the last decade or two, it is that valid new conceptions of giftedness have emerged from the research and theoretical literature. But if we continue to operate programs based largely on the older IQ cut-off score models and the advanced lesson learning models, we will stifle the development of new and innovative programs where pioneering research can take place.

It is also time to put aside the endless arguments about whether acceleration or enrichment is the best way of serving high-ability youth or whether special classes, special schools, or pull-out programs are the best way to organize services for the gifted. And it is time to stop debating whether content or process is the right and proper focus of curriculum for the gifted—as if one could conceivably be taught without the other! Most of all, we need to focus our research efforts on the core issue of education for the gifted and talented, *the process of learning how to become a creatively productive person*. The model presented in this paper represents what I believe are the key components for studying this process—the interactions between and among the learner, the curriculum, and the teacher. A better understanding of these components and interactions will lead to more effective ways of developing in young people not only high levels of competence, but also the within-discipline thinking, the *modus operandi* of the first-hand investigator, the self-understanding, and the passion for scholarship that has characterized the creative producers of our world.

NOTES

1. The work reported herein was supported under the Javits Act Program (Grant No. R206R00001) as administered by the Office of Educational Research and Improvement, U.S. Department of Education. The opinions expressed in this article do not reflect the position or policies of the Office of Educational Research and Improvement or the U.S. Department of Education.

2. The interestingness of a task or object is viewed as a property of the task or object rather than a property of the person. Interestingness does, however, have the power to promote personal interests in the learner.

3. At the University of Connecticut, all persons enrolled in our program for teachers of the gifted are required to take at least one course in research methods. Additionally, persons enrolled in a course dealing with curriculum development for the gifted are required to gain at least introductory college-level familiarity with an academic area in which they are planning to prepare curricular materials.

REFERENCES

Albert, R. S., & Runco, M. A. (1986). The achievement of eminence: A model on a longitudinal study of exceptionally gifted boys and their families. In R. J. Sternberg & J. E. Davidson, (Eds.), *Conceptions of giftedness* (pp. 332–357). New York: Cambridge University Press.

Amabile, T. M. (1989). The creative environment scales: Work environment inventory. *Creativity Research Journal, 2,* 231–253.

Barbe, W. B., & Swassing, R. H. (1979). *Teaching through modality strengths: Concept and practices.* Columbus, OH: Zaner-Bloser.

Bishop, W. E. (1981). Characteristics of teachers judged successful by intellectually gifted high school students. In W. B. Barbe & J. S. Renzulli (Eds.), *Psychology and education of the gifted* (pp. 422–432). New York: Irvington.

Bloom, B. S. (Ed.). (1985). *Developing talent in young people*. New York: Ballantine Books.

Board, J. (1991). *A special relationship: Our teachers and how we learned*. Wainscott, NY: Pushcart Press.

Briggs, J. (1990). *Fire in the crucible*. Los Angeles, CA: Jeremy P. Tarcher.

Chambers, J. A. (1973). College teachers: Their effect on creativity of students. *Journal of Educational Psychology, 65*, 326–339.

Dewey, J. (1913). *Interest and effort in education*. New York: Houghton Mifflin.

Dewey, J. (1929). *The quest for certainty*. New York: Milton, Balch, & Co.

Dunn, R., Dunn, K., & Price, G. E. (1975). *Learning style inventory*. Chappaqua, NY: Rita Dunn & Associates.

Feldhusen, J. F., & Hansen, J. (1988). Teachers of the gifted: Preparation and supervision. *Gifted Education International, 5*, 84–89.

Feldhusen, J. F., Hobson, S., & Treffinger, D. J. (1975). The effects of visual and verbal stimuli on divergent thinking. *Gifted Child Quarterly, 19*, 205–209, 263.

Feldman, D. H. (1988). Creativity: Dreams, insights, and transformations. In R. J. Sternberg (Ed.). *The nature of creativity* (pp. 271–277). Cambridge, MA: Cambridge University Press.

Gage, N. (1963). *Handbook of educational research on teaching*. A project from the American Educational Research Association. Chicago, IL: Rand McNally.

Gage, N. (1973). *Handbook of educational research on teaching* (2nd ed.). A project from the American Educational Research Association. Chicago, IL: Rand McNally.

Gear, G. (1979). Teachers of the gifted: A student's perspective. *Roeper Review, 1*(3). 18–20.

Goertzel, M. C., Goertzel, V., & Goertzel, T. G. (1978). *Three hundred eminent personalities*. San Francisco, CA: Jossey Bass.

Gowan, J. C., & Brunch, C. (1967). What makes a creative person a creative teacher? *Gifted Child Quarterly, 11*, 157–159.

Gregorc, A. (1985). *Inside style: Beyond the basics*. Maynard, MA: Gabriel Systems.

Gruber, H. F. (1986). The self-construction of the extraordinary. In R. J. Sternberg & J. E. Davidson (Eds.), *Conceptions of giftedness* (pp. 332–357). New York: Cambridge University Press.

Gruber, H. E., & Davis, S. N. (1988). Inching our way up Mount Olympus: The evolving systems approach to creative thinking. In R. J. Sternberg, (Ed.). *The nature of creativity* (pp. 247–263). Cambridge, MA: Cambridge University Press.

Hébert, T. P. (in preparation). A developmental examination of young creative producers.

Herbart, J. F. (1965). Outline of education lectures. In J. F. Herbart (Ed.). *Writing on education* (Vol. 3, pp. 157–300). Dusseldorf: Kuepper. (Original work published 1841)

Herbart, J. F. (1965). General theory of pedagogy, derived from the purpose of education. In J. F. Herbart (Ed.), *Writing on education* (Vol. 2, pp. 9–155). Dusseldorf: Kuepper. (Original work published 1806)

Hunt, D. E. (1971). *Matching models in education: The coordination of teaching methods with student characteristics*. Toronto, Canada: Ontario Institute for Studies in Education.

Hunt, D. E. (1975). Person-environment interaction: A challenge found wanting before it was tried. *Review of Educational Psychology, 45*, 209–230.

James, N. E. (1962). Personal preference for method as a factor in learning. *Journal of Educational Psychology, 53*, 43–47.

James, W. (1885). On the functions of cognition. *Mind, 10*, 27–44.

James, W. (1890). *The principles of psychology*. London: Macmillan.

Kolb, D., Rubin, I., & McIntyre, J. (1971). *Organizational psychology: An experimental approach*. Englewood Cliffs, NJ: Prentice Hall.

Krapp, A. (1989). The importance of the concept of interest in education research. *Empirische Pädagogik. 3*, 233–255.

Lindsey, M. (1980). *Training teachers of the gifted and talented.* New York: Teachers College Press.

Maker, C. J. (1975). *Training teachers for the gifted and talented: A comparison of models.* Reston, VA: Council for Exceptional Children.

McGreevy, A. (1982). *My book of things and stuff: An interest questionnaire for young children.* Mansfield Center, CT: Creative Learning Press.

McNary, S. R. (1967). *The relationship between certain teacher characteristics and achievement and creativity of gifted elementary school students.* Washington, DC: United States Department of Health, Education, and Welfare. (ERIC Document Reproduction Service No. Ed 060–479)

Mönks, F. J., van Boxtel, H. W., Roelofs, J. J. W., & Sanders, M. P. M. (1985). The identification of gifted children in secondary education and a description of their situation in Holland. In K. A. Heller & J. F. Feldhusen, *Identifying and nurturing the gifted: An international perspective* (pp. 39–65). Lewingston, NY: Hans Huber.

Mulhern, J. D., & Ward, M. (1983). A collaborative program for developing teachers of gifted and talented students. *Gifted Child Quarterly, 27*, 152–156.

Myers, I. B. (1980). *Gifts differing.* Palo Alto, CA: Consulting Psychologists Press.

Pascal, C. E. (1971). Instructional options, option preferences, and course outcomes. *The Alberta Journal of Educational Research, 17*, 1–11.

Phenix, P. H. (1964). *Realms of meaning.* New York: McGraw Hill.

Piaget, J. (Ed. and Trans.). (1981). Intelligence and affectivity: Their relationship during child development. *Annual Reviews Monograph.* Palo Alto, CA: Annual Review.

Pierson, D. M. (1985). Effective teachers of the gifted: Their characteristics and the relationship of self-selection. *Dissertation Abstracts International, 46*, 1596A. (University Microfilms No. DA85-17-550)

Reis, S. M., & Renzulli, J. S. (in preparation). A follow-up study of high creative producers who participated in an Enrichment Triad based program.

Renninger, K. A. (1989). Individual patterns in children's play interests. In L. T. Winegar (Ed.). *Social interaction and the development of children's understanding* (pp. 147–172). Norwood, NJ: Ablex.

Renninger, K. A. (1990). Children's play interests, representation, and activity. In R. Fivush & J. Hudson (Eds.). *Knowing and remembering in young children* (pp. 127–165). Emory Cognition Series (Vol. III). Cambridge, MA: Cambridge University Press.

Renzulli, J. S. (1977a). *The interest-a-lyzer.* Mansfield Center, CT: Creative Learning Press.

Renzulli, J. S. (1977b). *The enrichment triad model: A guide for developing defensible programs for the gifted.* Mansfield Center, CT: Creative Learning Press.

Renzulli, J. S. (1978a). What makes giftedness? Re-examining a definition. *Phi Delta Kappan, 60*, 180–184, 261.

Renzulli, J. S. (1978b). What makes a problem real? Stalking the illusive meaning of qualitative difference in gifted education. *Gifted Child Quarterly, 26*, 148–156.

Renzulli, J. S. (1986). The three-ring conception of giftedness: A developmental model for creative productivity. In R. J. Sternberg & J. E. Davidson (Eds.), *Conceptions of Giftedness* (pp. 53–92). New York: Cambridge University Press.

Renzulli, J. S. (1988). The multiple menu model for developing differentiated curriculum for the gifted and talented. *Gifted Child Quarterly, 32*, 298–309.

Renzulli, J. S., & Reis, S. M. (1985). *The school-wide enrichment model: A comprehensive plan for educational excellence.* Mansfield Center, CT: Creative Learning Press.

Renzulli, J. S., & Smith, L. H. (1978). *The learning style inventory: A measure of student preference for instructional techniques.* Mansfield Center, CT: Creative Learning Press.

Schiefele, U. (1988). Motivated conditions of text comprehension. *Zeitschrift für Pädagogik, 34,* 687–708.

Schwab, J. J., & Brandwein, P. F. (1962). *The teaching of science.* Cambridge, MA: Harvard University Press.

Smith, L. H. (1976). *Learning styles: Measurement and educational significance.* Unpublished doctoral dissertation, University of Connecticut.

Smith, L. H., & Renzulli, J. S. (1984). Learning styles preferences: A practical approach for classroom teachers. *Theory into Practice, 23,* 44–50.

Sternberg, R. J. (1988). Mental self-government: A theory of intellectual styles and their development. *Human Development, 31,* 197–224.

Sternberg, R. J., & Davidson, J. E. (1986). *Conceptions of giftedness.* New York: Cambridge University Press.

Sternberg, R. J., & Lubart, T. I. (1991). An investment theory of creativity and its development. *Human Development, 34,* 1–31.

Story, C. M. (1985). Facilitator of learning: A micro-ethnographic study of the teacher of the gifted. *Gifted Child Quarterly, 29,* 155–159.

Tannenbaum, A. J. (1983). *Gifted children: Psychological and educational perspectives.* New York: Macmillan.

Tannenbaum, A. J. (1986). Giftedness: A psychological approach. In R. J. Sternberg & J. E. Davidson (Eds.). *Conceptions of giftedness* (pp. 21–52). New York: Cambridge University Press.

Thorndike, E. L. (1935). *Adult interests.* New York: Macmillan.

Torrance, E. P. (1981). Predicting the creativity of elementary school children (1958–80)—and the teacher who "made a difference." *Gifted Child Quarterly, 25,* 55–62.

Walberg, H. J., Rasher, S. P., & Parkerson, J. (1980). Childhood and eminence. *Journal of Creative Behavior, 13,* 225–231.

Ward, W. C. (1969). Creativity and environmental cues in nursery school children. *Developmental Psychology, 1,* 543–547.

Whitehead, A. N. (1929). The rhythm of education. In A. N. Whitehead (Ed.). *The aims of education* (pp. 46–59). New York: Macmillan.

Whitlock, M. S., & DuCette, J. P. (1989). Outstanding and average teachers of the gifted: A comparative study. *Gifted Child Quarterly, 33,* 15–21.

Wittrock, M. C. (1986). *Handbook of educational research on teaching* (3rd ed.). New York: Macmillan.

Yando, R. M., & Kagan, J. (1968). The effect of teacher tempo on the child. *Child Development, 39,* 27–34.

7

The Interdisciplinary Concept Model: Theory and Practice

Heidi Hayes Jacobs

James H. Borland

Center for the Study and Education of the
Gifted Teachers College, Columbia University

A rationale for interdisciplinarity as a content modification for gifted learners is presented along with assumptions underlying the implementation of an interdisciplinary model. The importance of orientation to the disciplinary fields as a precursor to interdisciplinary studies is stressed. Finally, the Interdisciplinary Concept Model, a four-step plan for developing interdisciplinary units, is discussed.

Editor's Note: From Hayes Jacobs, H., & Borland, J. (1986). The interdisciplinary concept model: Theory and practice. *Gifted Child Quarterly*, *30*(4), 159–163. © 1986 National Association for Gifted Children. Reprinted with permission.

"Defensible, differentiated curriculum" is a phrase that brings to mind the words of Browning's Andrea del Sarto, that "man's reach should exceed his grasp." Most practitioners realize that differentiating the curriculum for the gifted, especially when the goal is enrichment, involves a number of curricular modifications in terms of thinking processes, student products, and curriculum content. In too many cases, however, these modifications result in an enrichment curriculum that is little more than a hodge-podge of unrelated topics and activities. Teachers faced with the task of preparing a separate course of study for the gifted but warned not to infringe on the content of the regular curriculum often see little alternative to offering their students an unstructured stream of minicourses, "creativity" kits and methods, and frequently abortive attempts at independent study. It is thus not surprising that the question, "What should the gifted learn?", especially when posed by a teacher responsible for developing an enrichment curriculum, is one of the most fundamental and intractable of those with which we have to wrestle.

For some, the answer has been interdisciplinarity. Faced with an explosion of knowledge in nearly every discipline and a school day and school calendar that reflect the agrarian age in which they were fashioned, some teachers have found the concept of interdisciplinary studies to be an attractive one. Unfortunately, despite the best of intentions, this frequently results in a potpourri rather than true interdisciplinarity, with students receiving a little English, a bit of math, and a dash of science. Such forced marriages may be a reason for the failure of interdisciplinary education to have a major impact on the educational system in this country (Petrie, 1976).

It is our belief, based on our experiences with a number of school districts around the country and our reading of the literature on interdisciplinarity in the schools, that interdisciplinary studies, when viewed as a conscious and comprehensive component of curriculum design, can and should play an important role in the special course of study of gifted learners. Further, we believe that properly designed interdisciplinary units can lessen the fragmentation that too often results from attempts at providing enrichment for the gifted.

In this paper, we will discuss the theoretical background and the implementation of the Interdisciplinary Concept Model, an approach to developing interdisciplinary enrichment units. We will also make a case for the importance of the peaceful co-existence of interdisciplinarity and disciplinarity, since we believe that a solid orientation to the disciplines is requisite for the success of interdisciplinary studies.

ASSUMPTIONS

First, we will outline some assumptions underlying our approach. These touch upon issues related to basic curricular concerns with respect to gifted students as well as the specific topic of interdisciplinarity itself.

1. *Gifted students should explore epistemological issues.* Knowledge, often referred to as "mere knowledge," has taken a beating in recent writings on the education of the gifted. Not only do we think that this is misguided, harmful, and perhaps anti-intellectual, we believe that knowledge is the proper object and goal of gifted education. Epistemological questions such as "What is knowledge?", "What do we know?", and "How is knowledge produced?" can and should be at the heart of our curricular efforts. Tannenbaum (1983) states that the gifted are producers, not merely consumers, of knowledge. If that is the case, what better focus is there for the education of the gifted than epistemology?

2. *A model of curriculum and instruction for the gifted should include a dimension that focuses on the development of thinking processes.* This is important, and it is also frequently misinterpreted. In reaction to the oft-maligned "old content-centered curriculum," many program developers have chosen to make "process development" the sole focus of their curricula. However, as Renzulli (1977) rightly asserts, process is a means, not an end of instruction. What is needed is a skillful blend of high-level thinking and high-level content. "Higher-level thinking skills" brought to bear upon trivial content produce trivial results, a major reason for the failure of the kits and games of which we as a field were so enamored a few years ago (Perkins, 1980). Process development is important, but it requires the proper context. Teachers of the gifted must forge epistemological links between cognitive processes and the presentation of content if either is to play a meaningful role in the overall curriculum.

3. *A special curriculum for the gifted should reflect both a discipline-field and an interdisciplinary orientation.* Too often, disciplinarity and interdisciplinarity are viewed as an either/or proposition (Hayes-Jacobs, 1981). This, in our opinion, is an unfortunate and unnecessary dichotomy. Gifted students need to acquire the unique knowledge, skills, and language of the various disciplines as well as the vantage point and integrating dynamic of the interdisciplinary approach. It is this dual emphasis, along with the conscious focus on epistemological issues, that provides a means for differentiating content in a defensible manner. Just as pioneering artists like Joyce and Picasso could not break the rules until they had fully mastered them, one cannot derive full benefit from interdisciplinary studies until one acquires a solid grounding in the various disciplines that interdisciplinarity attempts to bridge.

4. *The Interdisciplinary Concept Model should serve as a precursor to independent study.* Although independent study is hardly the panacea that some have claimed, it should play an important role in the special education of the gifted. The advantage of using this model as a springboard for independent study is that it provides practice in many of the skills necessary to complete independent study, especially those required for the production

of knowledge. In addition, one can provide sequential instruction in problem definition and research methodology, requisites for successful independent study that are not adequately structured and sequenced in many independent-study schemes. Moreover, there is room within this model for that student who is clearly in need of a special program but who is not ready, willing, or able to carry on a long-term independent project.

5. *Gifted Students can, and in many cases should, be involved in the development of interdisciplinary units.* The four-step process described below allows for student input at all stages. It will not be desirable for students to participate in every case, but we have found that student interest in the interdisciplinary units often is enhanced by their involvement in the unit-planning process.

ORIENTATION TO DISCIPLINE FIELDS

The Concept of Disciplinarity

The initial goal of the model is to allow students to examine how professionals in each discipline field approach problems in characteristics ways unique to their disciplines. By examining the manner in which field specialists create and transmit bodies of knowledge and how these are sanctioned by society, students are afforded the opportunity, rare in our educational system, to delve into basic epistemological questions. Probings of this sort tend by their very nature to be highly abstract and to focus on symbol systems, the manipulation of which, Gallagher (1975) claims, is the essence of giftedness.

This is also a practicable approach for the teacher concerned to design an enrichment curriculum. The alternative, presenting the students with a myriad of facts within each discipline, would require the teacher to become a content specialist in every discipline. It is far more valuable for students to look instead at what could be called the "meta-level" of the disciplines. Specifically, students should focus on the language used by specialists to transmit knowledge and the methodology specific to the production of knowledge in each discipline.

The Language of the Disciplines

Scheffler (1976) suggests that one of the major tasks facing teachers today is the teaching of foreign languages. By this he means not the familiar language groups but the specialized vocabulary, usages, and linguistic structures used by practitioners within the various disciplines. Each of these is a foreign tongue to the individual not conversant with the jargon of the tribe, and whether by design or not, each serves both to delimit the field and to distinguish those who belong from those who do not. It is not by accident that we commonly employ geopolitical metaphors in discussing such topics as "the world of mathematics."

It would not be possible for teachers to make their gifted students fluent in the language of every discipline. However, a certain conversational familiarity should be sought so that students do not have to view each discipline as a totally alien land. A feasible goal is for the students to be able to make their way, to recognize some landmarks, and to perceive the structure and concepts necessary for a basic orientation to the disciplines.

This is not simply an exercise in knowledge acquisition, as valuable as that may be, but a chance for students to begin to realize that there is a way of perceiving reality that is unique to each field. One manner in which this can be demonstrated to students is to have them view a common object, such as a book, through a series of "lenses." Students can be asked figuratively to look at the book using the lens of a historian and to ask questions about it. Common questions might include "How old is the book?", "Where did it come from?", and "Who has owned it?". The students then can "put on" the lenses of a chemist, a poet, a mathematician, and so forth, each time asking questions characteristic of the discipline in question.

Exercises such as this serve to introduce students to the idea that specialized languages not only function as delimiters of disciplinary space but as "ways of knowing" (Phenix, 1964) within the disciplines. This realization is a prerequisite for the adoption of a true interdisciplinary perspective.

The Methodology of the Disciplines

Bruner (1975) asserts that the ways in which a body of knowledge is generated and structured should be specified so they can be grasped readily by the learner. Focusing on this aspect of a discipline field, its methodological level, can give students valuable insights into the epistemological essence of a discipline field. It is important here to concentrate on the linkages between methodologies and the content of the disciplines. For example, students might investigate:

- the empirical methods used to generate scientific knowledge
- the quantitative methods used to generate mathematical knowledge
- the aesthetic methods used to create meaning in the arts
- the use of ethical argument to clarify philosophical issues.

To give this investigation of methodologies more immediacy, students might meet with professionals working in various fields under study to explore further the techniques they use in their work. This is in line with the suggestions of both Renzulli (1977) and Tannenbaum (1983) that gifted students can benefit from emulating the methodology of field specialists.

In this first phase of the model, there is a concentrated attempt to examine the various disciplines *qua* disciplines in order to lay the groundwork for advanced disciplinary and interdisciplinary work that will require the perspectives of the disciplines themselves. Huebner (1977) asserts that a familiarity with the language, symbols, and methods of the disciplines enables students to respond to and to recreate the world. "Knowledge becomes a way of conversing between the educator and students about the phenomena in the world" (p. 231). Far from being "mere knowledge," this becomes a powerful tool for restructuring problems in a manner that suggests solutions that derive from both a disciplinary and an interdisciplinary perspective.

DEVELOPMENT OF INTERDISCIPLINARY UNITS: THE INTERDISCIPLINARY CONCEPT MODEL

Once students acquire a familiarity with the dimensions of the disciplines mentioned above, it becomes feasible to develop carefully structured interdisciplinary units of study. Since this would be a daunting proposition for most of us, we are proposing a four-step method whereby one can undertake this task. We are not claiming that this is an absolutely original approach. Readers familiar with brainstorming techniques, webbing strategies, and the integrated day concept will recognize some familiar suggestions. Our intention is to synthesize these ideas with some of our own in order to produce a functional alternative to the patchwork efforts that often pass for interdisciplinary curricula.

Step I: Selecting a Topic

Since this is a unit approach, the first step entails the selection of a topic or theme around which a curriculum can be developed. The choice of a topic is a somewhat difficult process to describe or prescribe since the interests and capabilities of the teacher and students are major factors. However, there are certain guidelines that should be followed.

The topic should be appropriate in scope. A topic that is too broad, such as "life," could pose some difficulties with respect to manageability and focus. On the other hand, a topic that is too narrow, such as "the suppresion of the Albigensian heresies in the south of France in the thirteenth century," is difficult to approach from an interdisciplinary perspective and lacks proper resonance with what the students already know.

Topics of a conceptual nature, as long as they are somewhat circumscribed, lend themselves to this purpose due to their abstractness. In the past, topics such as intelligence, flight, observation, revolution, humor, light, and the future have provided the bases for successful interdisciplinary units.

Interest in the topic can be enhanced by having students participate in this step of the process. The class can brainstorm possible topics and then discuss their relative merits as unit themes. A caveat is in order here, however. Students have a habit of wanting to examine the same themes again and again. Defensible units can and have been structured around the topics of sports and rock and roll, but teachers of the gifted have a responsibility to expose students to areas of study with which they are unfamiliar. Clearly, students are not likely to suggest the investigation of a topic whose existence is unknown to them, so some units should probably be suggested by the teacher.

However the topic is selected, the next step is to begin to develop a unit around it. That process begins with the next step.

Step II: Brainstorming Associations

The choice of a good topic creates a major problem in terms of instruction. Let us assume that the topic of "intelligence" has been chosen as the basis for the planned unit. Where does one go from here? One cannot simply turn to the text because there is no intelligence text, nor is there a scope and sequence for this particular subject.

This is where one must rely on a divergent method, brainstorming, in order to produce some raw material for the task of curriculum development. A graphic device resembling a wheel is useful at this point. This can be reproduced on a blackboard or large sheet of paper with the unit theme written in a circle in the middle of the wheel. Each of the spokes emanating from the center represents a discipline, for example, language arts, mathematics, science, social studies, philosophy and the humanities, and the arts, to remind the participants in the brainstorming session that each of the disciplines should be considered.

Next, the participants in this step of the process— teachers, students, or both—should begin to associate freely in response to the unit theme. Whatever comes to mind—people, events, problems, creations, issues, controversies— should be stated and written on the board or paper, preferably in the area defined by the "spoke" representing the discipline to which it most closely belongs. The object of this brainstorming session is to dredge from whatever conscious and unconscious sources possible ideas and bits of information that could be of use in planning the unit. No attempt should be made to structure these associations or even to make much sense of them at this point. The fluent production of ideas is the object, and the process should continue until the participants run dry.

The result should be a graphic nightmare, the "wheel" all but obscured by the brainstormed associations. This welter of seemingly random bits of information, however, is the basis of the following step, an integrative one in which sense is made of what has gone before.

Step III: Formulating Guiding Questions for Inquiry

This step of the process requires the participants to perform the mental equivalent of a factor analysis. One should now examine the material on the chart, searching for commonalities or themes that emerge from related ideas. It is highly likely that ideas from a number of disciplines that have been brainstormed will begin to coalesce into or to suggest larger concepts. Taking our example of intelligence, one might find the following brainstormed associations from the following discipline areas:

Mathematics: IQ ratios

Philosophy: the ethics of testing

Science: physiological responses as measures of intelligence

Language arts: Galton's *Hereditary Genius*

Social studies: psychometrics.

These all suggest a single theme: the measurement of intelligence. We suggest that this be made into a simple question, which in this case might be "How is intelligence measured?"

This process of looking for common threads that emerge as themes and are then converted into inquiry questions should continue until most of the brainstormed associations are used at least once and no more themes emerge. Then, one can combine related themes into superordinate inquiry questions, eliminate redundant themes, rewrite those that do not suggest major issues, and generally try to refine the list of questions. The goal should be a list of four to six major questions in a logical order. Here are the guiding questions that emerged from the development of a unit based on theme of intelligence:

1. What is intelligence?

2. How did human intelligence evolve?

3. How is intelligence measured?

4. Is intelligence solely a human quality?

5. How is intelligence used and expressed by artists?

These guiding inquiry questions thus become the scope and sequence of the interdisciplinary unit. They represent the topics to be explored over the course of time (usually four to six weeks) in which the unit topic will be investigated. One is thus provided with a framework for instruction and the development of instructional activities.

Step IV: Designing and Implementing Activities

This is where most "methods" become vague, and in this approach, too, there is a step that relies on the teacher's ability to design activities and instructional strategies in the service of certain objectives. For once the guiding inquiry questions have been formulated, the means for exploring these questions must be developed. There are some guidelines that can be of assistance here, however.

As we stated above, one of the assumptions underlying this model is that there should be a conscious effort to develop students' higher-level thinking processes but that this has to be done within a meaningful context. This is the step in the development of an interdisciplinary unit where the introduction of process development makes sense. A content-process matrix can aid in further defining the task of activity planning. In the matrix, the rows represent the guiding inquiry questions developed in step III, and the columns can represent, for example, the classroom-outcome categories of Bloom's Taxonomy of the Cognitive Domain (Bloom, 1956). This suggests that there is a need to focus on what the students do as well as the content of the unit.

Activities should be developed using both dimensions of the matrix, keeping in mind that there is no need to develop one activity for each cell. In fact, if the unit represents true enrichment, it will be necessary to focus initially on the levels of knowledge and comprehension. Although these are often denigrated as "lower-level" processes, the students will have to internalize information about the topic under consideration before they can begin to analyze, synthesize, and evaluate information.

Well-stated objectives can assist in the planning of activities, and they can also reflect a dual concern for content and process. Using our unit on intelligence as an example, an objective for the first week might be "To become aware of various theories of intelligence" (What is intelligence?; knowledge and comprehension on the taxonomy) while one for a later week might be "To assess the validity of the Wechsler Intelligence Scale for Children (How is intelligence measured?; evaluation on the taxonomy).

It will probably prove useful to employ a number of modes of instruction including lecture, assigned readings, small-group discussions, activity cards, brainstorming, guest speakers, field trips, personal essays, and so forth. Opportunities for independent study can be provided for those students who show a particular interest in the area. Evaluation of the unit can be accomplished through pre- and post-tests of the unit content, written evaluations by students, an evaluation of student products, and other means.

This method of developing interdisciplinary units, although it has been used with success in a variety of types of programs and school districts, is not a panacea. Moreover, it should be clear that it is not an easy solution; it requires considerably more effort than is needed to reproduce a stack of ditto masters. It is not a kit or a game but a serious approach to the question of what gifted students should learn. It is recommended to those teachers of the gifted who believe in the value of knowledge as a means and an end and who take seriously their role as creators, not merely dispensers, of curriculum. For us, interdisciplinarity is a powerful tool for working with gifted, or indeed any, children. We urge other educators to explore this way of answering the question, "What do I do on Monday?"

REFERENCES

Bloom, B. (Ed.). (1956). *Taxonomy of educational objectives. Handbook I: Cognitive domain.* New York: Longman.

Bruner, J. R. (1975). *Toward a theory of instruction.* Cambridge, MA: Belknap.

Gallagher, J. J. (1975). *Teaching the gifted child* (2nd ed.). Boston: Allyn & Bacon.

Hayes-Jacobs, H. (1981). *A model for curriculum and instruction: Discipline fields, interdisciplinarity, and cognitive process.* Unpublished doctoral dissertation, Columbia University.

Heubner, D. (1977). Implications of psychological thought for the curriculum. In A. A. Bellack & H. M. Kleibard (Eds.), *Curriculum and evaluation.* Berkeley, CA: McCutchan.

Perkins, D.N. (1980). *General cognitive skills: Why not?* Paper presented at the NIE-LRDC Conference on Thinking and Learning Skills, Pittsburgh, PA.

Petrie, H. G. (1976). Do you see what I see? The epistemology of interdisciplinary inquiry. *Aesthetic Education, 10,* 29–43.

Phenix, P. (1964). *Realms of meaning.* New York: McGraw-Hill.

Renzulli, J.S. (1977). *The enrichment triad model.* Mansfield Center, CT: Creative Learning Press.

Scheffler, I. (1976). Basic mathematical skills: Some philosophical and practical remarks. *Teachers College Record, 78,* 205–212.

Tannenbaum, A.J. (1983). *Gifted children: Psychological and educational perspectives.* New York: Macmillan.

8

Curriculum for the Gifted and Talented at the Secondary Level

A. Harry Passow

Teachers College, Columbia University

Curriculum for the gifted and talented at the secondary level involves more than deciding whether to accelerate or enrich, to group or not, to offer an honors program or an advanced seminar, or to offer advanced placement courses. Rather, it consists of the total learning environment and encompasses the general education, specialized education, co-curricular, and education in non-school settings, together with the climate which is created in the school and classroom for pursuit of excellence. Curriculum planning begins with a clear concept of program goals and objectives. It consists of a number of decisions about content, scope, sequence, integration, articulation and balance, as well as about resource use, time, space, and organization.

Editor's Note: From Passow, A.H. (1986). Curriculum for the gifted and talented at the secondary level. *Gifted Child Quarterly*, *30*(4). 186–191. © 1986 National Association for Gifted Children. Reprinted with permission.

Most discussions of curriculum at the secondary level for the gifted and talented seem to focus on such topics as accelerated courses, honors courses, independent study, advanced placement, International Baccalaureate, advanced seminars, etc. While these programs and provisions are important, curriculum planning must begin with clear goals and objectives if curricular efforts are to be meaningful. Without a clear concept of what it is we expect that gifted and talented students to achieve, what it is we want them "to become," our curricular efforts will be directionless. We may implement programs and provide various learning opportunities but we can never know whether we have achieved our ends of helping the gifted to realize their potential if we are not clear about what those ends are. For many programs for the gifted, the lack of a clear concept of the goals and objectives is a major shortcoming in such efforts.

I have suggested elsewhere that regardless of their specific talents, interests, or degree of talent, there are some common goals for all gifted and talented youth. All gifted children and youth must acquire the knowledge, skills, insights, attitudes and motivations which will enable them to achieve the following:

1. To deal competently with themselves, their fellow men, and the world about them as human beings, citizens, parents, and participants in the "good life."

2. To build a sound liberal foundation to sustain the rigorous development of specialized competencies at the higher levels which they can handle.

3. To foster self-direction, independence, a love of learning, and a desire to create and experiment with ideas and things.

4. To provide the self-understanding, inner consistency, and ethical standards to see their own uniqueness in terms of responsibility to society.

5. To stimulate critical thinking and a scientific approach to solving their persistent problems.

6. To nurture an appreciation of the cultural heritage bequeathed by societies through the ages.

7. To motivate the desire to meet the special expectations society has for individuals with unique talents. (Passow, 1958, p. 194)

These goals are admittedly broad and general and differ from those for all youth only in the relatively greater emphasis placed on those characteristics and traits which we identify with the gifted and talented—intellect, initiative, creative effort, critical thinking ability, higher order analytical and synthesis skills, etc. When translated into instructional objectives in particular domains or discipline areas, some of these goals are more readily attained by gifted students who can then plunge deeper into learning, explore farther and deeper, and acquire more advanced concepts, meanings, and relationships. It is the *qualitative* emphasis, the levels of attainment, which helps differentiate these general goals for the gifted from that of other students, not that these goals are exclusive with the gifted student only.

In considering curricula for secondary school gifted and talented youth, there are other ways of stating some of the above objectives. It is important, for example, for gifted students to continue developing their potential in post-secondary institutions. Therefore, they must be enabled to meet the requirements at a sufficiently high level to be admitted to an appropriate institution of higher education and to succeed in a program there. It is important that a gifted student have a sound general education which means opportunities to engage in appropriate learning experiences in those disciplines and subject areas which we think contribute to a mastery of the cultural heritage but also nurture gifted students as creative participants and productive contributors to that culture. It is important that gifted students have opportunities to develop their particular areas of specialized talents, recognizing that in most areas the talents will not be fully nurtured in the secondary school. Gifted high school students should have developed their talents far beyond the level other students will reach but they recognize that, except in very rare instances, they are not "finished" scientists, mathematicians, writers, musicians, or historians. They should achieve at an advanced level but also should recognize how much more is needed if they are to perform as productive, creative, gifted persons in their talent areas. It is important that affective goals be attended to as well as cognitive and academic goals. Self concepts, attitudes, motives, values, interests, and emotions are components of positive self actualization and functioning fully in society and the curriculum must contribute to nurturing the affective domain as well as the cognitive domain. It is important that gifted students acquire the learning-how-to-learn skills so that they can function as "self-starters" with the motivation and the enthusiasm needed to sustain the intensive efforts needed to develop gifted potential.

If these considerations are kept in mind, decisions regarding curriculum for secondary school gifted youth are not as simple as many planners believe. Certainly, it is not simply a question of whether to provide for radical acceleration or enrichment; whether to schedule honors classes, independent study or advanced seminars; or whether to engage students in various individual or team competitions. All of these have merit and deserve consideration in planning high school programs for the gifted.

CURRICULAR DECISIONS TO BE MADE

Curriculum planning consists of a number of decisions to be made about content, scope, sequence, integration, articulation and balance. To some extent, the decisions at the secondary school level depend on curricular decisions made at the elementary, middle or junior high schools. Depending on the extent to which identification has taken place earlier and the nature of the learning opportunities provided at those earlier levels, decisions concerning the high school curriculum will—or should be—effected. High school curriculum should build on and be articulated with prior gifted education. If a student has been accelerated in mathematics or a foreign language in earlier grades, for example, the mathematics curriculum and the foreign language curriculum should build on those prior experiences and the articulation provided should affect other dimensions of the curriculum.

As mentioned above, one dimension of curriculum for the gifted in secondary school is to insure through good guidance that the student takes the courses which will enable him/her to be admitted to a college or university which has the programs and the resources which will contribute to the fullest development of that talent potential. A secondary school curriculum must fulfill a number of functions—general education, specialized education, and exploration, to name three of the most important.

It is the general education curriculum which helps build the sound liberal foundation needed to sustain development of specialized competencies at higher levels and which nurtures an understanding and appreciation of the cultural heritage. It is, as Phenix (1964) puts it, "the process of engendering essential meanings" (p. 5). The specialized curriculum is aimed at nurturing the special talent areas of the individual, at providing the knowledge, skills, insights and understandings which will enable the individual to grow towards becoming a gifted adult, a producer of knowledge and of creative products and performance. The exploratory curriculum provides opportunities for students to engage in learning experiences to determine how these match with the individual's skills and interests and whether he/she wishes to pursue an area further through the specialized curriculum. These curricula interact, of course, and learning opportunities may fulfill more than one of these functions.

Phenix sees six fundamental patterns of meaning emerging from the six possible modes of human understanding. He suggests that general education is the process of engendering essential meanings:

> If the six realms cover the range of possible meanings, they may be regarded as comprising the basic competences that general education should develop in every person. A complete person should be skilled in the use of speech, symbol and gesture, factually well-informed, capable of creating and appreciating objects of esthetic significance, endowed with a rich and disciplined life in relation to self and others, able to make wise decisions and to judge between right and wrong, and possessed of an integral outlook. These are the aims of general education for the development of whole persons. (Phenix, 1964, p. 8)

Most schools do not organize their programs along the lines of the realms of meaning which Phenix proposes, but their required, common or core curricula aim at providing a general education for students. Are traditional college preparatory courses the appropriate courses for a general education? Is there a place for the so-called non-academic or technical-vocational subjects in the program for gifted? Is there a minimum requirement which is appropriate for all students in the areas of English, social studies, mathematics, science, foreign languages, and the arts? Are the minima the same or do they vary depending on the students' areas of specialized talent and interest? Is there an appropriate balance between mathematics and science on the one hand and the humanities and art areas on the other? Should all gifted students be expected to achieve at an equally high level in all areas of general education? Depending on the goals and objectives which have been set for students identified as gifted, educational planners will deal with these issues in different ways. They are central issues, however, and are better dealt with directly than by default.

Most secondary school curricula deal with Phenix's realms of meaning under different rubrics, most within subjects tied to traditional disciplines. Within each of these discipline areas—if that is the organization—educational experiences and learning opportunities may be differentiated in at least three ways—in *breadth* and/or *depth*, in *tempo* or *pace*, or in *kind* or *nature*—or in combination. Within each subject area, the curriculum must be differentiated. A distinction must be made between that which is basic and that which is advanced and learning opportunities differentiated accordingly. The guiding principle concerning curriculum content is that it "should focus on and be organized to include more elaborate, more complex, and in-depth study of major ideas, problems, and themes that integrate knowledge with and across systems of thought" (Passow, 1982, p. 7).

Thus, one important component of the curriculum for gifted secondary school students consists of those disciplines which provide a sound general education. While this is often thought of as the college preparatory or academic curriculum, it is only appropriate for gifted students when differentiation is provided in terms of advanced content, instructional strategies, advanced resources and learning opportunities which match the characteristics and traits of identified gifted students. This curriculum differentiation may take place within the regular classroom, in separate classes or sections, or in specially designed courses. The organizational or administrative arrangements depend on other factors—such as the number of gifted students, the overall provisions for gifted, etc. In any event, administrative differentiation should not be confused with curriculum differentiation.

The specialized curriculum, the curriculum in which individual talents are developed and potential realized, may be implemented through differentiation in the general education program plus separate courses, study areas or learning opportunities. That is, through acceleration (increased tempo or pace) or enrichment (breadth and/or depth of study), gifted students may engage in learning experiences which are more advanced, stimulate higher order cognitive development, and develop individual talent areas. By differentiating goals and objectives, content, resources, assignments, learning and teaching methods, and evaluation procedures, gifted students are enabled to acquire the knowledge, skills, and understandings which make it possible for them to perform or behave at outstanding levels. In those areas where they have outstanding potential coupled with interest and motivation, curricular conditions need to be created which enable gifted students to pursue those areas as deeply, as broadly, and as rapidly as possible—to go as far and as fast as the student is capable of and wishes to. Some disciplines—mathematics and foreign languages, for example— lend themselves to accelerated study while other disciplines—history, literature and art, for example—lend themselves to study in breadth and/or depth, to reflection and playing around with ideas and things. Still other disciplines—the sciences, for example—may be pursued through both acceleration and study in breadth and depth. Schools should provide for these individual, specialized pursuits by making learning opportunities available through whatever administrative arrangements are required—differentiation within the regular classroom, special classes or seminars, or independent study.

The variety of ways in which differentiated curriculum and instruction may be delivered can be seen from the elements of the program offered at one large four-year comprehensive high school located in a well-established suburb. These elements are the administrative provisions; the curricula and instructional differentiations are planned and implemented within this framework. This high school's program for the gifted includes:

1. *Honors Classes* in all of the school's academic departments. A few such courses are offered at the ninth grade level to identify the talented. In grades 10 through 12, honors classes are set up in English, social studies, mathematics, science, French and Spanish. Because there tends not to be a wide range of ability in chemistry, German and Latin, no honors classes are offered in those subjects. Honors classes aim at providing appropriate instruction for students who cannot be fully provided for within the regular classes. Intellectually able students are challenged by learning activities which may not be as meaningful or as appropriate to other students.

2. *Combined Studies* is a four-year elective that "features pupil participation and planning within defined areas of content, guidance and accompanying extra class activities." This elective is basically an interdisciplinary study, developed by the school's faculty. A wide range of subject matter is encompassed during a double period, with considerable emphasis on reading and research. The opportunities in planning, discussing, and class management are seen as especially appropriate for the talented pupil. A special feature has been the concept of intellectual leadership with honors students expected "to make a significant contribution to creative individual and group progress" (p. 223).

3. *Advanced Placement Program* offers college level courses in a variety of subjects.

4. *Special Interest Courses* are available in a variety of areas such as: "playing in the band or orchestra, singing in a chorus, individual voice or instrument lessons, or studying music as a listener; speech arts of some sort;

arts and crafts, painting, designing; typing, shorthand, preparatory accounting, or other business education; shop courses such as mechanical drawing, metalwork, electricity, or auto mechanics; home economics classes; or a short driver training course" (pp. 224–225).

5. *Extracurricular Activities* abound, and the very able are often the leaders in many areas. Some talented students add a leadership training course to their program of academic courses and extracurricular responsibilities.

As viewed by the school's curriculum planners, "the heart of the program lies in the quality of learning experiences expected of the talented" (p. 232) students. In their view, "a better quality of learning involves not a mere collection of facts, but the development of abstract concepts and generalizations, the organization and integration of ideas, and a deep analysis of large and more complex phenomena" (p. 233). The school gives attention to the nature of staff members who work with the gifted, to the instructional resources needed to promote many kinds of interests and abilities, to the particular guidance needs of the talented, and to appropriate research and evaluation focusing on the programs for the talented (see Michael and Fair, 1961).

There are other programs which are designed to provide a specialized curriculum. The College Board operated Advanced Placement Program, mentioned above, now provides syllabi and examinations in 24 specific subject areas, offering college-level studies in high schools. The program is based on the idea that able high school students are challenged by engaging in academically advanced courses. On a much smaller scale, the International Baccalaureate is being viewed as providing an appropriate curriculum for gifted students. The IB program provides a two-year course structure followed by an international set of examinations. The program aims at offering "a comprehensive and cohesive curriculum of general education that responds to the need for greater challenge on the upper secondary level and for new opportunities to achieve excellence in education," aims which correspond with those for gifted programs. In the eleventh and twelfth grades, students study six subjects—three for five periods per week for two years and three for half the total time for one or two years. Students select one course from each of the areas: (1) Language A, the student's native language; (2) Language B, a second language; (3) Study of Man, chosen from seven options including history, geography, economics, philosophy, psychology, social anthropology, or business studies; (4) experimental sciences, chosen from the options of biology, chemistry, physics, physical science, or scientific studies; (5) mathematics; and (6) a choice of one from art, music, a classical language, computer studies, a second language B, and additional options from 3, 4, or 5, or special syllabi developed by the schools, including theater arts. In addition to the six courses, IB diploma candidates are required to take an interdisciplinary course on the philosophy of knowledge, called the Theory of Knowledge; to prepare a research paper; and to participate in a creative, aesthetic, or social service activity. Because the International Baccalaureate is intended to be academically rigorous and challenging, it is seen as affecting curriculum in the earlier grades as students are prepared to engage in the advanced studies in grades 11 and 12. The IB prospectus observes: "In providing a comprehensive and cohesive framework for already existing honors courses, the IB gives them added meaning in the context of a curriculum with both breadth and depth" (International Baccalaureate, 1984).

Two contrasting examples of curriculum differentiation in a specialized curriculum can be found in the Johns Hopkins Studies of Mathematically Precocious Youth (SMPY) (Stanley, 1977) and CEMREL's project, (Kaufman, et al., 1981) Mathematical Education for the Gifted Secondary School Student (MEGSSS). SMPY involves what its originator calls "radical acceleration" or "fast paced academic programs." SMPY offers such courses as: Fast-Paced Precalculus Mathematics, Probability and Statistics, Quantitative Economics, Problem-Solving Strategies with Mathematics, Supplemental Calculus: AB Level, Supplementary Calculus: BC Level, Computer Science, and Advanced Computer Science. Through the Center for the Advancement of Academically Talented Youth (CTY) courses are offered in humanities, science, and mathematics, courses which are "demanding and especially designed to match the gifted adolescent's intellectual requirements and rate of learning." (Center for the Advancement of Academically Talented Youth, 1984) MEGSSS is an integrated, articulated seventh- through twelfth-grade mathematics program especially designed for students with excellent reading and reasoning ability who are in the upper 5% of the school population. One of its aims is to explore the upper content limits of mathematics which gifted students can understand and appreciate. Some of the more advanced parts of the program are not teacher-taught; students read the upper-level books on their own and then engage in discussions with the teacher. While there is accelerated content, the aim is to provide a breadth of mathematical knowledge so that the topics are chosen from a wide variety of mathematical fields. MEGSS is designed to familiarize the gifted student "with important mathematical problems, ideas, and theories that have at any time engaged the attention of serious mathematicians and serious users of mathematics . . . to bring the student as close as possible to the kinds of things that are of interest to contemporary mathematicians and contemporary users of mathematics" (Kaufman, Fitzgerald, and Harpel, 1981, p. 5). During the Era of Curriculum Innovation of the 1960s, programs like the Biological Sciences Curriculum Study (BSCS) not only made significant revisions in the biology curriculum but also prepared a special program for gifted students with more advanced concepts and content, more complex laboratory work, and more opportunities to undertake original, creative biological research. Like MEGSSS, the BSCS program for gifted students is not fast-paced, but does have an element of acceleration in providing advanced biological content at an earlier age than is usual.

Another aspect of differentiated curriculum aimed at developing the specialized talents of gifted students is found in the opportunities provided for independent study and research. They involve the individual, under the guidance of a teacher or a mentor, in identifying a problem or study area which he/she pursues and shares or communicates what has been learned. For independent study to be of value, the student must acquire necessary research and learning-how-to-learn skills, the modes of inquiry appropriate to the discipline area being studied, and the skills of identifying and using resources appropriate to the problem or area of inquiry. Independent study is not simply a student "going off on his/her own" but involves a particular kind of relationship with a teacher or mentor who provides guidance and feedback.

The focus of independent study and research obviously varies considerably. A student may undertake a research project in a particular discipline area, or study a problem or topic on an interdisciplinary basis, or prepare a work of art, or write a poem or short story. A student may undertake a self-study project in an advanced course such as an Advanced Placement program subject. A student may prepare a research project for competition such as the Westinghouse Science Talent Search. For maximum benefit, the independent study or research should involve opportunities for sharing, communicating, and critiquing the products or performances which result from such study activities.

Still another part of the specialized curriculum may be provided by cooperation between the high school and a college or university. Gifted students may attend regular classes or special classes during the day, after school, weekends or during the summer. They may attend classes with college/university students or special classes offered for high school students only. The programs may or may not carry college credit. Many such programs have been operating for a number of years while others have just been started recently. Columbia University, for example, has operated a Saturday Science Program for over 30 years with 500 gifted students selected from the metropolitan New York area attending special lectures and seminars and engaging in advanced laboratory research. Saturday and summer programs on campus are becoming increasingly popular as colleges and universities make their personnel and facilities available to gifted students to accelerate or enrich their curricula and to make learning opportunities available that cannot be or are not provided by the high schools.

Competitions and contests provide another way of extending the development of individual talents. Opportunities to participate in programs such as the Westinghouse Science Talent Search, Mathematics Olympiads, OM (formerly Olympics of the Mind), Future Problem Solving, poetry or essay contests, dance and music performances, etc. enable interaction, competition, and cooperation with gifted peers under conditions which push individuals to perform at their best.

What is called the extracurricular or cocurricular program of the high school also provides opportunities for talent development. This component of the school curriculum provides a wide range of learning opportunities in both formal and informal settings. The student government enables the development of leadership skills. Through a variety of teams, clubs, and other organizations, students are provided with learning opportunities which are usually not available in more formal curriculum offerings. Thus, the cocurricular activities represent a means of extending and enriching the curriculum for the gifted as well as other students.

The guidance process in the high school represents still another curriculum component in the sense of counseling affecting the learning of the student. Rothney and Koopman (1958) observed that guidance for the gifted varies from guidance of others in three respects:

1. Educational and occupational opportunities for the gifted are usually greater than for others.

2. Gifted pupils become ready for self-appraisal and self-conceptualization at higher levels and at earlier ages.

3. Gifted children may be subject to unusual pressures by parents, teachers, peers, and others. (p. 348)

A considerable amount of affective and cognitive development takes place in the individual and group counseling experiences provided gifted students. The guidance process constitutes a curriculum which is both structured and unstructured, formal and informal. It provides both substantive cognitive growth as well as affective development.

Education and socialization take place through a variety of non-school educational settings. There is a growing body of literature on the educating and socializing roles and functions of non-school agencies and institutions. For the gifted, as for other students, the non-school setting represents a rich resource for extending the curriculum. There are both personnel and material resources outside the school which can provide learning opportunities far beyond those which the school can offer. Mentor programs represent one kind of program enrichment. Museums, libraries, laboratories, studios, and agencies constitute learning settings with their own curricula. Community-based experiential learning uses human and material resources. Some schools have formalized such learning opportunities while others do little to integrate such experiences with curricular experiences. One school system has a Leadership Training Program in which juniors and seniors spend a semester with leaders in government, industry, media, social service or other areas and participate in a biweekly seminar during which the experiences are shared, analyzed, and critiqued and the learnings mediated. Other programs make it possible for gifted students to interact with gifted performers and producers. Other programs make resources available which a high school may be unable to provide.

PROVIDING A TOTAL LEARNING ENVIRONMENT

Curriculum for the gifted and talented at the secondary level involves more than deciding whether to accelerate or enrich, to group or not, to offer honors programs, advanced seminars, or Advanced Placement. All curriculum planning begins with determining what the goals and objectives are so that learning opportunities can be provided for the attainment of these ends. Curriculum for the gifted does not consist only of that portion which we label as honors courses, Advanced Placement, or by some clever acronym. Education of the gifted consists of the total learning environment and encompasses general education, specialized education, cocurricular, and education in non-school settings plus the climate which is created in the school and classroom. Students' affective and cognitive growth are strongly influenced by relationships, feeling-tone, and values which pervade the learning environment. The climate for learning constitutes a subliminal or covert curriculum. Self-concepts, perceptions of excellence and outstanding performance, attitudes, and motivation are all affected by the climate which is created. Pressey (1955) observed: "At any age, development of any ability is fostered by a favorable immediate environment, expert instruction, frequent and progressive opportunities for exercise of the ability, social facilitation and frequent success experiences" (p. 125). Curriculum for the gifted should contribute to the total learning environment of which Pressey spoke but it can only do this if all the curricula are considered and the issues concerning them resolved.

REFERENCES

Center for the Advancement of Academically Talented Youth. (1984). *Summer Programs 1984*. Baltimore, MD: Johns Hopkins University Press.

International Baccalaureate North America (IBNA). (1984). *Prospectus on IBNA Seminars 1983-84*. New York: International Baccalaureate North America.

Kaufman, B., Fitzgerald, J., & Harpel, J. (1981). *MEGSSS in Action*. St. Louis, MO: CEMREL.

Michael, L. S., & Fair, J. (1961). Program in a large comprehensive high school. In S. Everett (Ed.)., *Programs for the gifted: A case in secondary education*, Fifteenth Yearbook of the John Dewey Society (pp. 216–241). New York: Harper.

Passow, A. H. (1958). Enrichment of education for the gifted. In N. B. Henry, (Ed.), *Education for the gifted*. Fifty-Seventh Yearbook Part II of the National Society for the Study of Education (pp. 193–221). Chicago: University of Chicago Press.

Passow, A. H. (1982). Differentiated curricula for the gifted/talented, *Curricula for the Gifted* (pp. 1–20). Ventura, CA: Ventura County Superintendent of Schools Office.

Phenix, P. H. (1964). *Realms of meaning: A philosophy of the curriculum for general education*. New York: McGraw-Hill.

Pressey, S. L. (1955). Concerning the nature and nurture of genius. *Scientific Monthly*, *81*, 123–129.

Rothney, J. W. M., & Koopman, N. E. (1958). Guidance of the gifted. In N. B. Henry, (Ed.), *Education for the gifted*. Fifty-Seventh Yearbook Part II of the National Society for the Study of Education (pp. 347–361). Chicago: University of Chicago Press.

Stanley, Julian C. (1977). Rationale of the Study of Mathematically Precocious Youth (SMPY) during its first five years of promoting educational acceleration. In J. C. Stanley, W. C. George, and C. H. Solano, (Eds.). *The gifted and the creative: A fifty-year perspective*. Baltimore, MD: The Johns Hopkins University Press.

9

The Multiple Menu Model for Developing Differentiated Curriculum for the Gifted and Talented

Joseph S. Renzulli

University of Connecticut

The history of curriculum development for the gifted has witnessed a seesaw effect rather than an appropriate balance between authentic knowledge (content) and instructional techniques (process). The Multiple Menu Model

Editor's Note: From Renzulli, J. (1988). The multiple menu model for developing differentiated curriculum for the gifted and talented. *Gifted Child Quarterly*, 32(3), 298–309. © 1988 National Association for Gifted Children. Reprinted with permission.

is a practical set of planning guides that can assist curriculum developers in combining content with instructional strategies. Menus are provided in the areas of Knowledge, Instructional Objectives and Student Activities, Instructional Strategies, Instructional Sequences, and Artistic Modification. Each of the five planning menus is designed to provide specific forms of guidance for the construction of curricular material that is consistent with generally agreed upon goals of gifted education. A lesson planning guide is designed to synthesize and insure representation of the content and process selected from the respective menus.

Thinking ability is not a substitute for knowledge; nor is knowledge a substitute for thinking ability. Both are essential. Knowledge and thinking ability are two sides of the same coin.

—R.S. Nickerson

A nyone who sets out to develop curriculum for the gifted will invariably come face to face with two unavoidable realizations. First, the development of truly differentiated curricular material is a difficult and demanding process. It involves far more thought and work than "slapping together" a few process development activities, no matter how exciting these activities may be. An extraordinary amount of effort is necessary to produce material that will respect the curricular principles that have been set forth by various theorists and withstand the kinds of criticism leveled at many of the activities commonly used in programs for the gifted (Stanley, 1980, p. 234; Renzulli, 1977, Preface and Chapters 1 and 2).

A second realization is that there is a good deal of consensus among present day writers about underlying principles for developing differentiated curriculum. Although various approaches are recommended, the fact that there have been few if any "small wars" among theorists is testimony to the general acceptance of principles that can be found in the literature. Most of these principles, invariably phrased as "should statements," point out the need for curricular experiences that focus on thinking skills, abstract concepts, advanced level content, interdisciplinary studies, and a blending of content, process, and product (*NSSE Yearbook*, 1958; Passow, 1982). These same should-lists typically include principles that call for cooperative efforts between content scholars and teachers or instructional specialists.

From the vantage point of an idealist, the principles are worthy because they represent ultimate goals, and these goals have been widely accepted. Indeed, the principles form the veritable "gifted gerberfood" of the field because they represent the basic kind of information that forms the foundation of curriculum development. But from the perspective of a pragmatist, the principles are far too general to provide the kinds of specific guidance necessary for the practical job of actually writing differentiated curricular material. Curriculum developers are, by definition, pragmatists, because they must come up with tangible, practical outcomes. They also need guidance in overcoming the practical problems that are typically encountered in curriculum development. To do this they need both the principles of the idealist *and* the practical models that will allow them to translate principles into concrete products.

OVERVIEW OF THE MULTIPLE MENU MODEL

Experience gained through various curriculum projects has led to the development of the Multiple Menu Model for Developing Differentiated Curriculum for the Gifted (see Figure 1). The purpose of this model is to provide a practical set of planning guides that can assist curriculum developers in the process of combining authentic knowledge with several dimensions of instructional technique. The concept of a "menu" was selected because it conveys the idea of choices that can be made within each of the several components of the model. Each menu provides a range of options from which the curriculum developer can select the knowledge segments that will form the basis for a curricular unit, lesson, or lesson segment, and the various instructional techniques that will enable the knowledge to be taught in an interesting and effective manner. In later sections, we will examine each menu in detail and the specific procedures that are recommended for using the menus.

Putting the Research to Use

The model presented in this article is designed to provide curriculum developers with a concrete "blueprint" within which content and process can be applied in classroom or resource room settings. A broad range of specific dimensions of knowledge and instructional objectives are arranged into a series of "menus" from which curriculum authors can make choices based on the particular types of emphasis they would like to place on an instructional sequence. A *Lesson Planning Guide* that is designed to synthesize several components of a lesson is provided, and procedures for cross-referencing content and process are suggested.

RATIONALE

The rationale underlying this model is divided into the following four parts: a brief theory of knowledge, selected concepts from theories of curriculum and

Figure 1 The Multiple Menu Model for Developing Differentiated Curriculum

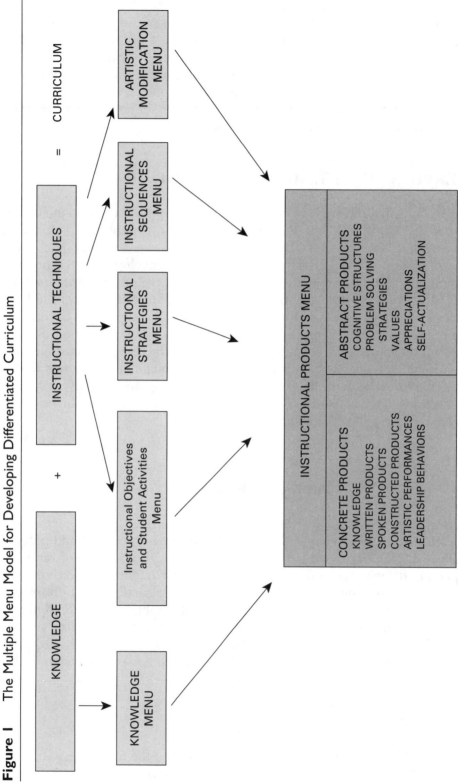

instruction, issues related to curricular differentiation, and the goals of special programming for the gifted.

A Brief Theory of Knowledge

Untold numbers of books have been written about theories of knowledge, and various authors have proposed several organizational systems for classifying knowledge and studying it in a systematic manner. Although any one of these organizational systems might serve as the rationale underlying a particular approach to curriculum development, the theory of knowledge that I have selected as a rationale for the Multiple Menu Model is one that focuses on both levels and functions of knowledge within any given content field.

The theory of knowledge underlying the Multiple Menu Model is based on three levels of knowing first suggested by the American psychologist and philosopher, William James (1885). These levels are: knowledge-of, knowledge-about (also referred to as knowledge-that), and knowledge-how. Before going on to describe these levels, it must be pointed out that each of the three levels, and especially the second and third levels, also exists on a continuum from the simple to the complex. It remains the responsibility of the curriculum developer to determine the degree of complexity within each level that might be appropriate for a given age or ability group. In the final analysis, it is the curriculum developer's understanding of the content field and instructional techniques, plus an understanding of cognitive, developmental, and differential psychology that will determine decision making with regard to the level of knowledge that might serve as appropriate content for a particular unit to be taught to a given age group. I also might add that a good deal of this understanding is undoubtedly the result of teaching experience gained through work with various age and ability groups combined with formal study in the three psychologies mentioned above.

Knowledge-Of. This entry level of knowing might best be described as an awareness level. Knowledge-of consists of being acquainted with rather than familiar with an area of study, a piece of information, or a person, place, object, or event. James (1885) referred to this level as "knowledge by acquaintance" to distinguish it from more advanced levels, which he referred to as "knowledge by systematic study and reflection." Thus, for example, I may be knowledgeable of a field of study called astrophysics, and I might even add that I know a little bit about what astrophysicists study. But it would be inaccurate to say that I am knowledgeable *about* astrophysics in any way other than a very superficial or awareness level.

Knowledge-of involves remembering (storage of knowledge), recollecting (retrieval of knowledge), and recognizing, but this level does not ordinarily include more advanced processes of mind that will be described below when we discuss knowledge-about. Most curriculum development efforts automatically begin with the knowledge-of level, but they proceed quickly to the knowledge-about level because this level represents the systematic study and reflection that James used to distinguish between lower and higher levels of knowing.

Knowledge-About. Knowledge-about represents a more advanced level of understanding than merely remembering or recalling information that has been learned. Knowledge-about builds upon remembering and recalling, but it also includes more advanced elements of knowing such as distinguishing, translating, interpreting, and being able to explain a given fact, concept, theory, or principle. Being able to explain something might also involve the ability to demonstrate it through physical or artistic performance (e.g., demonstrating a particular dance movement) or through a combination of verbal and manipulative activities (e.g., demonstrating how a piece of scientific apparatus works).

The amount of knowledge about a particular topic that should be included in a unit, lesson, or lesson segment, and the depth or complexity of coverage are among the most important decisions to be made in curriculum development. Persons who do not have an extensive background in the knowledge area in which they plan to develop curricular materials will undoubtedly need to acquire the knowledge necessary for their curriculum development efforts through formal courses, independent study, or by teaming up with specialists in the area in which they plan to develop curricular materials. A carefully selected introductory college textbook in a content field is usually the most economical way to begin acquiring the knowledge base necessary for curriculum development in a given field.

Knowledge-How. This level represents types of knowledge that enable persons to make new contributions to their respective fields of study. It deals mainly with the *application* of investigative methodology to the generation of the knowledge-about aspects of a given field of study. Scholars generally view knowledge-how as the highest level of involvement in a field. It represents the kind of work that is pursued by researchers, writers, and artists who are making new contributions to the sciences, humanities, and arts.

The theory of knowledge represented by James's three levels is used in this rationale in harmony with Alfred North Whitehead's (1929) concepts of romance, technical proficiency, and generalization. According to Whitehead, we first develop an interest in or romance with a particular field. A young person might, for example, develop a romance with the field of medicine as he or she explores the field at the knowledge-of level. Some people follow up this romance by pursuing a field or career to the point of becoming a proficient practitioner in one of the medical professions. Most professionals within a field reach their maximum involvement at this level; however, there are some persons who go on to the generalization level. It is these persons who say, in effect, "I want to add new information and contribute new knowledge to the field of medicine." This third level is, in many respects, consistent with one of the major goals of special programming for the gifted and talented. This point is further developed in the third part of this rationale.

Selected Concepts From Theories of Curriculum and Instruction

Because of space limitations, a disproportionate amount of the material that follows will focus on issues related to the above theory of knowledge; however, an important part of the rationale underlying the model draws upon the work of several persons who have made important contributions to curricular and instructional theory. These persons include Jerome Bruner (1960, 1966), A. Harry Passow (1982), Virgil Ward (1961), Philip Phenix (1964), Robert Gagne and Leslie Briggs (1979), Sandra Kaplan (1986), David Ausubel (1968), Albert Bandura (1977), and Benjamin Bloom and his colleagues (1954). Except in those instances where specific citations have been made, the work of these theorists is reflected in a blended way in most of the material that follows. Although these writers have influenced my overall thinking about the Multiple Menu Model, some of them might disagree with the applications of their work. I have, for example, relied heavily on Bloom's *Taxonomy* for major sections of the Knowledge and Instructional Objectives Menus, but I have also made some changes related to the placement of certain segments in the *Taxonomy*. The largest change deals with the category of Application (Bloom's Level 3.00), which I have always thought to be a product or outcome of *all* of the other processes listed in the *Taxonomy*.

Issues Related to Curricular Differentiation

A major part of the rationale underlying gifted education is that special programs will contribute to the development of persons who will be the inventors, leaders, and creative producers of the next generation. The Multiple Menu Model has been developed in a way that places a premium on both the organization and pursuit of authentic knowledge and the application of investigative methodology to problem areas within various content domains. As will be pointed out in a later section, three-fourths of the knowledge menu deals with the kinds of complex structures, principles, concepts, and research methods that characterize the *modus operandi* of the first-hand inquirer. Suggestions for using the instructional technique menus emphasize higher level thinking skills, less structured teaching strategies, and a concern for controversial issues, values, and beliefs. These areas of emphasis differ from the more factual, assimilative, and noncontroversial nature of most regular curricular materials.

Another issue related to curricular differentiation is concerned with content selection and procedures that will help to maximize the transfer of that which is learned. This issue is especially relevant today because of the accelerated rate at which knowledge is expanding. Futurists tell us that the amount of accumulated knowledge now doubles every twenty months, and a recent book (Naisbitt, 1982) reported that approximately 600 new scientific and professional articles are published each day in English! These awesome figures might suggest a potentially dangerous approach when it comes to curriculum development for highly able youth. The fact that brighter students can learn more material faster might lead us to become seduced by the quantitative (i.e., more-of-the-same) approach to curriculum development.

The Multiple Menu Model deals with this issue by concentrating on the various structural elements of a field and the basic principles and functional concepts (Ward, 1960) of given fields. Information of this type might best be referred to as enduring knowledge, as opposed to timely topics or transitory information. Principles and concepts should be viewed as tools that help the learner understand any and all of the selected topics of a content field. Thus, for example, understanding the concept of reliability is central to the study of psychological testing and therefore may be considered an example of an enduring element of that field.

In a similar fashion, the model deals with content selection by focusing on what Phenix calls representative topics (Phenix, 1964, p. 11). These topics consist of any and all of the content of a field that the curriculum developer might choose as the focus of a unit, lesson, or lesson segment. For example, a representative literary selection such as *The Merchant of Venice* can be used to illustrate (among other things) the key concept of a tragic hero. Reference to other selections that employ this key concept can be integrated into the unit of study, and a second or third selection might be necessary if an instructional objective is to compare and contrast tragic heroes. But it is not economical or feasible to cover an extensive list of selections if the concept can be dealt with through one or a few representative literary selections.

In view of the general goals of the model set forth above, I am not as concerned with the issue of knowledge-as-product as I am with the process objectives that have broader transfer value, such as application, appreciation, self-actualization, and improved cognitive structures. In other words, this model views representative topics as vehicles for process development. The structural dimensions and key concepts mentioned above provide the learner with tools for examining any or all of the vast number of topics in a given discipline. This model views the learner as one who is developing, practicing, applying, and (hopefully) gaining an appreciation of a particular segment of knowledge by studying Topic A, so that he or she may then use the same strategies to examine any one or a combination of Topics B through Z.

This model also places a great deal of emphasis on the appropriate use of methodology within content fields. All content fields can be defined, in part, by the research methods and investigative techniques that are used to add new knowledge to a given field of study. Most knowledge experts consider the appropriate use of methodology to be the highest level of competence in a content field. Indeed, this is the level at which research scientists, composers, authors, and academicians who are making new contributions to their fields typically operate. Although this level undoubtedly requires advanced understanding of a field, and sometimes requires the use of sophisticated equipment, young students can successfully learn and apply some of the entry level methodologies associated with most fields of knowledge (Bruner, 1960). The methodology dimension is also an important consideration for the development of differentiated curriculum because one of the major goals of education for the gifted is to develop a positive attitude toward the creative challenges of investigative activity and knowledge production. A focus on the acquisition and application of methodology also forces the issue of more active learning and a "hands on" involvement with a content field.

The Goals of Special Programming for the Gifted

The final part of the rationale underlying the Multiple Menu Model deals with the overall mission and the goals of providing special programs for the gifted. Although unanimous agreement on goals probably will never be achieved, it is nevertheless important for the curriculum developer to have some idea about the outcomes or products that are intended by a particular model. Persons who disagree in major ways with the stated goals of a given model should obviously seek other approaches to curriculum development.

The Multiple Menu Model is based on the belief that a curriculum for the gifted should result in both concrete and abstract products. These outcomes are reflected in the Instructional Products Menu that appears at the bottom of Figure 1. These two kinds of products generally work in harmony with one another and are separated here for analytic purposes only. The concrete products consist of the acquisition of specific segments of knowledge plus a broad range of tangible things that are actually produced by students (e.g., reports, stories, time lines, dances, musical compositions, etc.). It is important to emphasize that these concrete products are not considered ends in and of themselves. Rather, they are viewed as means or vehicles through which the various abstract products can be developed and applied (Renzulli, 1982).

The abstract products consist of more enduring and transferable outcomes of the learning process. In most cases, the abstract products take many years to reach full maturity; however, each curricular experience should make a contribution to one or a combination of these more enduring goals of instruction. The abstract products include improved cognitive structures and problem solving strategies, (Renzulli, 1977, pp. 64–68), the development of a value system (including new appreciations for knowledge, methodology, and the aesthetic aspects of knowledge), and the development of self-actualization. This final category includes specific affective components of development such as self-concept, self-efficacy (Bandura, 1977), and social and emotional adjustment. Taken collectively, concrete and abstract products of curriculum represent the overall goals of providing special programs for the gifted.

THE MENUS AND HOW TO USE THEM

This section will present a brief description of each menu and point out how the menus can be used for selecting the knowledge and instructional techniques that might be considered for the differentiated curricular unit, lesson, or lesson segment. Since the target audience of this article is professional educators, it is assumed that they will have a greater familiarity with the instructional technique menus that follow. For this reason, a disproportionate amount of descriptive information will be provided for the Knowledge Menu, and the discussion of the Instructional Technique Menus will focus more on application than description.

Figure 2   The Knowledge Menu

Content Field _____ Subdivision _____

I. Location, Definition, and Organization

II. Basic Principles and Functional Concepts

III. Knowledge About Methodology
    A. How to Identify a Problem Area Within a Content Field
    B. How to Find and Focus a Problem Within an Area
    C. How to State Hypotheses or Research Questions
    D. How to Identify Sources of Data
    E. How to Locate and Construct Appropriate
        Data Gathering Instruments
    F. How to Classify and Categorize Data
    G. How to Summarize and Analyze Data
    H. How to Draw Conclusions and State Generalizations
    I. How to Report Findings

                                                                                          "Tools"

IV. Knowledge About Specifics
    A. Facts
    B. Conventions
    C. Trends and Sequences
    D. Classifications and Categories
    E. Criteria
    F. Principles and Generalizations
    G. Theories and Structures

                                                                                         Applications

The Knowledge Menu

The Knowledge Menu (see Figure 2) is divided into four parts, the first three of which are considered "tools." The final part represents the vast number of specific topics within any field to which the tools may be applied as one goes about the process of "studying" a topic.

1. Location, Definition, and Organization [of a Field of Knowledge]

The first task in analyzing a given field of knowledge is to provide learners with information about where a field is "located" within the broad spectrum of knowledge, the general nature of a field, the various subdivisions of knowledge within that field, and the specific mission and characteristics of any given subdivision. This "knowledge about knowledge" dimension of this menu is designed to help the learner locate where, within any given organizational system, she/he may be working. The information is best conveyed by developing a knowledge tree and organizing a series of instructional activities that are designed to answer several of the following questions:

1. What is the overall purpose or mission of this field of study?
2. What are the major areas of concentration of each subdivision?
3. What kinds of questions are asked in the subdivisions?
4. What are the major sources of data in each subdivision?
5. How is knowledge organized and classified in this field or subdivision?
6. What are the basic reference books in the field or subdivision?
7. What are the major professional journals?
8. What are the major data bases? How can we gain access to them?
9. Is there a history or chronology of events that will lead to a better understanding of the field or subdivision?
10. Are there any major events, persons, places, or beliefs that are predominant concerns of the field, or best-case examples of what the field is all about?
11. What are some selected examples of "insiders' knowledge" such as field-specific humor, trivia, abbreviations and acronyms, "meccas," scandals, hidden realities, or unspoken beliefs?

Information on the Location, Definition, and Organization section of the Knowledge Menu can be very useful in selecting introductory activities that are designed to gain attention, develop interest, and stimulate motivation (cf., first category of Instructional Sequence Menu). For example, in a high school psychology course, the instructor always began by showing some slides of Sigmund Freud and other early leaders and telling the students a few anecdotes related to their most famous cases. Even the following list of titles, in and of itself, had great motivating power, as well as providing information related to Question No. 10 above.

The Girl Who Couldn't Breathe

The Man Who Loved Corsets

The Girl Who Couldn't Stop Eating

The outcome of this particular segment of the Knowledge Menu should lead to a general understanding of the structure of the field and a localization in one of the subdivisions of a particular field. Although there undoubtedly will be some overlap of information between subdivisions, and there will also be certain commonalities in information about the field in general, an instructional goal should be to lead students into an examination of the above questions with regard to the specific subdivision of the field being studied. Not every question on the list need be dealt with, nor should this segment of the Knowledge Menu necessarily be considered a major focus of the unit of study. Rather, our purpose is to help the learner see the "big picture" and the interrelationships that might exist among a field in general and its various subdivisions. This section of the Knowledge Menu is also designed to provide an overview or survey function. We might, for example, deal with Question No. 3 in a relatively superficial way during the early stages of a unit, but when we reach Section V of the Knowledge Menu (i.e., Methodology), this topic may become a major area of concentration in the study of a particular subdivision.

II. Basic Principles and Functional Concepts

Every field of knowledge is built upon a set of basic principles and key concepts that help to facilitate comprehension, information processing, and communication of information that is representative of the essence of the field. Some of these principles and concepts are applicable to several subdivisions within a given field, but, ordinarily, even the subdivisions have small numbers of concepts that are unique to that branch. Indeed, subdivisions of major fields of knowledge probably come into being because of unique concepts (as well as other factors) that result in the establishment of an individual identity.

Basic principles are generally agreed upon truths that have been arrived at through rigorous study and research. Principles may be factual and concrete (e.g., The earth revolves around the sun once every 365 and ¼ days), or they may be abstract and open to various interpretations (e.g., The major social institutions of a society are home, church, school, government, business/industry).

Functional Concepts (Ward, 1960) are the intellectual instruments or tools with which a subject area specialist works. In many ways these concepts serve as the vocabulary of a field and the vehicles by which scholars communicate precisely with one another. A good way to identify the functional concepts of a field is to examine the glossary that might be included in a basic textbook in that field. Like principles, there is usually a high degree of general agreement among scholars in a particular field about the meaning of functional concepts.

Perhaps the best way to understand the meaning of functional concepts is to provide specific examples from a number of different fields.

Field	Functional Concepts
Psychology	Selectivity of Perception
Mythology	Oral Transmission
Literature	Genre
Music	Tone
Dance	Rotation, Flexation, and Extension
Cinematography	Storyboarding
Chemistry	The Periodic Table
Biology	Tropisms

III. Knowledge About Methodology

The subcategories dealing with methodology represent a generally standard listing of investigative procedures that are followed in most fields of inquiry. Although general college level textbooks have been found to be a useful and economic source of information for locating knowledge about the other three sections of the Knowledge Menu, experience has shown that information about methodology is seldom included in these sources. For this reason, we have identified a fairly comprehensive collection of methodological resource (How-To) books that can be used to teach students the skills necessary for acquiring knowledge about methodology.* Another useful source consists of the laboratory manuals that frequently accompany college level textbooks.

This section of the Knowledge Menu is especially important for curriculum development because it has important implications for more active kinds of instructional techniques. By providing students with the know-how of investigative methodology, we increase the probability of more inductive or "hands on" kinds of learning experiences. Once students have learned basic information about a field or topic and the procedures for doing some kind of research related to that topic, we can proceed to the application level, which is considered by many to be the highest level of involvement in a field of study. Student investigations may be limited in scope and complexity, and they frequently may follow prescribed scenarios, such as the ones typically found in laboratory manuals. At the same time, however, the inclusion of even junior level investigative activities in curricular materials forces us to go beyond the omnipresent didactic mode of instruction that has been the subject of so much criticism of education in recent years (Goodlad, 1984).

IV. Knowledge About Specifics

This section of the menu encompasses the main body of knowledge that makes up the content of any given field. It is from this area that curriculum developers should select representative topics illustrative of basic principles, functional concepts, or certain methodologies. Knowledge about specifics provides a vast warehouse of information from which selected aspects of content may be drawn and to which the "tools" described above may be applied. The size and diversity of knowledge about specifics provides the curriculum developer with an almost limitless opportunity to select interesting and dynamic topics that will maximize student interest, motivation, and enthusiasm about a particular field of study.

The several subcategories listed under Knowledge About Specifics are based on the first level of Bloom's *Taxonomy* (1954). This analysis of

---

*A copy of this book list can be obtained by writing to the author

various ways in which knowledge is organized is helpful in identifying organized components of a particular field. I have found, however, that when examining a content area for curriculum development, it may not always be easy to classify a topic according to the subcategories in this section of the Knowledge Menu. For this reason, it is recommended that curriculum developers also consider selecting content on the basis of the ways in which topics are organized in standard (college level) text and reference books. After a unit has been developed, it is a good idea to review the material in an effort to identify facts, conventions, trends and sequences, etc. It is also a good idea to call these subcategories to the attention of students, either through direct instruction or by asking them to analyze material according to the ways in which Knowledge About Specifics is classified.

The Instructional Objectives/Student Activities Menu

This combined menu (see Figure 3) of instructional objectives and student activities is designed to provide the curriculum developer with a wide range of both general statements and specific behaviors that are associated with various aspects of learning. The first section of the menu (Assimilation and Retention) deals with information input or pickup processes. The second section (Information Analysis) focuses on a broad range of thinking skills that describe the ways in which information can be processed in order to achieve greater levels of understanding. The third section (Information Synthesis and Application) deals with the output or products of the thinking process. The final section (Evaluation) is also an output process, but in this case the focus is on the review and judgment of information in terms of aesthetic, ethical, and functional qualities.

There are three important considerations that the curriculum developer should keep in mind when using this menu. First, the four categories on the menu are not intended to be followed in a linear and sequential fashion. In the real world of thinking and problem solving, we must often cycle back to more advanced levels of information input and analysis activities in order to improve the scope and quality of our products and judgments. The overall process, therefore, must be viewed as a cyclical or spiraling sequence of interrelated activities rather than a linear chain of events.

The second consideration relates to the general goal of achieving both specificity and comprehensiveness in the overall process of curriculum development. Each unit and lesson should be developed in such a way that we are as certain about the process objectives as we are about the content to be taught. And over a given period of time, we should attempt to achieve comprehensiveness in process development by selecting a diverse range of objectives and student activities. In this regard, this and other menus should be used as checklists that will help us to achieve balance as well as a catalogue of processes from which selections can be made.

Figure 3   The Instructional Objectives/Student Activities Menu

I. Assimilation and Retention

Listening	Reading
Observing	Sensing
Touching	Smelling
Counting	Manipulating
Sketching	Note Taking
Naming	

Identifying Information Types (e.g., Raw Data, Opinion, etc.)
Identifying Information Sources (e.g., Encyclopedias, Almanacs, etc.)
Identifying Information Retrieval Systems

II. Information Analysis

Classifying:
  Sorting into Component Parts
  Matching Properties
  Organizing and Reorganizing
  Distinguishing and Comparing

Interpreting:
  Questioning
  Discussing
  Debating
  Inferring
  Translating (Transforming)

Sequencing and Patterning:
  Ordering
  Tabulating
  Graphing and Charting
  Measuring

  Interpolating
  Extrapolating
  Interrelating
  Restating
  Speculating (Trial and Error)

Data Gathering:
  Interviewing
  Using Instruments
  Experimenting

Concluding and Explaining
  Critiquing
  Summarizing
  Defending a Position
  Hypothesizing

Exploring Alternatives:
  Estimating
  Brainstorming
  Creative Problem Solving
  Problem Finding
  Problem Focusing

  Generalizing
  Practicing
  Demonstrating
  Presenting

III. Information Synthesis and Application
  Writing:
    Literary (Fictional), Musical Composition
    Technical, Editorial, Journalistic (Non-fictional)

Speaking/Presenting:
  Artistic
  Functional/Informative
  Opinionative

Constructing:
  Artistic
  Functional

(Continued)

Figure 3   (Continued)

Painting, Drawing, Designing:	Performing:
Artistic	Dance
Functional	Drama
Managing:	Movement
Producing	Music
Directing	
Leading	
Arranging	
Conducting	

IV. Evaluation

Judging According to Internal Sets of Criteria (Personal Values, Aesthetic Preferences, Individual Beliefs and Attitudes)

Judging According to External Sets of Criteria (Conventional Standards for Judging Quantitative or Qualitative Ideas or Products)

Finally, the objectives and activities on this menu are designed to embrace the full range of affective processes. It is assumed that processes such as attending, receiving, and valuing take place in an integrated fashion when students pursue activities set forth in this menu and when such activities are combined with certain topics (knowledge) that enhance the development of affective processes. For this reason a separate affective menu was not included in the model. This decision was also made in order to simplify the process by avoiding the addition of another layer of complexity to the curriculum developer's task.

Instructional Strategies Menu

This menu (see Figure 4) provides a broad range of strategies that represent the ways in which teachers organize learning situations.** The strategies range from highly structured situations to those in which greater degrees of self directedness are placed upon the learner. Many of the strategies are, of course, used in combination with one another.

As is the case with menus discussed earlier, an effort should be made to achieve a balance in the use of these strategies. An effort also should be made to develop curricular experiences for brighter students that favor the less structured end of the instructional strategies continuum. This recommendation is consistent with the overall goals of gifted education and the emphasis that most

---

** A small book could undoubtedly be written on each of the instructional strategies included on this menu. Space does not permit adequate coverage of the strategies in this article; however, most general textbooks on instruction contain descriptive information about these topics.

Figure 4   Instructional Strategies Menu

   I. Recitation and Drill
  II. Peer Tutoring
 III. Programmed Instruction
 IV. Lecture
  V. Lecture and Discussion
 VI. Discussion
 VII. Guided Independent Study or Exploration (With or Without a Teacher or Mentor)
VIII. Learning or Interest Center Activity
 IX. Simulation, Role Playing, Dramatization, Guided Fantasy
  X. Learning Games
 XI. Replicative Reports or Projects
XII. Investigative Reports or Projects
XIII. Unguided Independent Study or Exploration
XIV. Internship or Apprenticeship

---

special programs place on both self-directed learning and creative productivity. Finally, attention should be given to matching certain strategies with particular types of knowledge. Thus, for example, the simulation or role playing strategy might "fit" more appropriately with content dealing with a controversial issue, and the programmed instruction strategy would undoubtedly work well with content designed to teach computer operation skills.

Instructional Sequence Menu

This menu (see Figure 5) is based on the work of major learning theorists such as Gagne and Briggs (1979) and Ausubel (1968). The specific aspects of their work reflected in this menu deal with the organization and sequence of events that help to maximize the outcomes of a preplanned learning activity. This menu differs from the others in that the items are likely to be followed in a sequential fashion. It is important to point out, however, that the sequence may be "recycled" several times in a single unit and sometimes even within a given lesson.

According to Gagne and Briggs, an important consideration in sequencing instruction is to organize material in such a way that the learner has mastered necessary prerequisites. Prerequisites are broadly interpreted to include a favorable attitude toward the material to be learned as well as essential terminology, functional concepts, and basic factual information. For this reason the Instructional Sequence Menu begins with an item that calls attention to the need for gaining attention and developing motivation. Gagne and Briggs also emphasize the value of relating present topics to relevant previously learned material and, whenever possible, integrating present topics into a larger framework that will add greater meaning to the topic at hand. This concern is dealt with, in part, through the strategies recommended in the first section of the

Figure 5   Instructional Sequence Menu

I.   Gaining Attention, Developing Interest and Motivation
II.   Informing Students About the Purpose or Objective of a Given Unit, Lesson, or Lesson
       Segment, and Providing Advanced Organizers About the Material that will be Covered.
III.   Relating the Topic to Relevant Previously Learned Material
IV.   Presenting the Material Through One or a Combination of Instructional Strategies and
       Student Activities. (Note: Emphasize Distinction Between the Following Two *General*
       Student Roles:
       A. Listening, Observing, and Notetaking
       B. Participating, Interacting, and Receiving Feedback)
V.   Providing Options and Suggestions for Advanced Level Follow-Up Activities on an
       Individual or Group Basis
VI.   Assessing Performance and Providing Feedback
VII.   Providing Advanced Organizers for Related Future Topics
VIII. Pointing Out Transfer Opportunities and Potential Applications.

Knowledge Menu. Finally, Gagne and Briggs recommend that transfer not be left to chance but rather that curriculum developers provide linkages between information learned and other situations in which such information may be applied. In a similar fashion, Ausubel's theory of meaningful learning maintains that learning is enhanced when students are provided with a preview or overview of the material to be taught and the ways in which the material is organized. These "advanced organizers" can be most easily dealt with by making students aware of content and process objectives at the beginning of the instructional sequence.

The Artistic Modification Menu

Most teachers have had the experience of teaching a lesson that was so successful and satisfying that at its conclusion they might have signed it (figuratively speaking) in much the same way that an artist signs a painting. This kind of personal involvement and excitement is more likely to occur when curriculum developers teach their own material. When the same material is used by other teachers, some of the effervescence is likely to be lost. The curriculum developer can take steps to stimulate or recapture intended excitement about a particular topic by encouraging teachers to approach a unit or lesson with some degree of artistic license. This license should include the right and the responsibility to criticize and interpret curricular content, to examine content in relation to the teacher's own values, and to add content of the teacher's own choosing, even if additional material is in conflict with the prescribed content of a unit of study. In other words, this menu (see Figure 6) asks curriculum developers to invite teachers to make their own creative contribution to a previously developed piece of curricular material.

Figure 6   The Artistic Modification Menu

___

I. Sharing with students a personal experience that is directly or indirectly related to the content (e.g., Showing slides of the trip you took to the Globe Theater and Stratford-on-Avon in connection with a unit on Shakespeare)

II. Sharing personal knowledge or insiders' information about a person, place, event, or topic. (e.g., Pointing out a *Time* magazine article on the controversy surrounding the authenticity of Margaret Mead's research in connection with a unit on anthropology)

III. Sharing personal interests, hobbies, independent research, or significant involvements in personal activities. (e.g., Showing students your own family tree in connection with a unit on genealogy)

IV. Sharing personal values and beliefs. (e.g., Describe events related to your participation in a civil rights demonstration in connection with a unit on contemporary American history.)

V. Sharing personal collections, family documents, or memorabilia. (e.g., Bringing to class your collection of newspapers, magazines, etc. that describe the events surrounding the assassination of John F. Kennedy in connection with a unit dealing with the Civil War and the death of Abraham Lincoln)

VI. Interpreting and sharing your own enthusiasm about a book, film, television program, or artistic performance that is related to a topic you are covering. (e.g., Telling a "spy story" from a book such as *The Man Called Intrepid* in connection with the study of World War II)

VII. Pointing out controversies, biases, or restrictions that might be placed on books, newspapers, or other sources of information. (e.g., Magazines that depend heavily on advertising by tobacco and liquor corporations might tend to avoid publishing articles on the dangers of smoking and alcohol)

VIII. Other (Suggest additional ways in which teachers might personalize the material that you have included in a particular unit or lesson)

___

From a practical standpoint, the purpose of the menu is to provide teachers with a series of suggestions that will enable them to add their own artistic interpretation to curricular material that has been prepared by others. The concept of artistic interpretation is based (in part) on an extremely insightful paper by Phenix (1987) in which he points out that instructional material can be either alive or dead, depending on the ways in which it is used or misused in the teaching-learning process. When material is imported from sources other than the teacher's own experience, it may assume an alien quality when not properly mediated by the teacher. Proper mediation means that the teacher is able to personalize and interpret curricular material in such a way that he or she brings life and meaning to the content.

Suggestions for artistic modification can be general or specific, but they must always be personal (rather than prescribed motivational activities) because the purpose is to encourage teachers to put *themselves* into the material rather than drawing on the experiences of the curriculum developer. The goal of this aspect of the model is to create excitement and involvement in the teacher so that she or he can, in turn, arouse interest, curiosity, and motivation on the part of students. Reflecting upon material before it is taught, even if it has been taught many times before, is as important to the teaching process as warm-up activities are for creating physical readiness and a positive mental attitude for the athlete. The interaction of prepared curricular material with the personal involvement of teachers will result in a "spontaneous combustion" that helps to bring the material to life.

In some cases teachers may already be prepared to inject their own personal involvement into prepared material, but in others some background reading or other types of preparation may be necessary. The curriculum developer can assist in the process by recommending background reading material for the teacher that contains unusual insights, controversies, little known facts, or insiders' information that is not likely to be included in the regular material prepared for students. Although curriculum developers will want to include effective motivational activities in their regular materials, this menu should not be interpreted as another opportunity to give the teacher a favorite activity. Background material can be recommended, but any instructional activity emanating therefrom must be created by the teacher because the goal is for teachers to "psych themselves up" to approach any teaching situation with the mind set of a creative artist.

Curriculum by Design: Putting It All Together

The goal of the Multiple Menu Model is to achieve balance and coordination between knowledge and instructional technique and to proceed from the abstract to the practical in the process of curriculum development. The complexity of the task defies simplification, but a certain amount of efficiency can be introduced into curriculum development by specifying the options that are available with regard to content and process and by pointing out procedures that can be used for blending together several factors that need to be considered simultaneously when developing curriculum.

Although the several options that represent the structure of this model are presented in the respective menus, two other conditions are necessary for the effective use of this or any other planning guide. First, the curriculum developer must understand the concepts presented on the menus. The appropriate use of an instructional activity such as extrapolating, or an instructional strategy such as simulation will elude us if we do not have a practical understanding of both the concepts and how we can put them to work in a learning situation.

The second condition for successful use of this model involves some kind of plan or guide for synthesizing the respective menus at the practical or output level (i.e., actually writing curricular material). Although there is still some controversy about whether knowledge (content) or instructional technique (process) should be the focus of curriculum planning, this model has chosen to place knowledge at the center of the planning process. At the same time, however, the planning guide presented in Figure 7 is structured in a way that encourages

Figure 7   Multiple Menu Model Lesson Planning Guide

Unit Title ——————————————— Author ———————————————————

Lesson Block Title ————————————— Lesson No. ———————————————

Instructional Objectives & Activities	Instructional Strategies
Artistic Modifications	Instructional Products
Previous Lessons or Necessary Backgound Material	
"Storyboarding" the Lesson: Provide a sequential outline of the knowledge (content) to be covered in this lesson. Include chapter or page references to textbooks or other sources, and attach resource material that the teacher will need in order to prepare for and/or teach this lesson. Cross reference the content with the instructional techniques listed above by underlining all words and phrases that refer to objectives, strategies, and products. Use additional pages if necessary.	

curriculum developers to consider each of the instructional technique menus in conjunction with the preparation of content. Taken collectively, the several menus and the planning guide direct us to consider a broad range of options and to interrelate the many factors that must be considered when attempting to achieve balance and comprehensiveness in curriculum development.

REFERENCES

Ausubel, D.P. (1968). *Educational psychology: A cognitive view*. New York: Holt, Rinehart and Winston.

Bandura A. (1977). Self-efficacy: Toward a unifying theory of behavioral change. *Psychological Review, 84*, 191–215.

Bloom, B.S. (Ed.) (1954). *Taxonomy of educational objectives. Handbook I: Cognitive domain*. New York: Longman.

Bruner, J.S. (1960). *The process of education*. Cambridge, MA: Harvard University Press.

Bruner, J.S. (1966). *Toward a theory of instruction*. Cambridge, MA: Harvard University Press.

Gagne, R.M., & Briggs, L.J. (1979). *Principles of instructional design* (2nd ed.). New York: Holt, Rinehart and Winston.

Goodlad, J.I. (1984). *A place called school: Prospects for the future*. New York: McGraw-Hill.

James, W. (1885). On the functions of cognition. *Mind, 10*, 27–44.

Kaplan, S.N. (1986). The grid: A model to construct differentiated curriculum for the gifted. In J.S. Renzulli (Ed.). *Systems and models for developing programs for the gifted and talented*. Mansfield Center, CT: Creative Learning Press.

Naisbitt, J. (1982). *Megatrends*. New York: Warner Books.

National Society for the Study of Education. (1958). *Education for the gifted* (57th Yearbook). Chicago: University of Chicago Press.

Passow, A.H. (1982). *Differentiated curricula for the gifted/talented.* Ventura, CA: Leadership Training Institute on the Gifted and Talented.

Phenix, P.H. (1964). *Realms of meaning.* New York: McGraw-Hill.

Phenix, P.H. (1987). Views on the use, misuse, and abuse of instructional materials. Paper presented at the Annual Meeting of the Leadership Training Institute on the Gifted and Talented, Houston.

Renzulli, J.S., & Nearine, R. (1968). Curriculum development for the gifted. *Accent on Talent (NEA), 2,* 9–12.

Renzulli, J.S. (1970). A curriculum development model for academically superior students. *Exceptional Children, 36,* 611–615.

Renzulli, J.S. (1977). *The enrichment triad model: A guide for developing defensible programs for the gifted.* Mansfield Center, CT: Creative Learning Press.

Renzulli, J.S. (1982). What makes a problem real? Stalking the illusive meaning of qualitative differences in gifted education. *Gifted Child Quarterly, 26,* 4, 49–59.

Stanley, J.C. (1980). On educating the gifted. *Educational Researcher, 9,* 10.

Ward, V.S. (1960). Systematic intensification and extensification of the school curriculum. *Exceptional Children, 28,* 67–71, 77.

Ward, V.S. (1961). *Educating the gifted: An axiomatic approach.* Columbus, OH: Merrill.

Whitehead, A.N. (1929). The rhythm of education. In A.N. Whitehead (Ed.) *The aims of education.* New York: Macmillan.

10

A Mathematics Curriculum for the Gifted and Talented

Grayson H. Wheatley

A mathematics program for the gifted and talented should provide for the diverse needs of individuals and a changing society as well. With the impact of information technology, the nature of knowledge is shifting. Schools must adjust or face obsolescence. Actually, many (most) schools will not change, in my judgment, and thus our youth will be "miseducated."

The curriculum being used in schools today was developed for an industrial society and requires major restructuring to prepare children for a future where computers will be the major tool for all areas of work and thought. In an industrial society, it is assumed that work will be done by machines being controlled by man. Many repetitive tasks are required. In the present information-based society, the focus is on access and transmission of information. Many routine tasks will

Editor's Note: From Wheatley, G. (1983). A mathematics curriculum for the gifted and talented. *Gifted Child Quarterly*, 27(2), 77–80. © 1983 National Association for Gifted Children. Reprinted with permission.

be performed by automated machines, freeing workers for more interesting and varied tasks. Furthermore, in almost every aspect of life the computer is a tool for thought and work. The present curriculum was developed for a society very different from the present; it is time changes were made.

During this century, the demands of an industrial society led to the rise in influence of behavioristic psychology on American education. Within the past few years there has been a surge of interest in cognitive psychology with emphasis on motivation, attention, thought processes, and other patterns of human cognition. While behavioristic approaches are appropriate for certain types of knowledge such as skill learning, programs for the gifted must break out of rule-oriented instruction.

The gifted are capable of mathematical achievement many times greater than we see in today's schools under existing curriculum. For example, sixth graders are capable of performing at the level of many university courses. Through several talent search programs, sixth-, seventh-, and eighth-grade pupils are taking the Scholastic Aptitude Test (SAT). Often, gifted and talented children in these grades score above the national average for college-bound seniors. The gifted are often blocked from rapid advances in conceptual thought by the almost exclusive emphasis on skill learning. The bright child can become mired in the details of skill acquisition and never experience the thrill of soaring with intellectual ideas. We must reorient the mathematics curriculum with attention to principles and concepts. Skill acquisition can be achieved quite efficiently when seen from a perspective of problem solving and application.

In today's schools, children expect to apply a rule. All of their experience has lead them to this expectation. Children think, "What am I expected to do with this task?", rather than focusing on the important ideas and relationships involved. This can be overcome only by changing content and approaches. In a recent study, we found that by studying problem solving, sixth-grade children can break out of such a rule orientation (problem solving is what you do when you don't know what to do). In the study (Wheatley & Wheatley, 1982), children learned heuristics for solving nonroutine problems. They worked in small groups to solve a variety of problems using such heuristics as look for a pattern, draw a diagram, and guess and test. After one semester the children in the experimental group were much more effective in solving problems; their scores were more than three times that of the control group. Furthermore, they did not respond with "I don't know how to do this problem," realizing that they had tools for exploring the problem which could lead to an understanding and solution.

In designing a mathematics curriculum for the gifted and talented, many factors must be considered. Certainly the gifted and talented must have good computational skills. But computational skill must not be the beginning point. This is a fatal error that has been made in the past. Teachers have reasoned that they would introduce problem solving and advanced topics only *after* the computations had been mastered. This approach fails, for a variety of reasons, among which is the very nature of skill learning. Skills must be practiced and maintained. A teacher can always justify devoting more time on a particular skill unless every child shows mastery. Of course this never happens. Furthermore, learning computational skills is just plain boring. In contrast, mathematics is exciting and alive. By emphasizing problem solving, children can see the reason for computational skills and learn them much more efficiently. Thus computational skills need not be mastered *before* using mathematics but should be learned simultaneously with the consideration of ideas and reasoning patterns. We must also recognize that alternatives now exist for performing complex computations. With the broad availability of calculators and computers, certain time consuming computational topics may no longer warrant the time allocated to them. After all, "Scaring the saber-tooth tiger" continued to be taught long after the tigers had vanished (Peddiwell, 1939).

Some worry that the use of calculators and computers will interfere with learning the "basics." We often read that calculators in the schools will lead to a nation of mindless button pushers. On the other hand, emphasis on computation will result in a nation of mindless pencil pushers. Ideally, we want adults that can reason and make effective use of the available tools.

Educators must not wait for textbooks which will contain mathematics content appropriate for gifted and talented students; they will probably never be widely available. A local school district can, however, build a program using available materials. Listed below are ten elementary school mathematics strands for the gifted and talented with suggested percentage of time. The allocation of time to the strands is intended as a guide, to convey relative importance. The relatively small percentage allocated to facts and computation is likely to be controversial but I feel there is merit in limiting this strand. Much computational skill practice occurs in other strands, especially problem solving.

1. Problem solving 20%

2. Estimation and mental arithmetic 6%

3. Numeration 6%

4. Geometry and measurement 15%

5. Spatial visualization 5%

6. Probability and statistics 6%

7. Arithmetic & algebra concepts 12%

8. Facts and computations 15%

9. Applications 5%

10. Computer programming 10%

Each of these strands will now be discussed.

PROBLEM SOLVING

Of all the units of study, problem solving may be the most fundamental. Typically, schools are very careful to make sure students know exactly what to do with each assignment. Yet outside of school we often face tasks and problems where we don't know what to do. There are general ways of proceeding when we don't know what to do. Children can learn to apply problem-solving heuristics. Problem solving can be the organizer which gives meaning to all that is studied. It can have a thermostatic effect in balancing the study of skills and memorization of facts.

An excellent way to teach problem solving is to introduce problem-solving heuristics. Heuristics appropriate at the elementary school level are: make a list, look for a pattern, guess and test, draw a diagram, and work backwards. As these heuristics are taught, nonroutine problems can be assigned for small groups of students to solve. Students profit greatly by discussing their ideas with others. After the groups have solved the problems, it is a good idea to have each group describe how they solved a problem. In this way students become more aware of their thought processes and thus able to make conscious decisions in attacking a new problem. For more information on teaching problem solving, see Charles and Lester (1982).

ESTIMATION AND MENTAL ARITHMETIC

While esimation skill has always been important, increased emphasis on this topic is warranted because of societal changes. With increasing frequency, number manipulation is being accomplished by calculators and computers. While the user may not have as great a need for paper and pencil computational skills, the need for evaluating results is increased. Children need to develop a facility and sensitivity for the reasonableness of an answer. Thus, increased emphasis must be placed on this topic. Throughout the elementary school years children should learn techniques for estimating and be taught the importance of estimating results.

In the GUESS materials (Reys & Reys, 1983), five strategies for numerical estimation are developed. These strategies, front ends, rounding, compatibles, averaging, and adjusting have proven quite effective in building estimation skills.

NUMERATION

At beginning levels, the concept of place value looms large in importance. Extensive use of manipulatives, such as Unifix Cubes, are invaluable to the young child in developing a sound concept of place value. At the intermediate level other numeration systems should be introduced. By studying other numeration systems, a child can better understand the base ten system. Also, and most importantly, increased use of computers suggests the value of learning the binary and hexadecimal systems. A mathematics program for the gifted and talented should place emphasis on numeration systems.

GEOMETRY AND MEASUREMENT

Over the past 25 years, geometry has joined arithmetic as a component of the elementary school mathematics program. Because Euclidean geometry was so firmly entrenched as a high school mathematics course, it has taken time to sort out the geometry topics and approaches for the elementary school. Much has been learned about teaching geometry but little has been implemented. By emphasizing concepts and principles rather than proof or computations of areas, a foundation in geometry can be established. Graphical representation of information is of increasing importance, thus, this topic should be fully developed.

SPATIAL VISUALIZATION

While children are learning to reason analytically and logically, it is important they also learn to reason spatially. The theory of hemispheric specialization (Wheatley, Frankland, Mitchell, & Kraft, 1978) suggests that the brain divides its work. Bogen (1969) suggests that the two modes of thought are appositional. It is becoming increasingly apparent that the ability to visualize spatial transformations is important in mathematics, science, and engineering. In the elementary school, children should have the opportunity to develop their spatial ability.

PROBABILITY AND STATISTICS

In the past 25 years probability has greatly increased in importance. Many aspects of chemistry and physics have been reconceptualized in terms of probability. From economics to archeology, probabilistic thought plays an important part in the formulation of ideas. Young minds need to begin to consider the chance of an event occurring rather than thinking in absolute terms. For these reasons it is important that the gifted and talented learn early to think probabilistically while they are forming their patterns of reasoning.

ARITHMETIC AND ALGEBRAIC CONCEPTS

There are numerous arithmetic principles and concepts which are essential for an educated person. Such topics as prime, composite, factor, divisibility, ratio, and proportion are but some of the important arithmetic concepts which should be in the curriculum of gifted and talented students. Additionally, certain algebraic ideas are appropriate for elementary school children. Too long we have considered algebra only as a high school course, just as we once did with geometry. It is time that the gifted and talented study the concept of variable, signed numbers, equations of curves in a plane, and intuitive solutions of number sentences.

FACTS AND COMPUTATIONS

A survey of current texts will show that more than 50% of the school year is spent on computation and memorization of facts. In practice, most teachers spend closer to 70% of the year on these topics. A key to providing for the gifted and talented is limiting the time on computation. Gifted children not only learn faster but they retain what they learn. The current texts are built on the assumption that topics will be repeated from year to year. Typically, a sixth-grade text will contain extensive review and reteaching of each topic. In fact, little prior knowledge is assumed. This approach is particularly devastating for the gifted. They are forced to study material they already understand. The time for facts and computations can be reduced providing time for other topics. A diagnostic-prescriptive instructional strategy is particularly appropriate for this strand.

APPLICATIONS

Mathematics is studied so that it can be applied. As students learn concepts and skills, it is important that they learn also to apply these ideas. The typical mathematics word problem, not to be confused with problem solving, should be considered. In applications, children may learn specific methods for solving certain classes of problems, but primarily, applications give meaning to the ideas studied.

COMPUTER PROGRAMMING

Knowledge about computers is becoming essential. Many colleges include computer literacy as part of their entrance requirements. The gifted and talented must have the opportunity to become computer literate. Furthermore, computer programming is an excellent context for problem solving. The reasoning patterns and discipline developed in writing and debugging a computer program are important educational experiences. Because young children seem to learn to program computers with such ease, the elementary school is a prime time for the gifted to learn their use.

SUMMARY

Developing a mathematics program for the gifted is more than setting a faster pace through existing textbooks. It is important to step back and take a broad view of the problem. What type of thinking do we want to encourage? What do we want children to know? What modes of instruction are appropriate? This paper has outlined ten major strands in elementary school mathematics. The mathematics needs of the eighties and nineties will be different from the fifties and sixties. We must plan for the future. Certainly the gifted should be encouraged to reason and relate ideas. Problem solving is an excellent tool for this purpose. Computers are rapidly becoming a standard tool for thought and work. The gifted must learn to use them and this should include writing computer programs. With increased use of computers and calculators it is important that estimation skills be strong. Additionally, there is the necessity for acquiring concepts, principles, facts, and mathematical rules. We must strive to achieve the proper balance between computational skill and higher level thinking; both are important. A major thesis of this paper is that present textbooks do not develop higher level reasoning but over-emphasize computational rules. The ten strands described can form the basis for a balanced mathematics program for the gifted.

MATERIALS

Problem Solving

Four booklets for the gifted are available from the Matteson School District. One of the booklets is devoted to problem solving in four content subjects.

Curriculum Concept Units for the Gifted K-8 Matteson School District # 162, 21244 Illinois Street, Matteson, IL 60441.

Dale Seymour Press publishes a variety of excellent materials for teaching problem solving. Write for a catalog. P.O. Box 10888, Palo Alto, CA 94303. Among the materials are:
Techniques of Problem Solving. A box of 200 problems specially selected for the gifted.
Problem of the Week. A collection of problems available on a wall poster.

Other Sources of Good Problems

Problem Solving: A Basic Mathematical Goal. A two-book resource on techniques of teaching heuristics; also includes good problems.

Estimation

The GUESS materials written by Robert and Barbara Reys and published by Dale Seymour Press are organized in two sequential boxes of cards. There are teaching and practice cards.

Numeration

One of the Curriculum Concept Units (see above) called Symbols treats numeration, especially base two and base 16.

Geometry and Measurement

Existing textbook materials can be adapted to teach geometry. Excellent supplements are available from Creative Publications, P.O. Box 10328, Palo Alto, CA 94303. If your school does not have a catalog, write for one.

Spatial Visualization

Creative Publications is a source of materials. See particularly Tessellations, Tangrams, Pattern Blocks, and Parquetry.

Probability and Statistics

The Curriculum Concept Units mentioned above include a booklet on Reasoning which contains units on probability for the gifted. Most textbooks have units on probability and statistics. These can be adapted. The National Council of Teachers of Mathematics has an excellent Yearbook which contains activities and suggestions for teaching probability and statistics.

National Council of Teachers of Mathematics, *Probability and Statistics*. Reston, VA: National Council of Teachers of Mathematics, 1981. Write: NCTM, 1906 Association Dr., Reston, VA 22091.

Arithmetic and Algebraic Concepts

Carefully selected topics from existing texts can be used.

Facts and Computations

Existing textbooks are excellent for teaching facts and computations. Care must be exercised to tailor the pace and coverage to the individuals. A diagnostic-prescriptive approach can be quite effective.

Applications

Mathematics textbooks contain problems which are designed to have pupils apply what they have learned. Additional efforts should be made to identify other applications as situations in the classroom arise. Projects can be encouraged which involve the application of mathematics.

Computer Programming

There are many new materials becoming available for teaching programming and computer literacy. For the gifted, the emphasis should be on computing rather than just learning about computers. One excellent set of materials available from the Math Group stand out.

Computer Conversations, More Computer Conversations, The Math Group, 3996 East 79th Street, Minneapolis, MN 55420.

REFERENCES

Bogen, J. (1969). The other side of the brain. *Bulletin of the Los Angeles Neurological Society II, 34*, 135–162.

Charles, R., & Lester, F. (1982). *Teaching problem solving: What and how.* Palo Alto, CA: Dale Seymour Press.

Peddiwell, J. A. (1939). *The saber-tooth curriculum.* New York: McGraw-Hill.

Reys, R., & Reys, B. (1983). *Guide to using estimation skills and strategies.* Palo Alto, CA: Dale Seymour Press.

Wheatley, G., Frankland, R., Mitchell, R., & Kraft, R. (1978). Hemispheric specialization and cognitive development: Implications of mathematics education. *Journal for Research in Mathematics Education. 9,* 20–32.

Wheatley, G., & Wheatley, C. (1982). *Calculator use and problem solving strategies of grade six pupils.* Final Report. IN: Purdue University Press.

11

A National Study of Science Curriculum Effectiveness With High Ability Students

Joyce VanTassel-Baska, George Bass, Roger Ries, Donna Poland, and Linda D. Avery
College of William and Mary

This study assessed student growth on integrated science process skills after being taught a 20-36 hour science unit. The prototypical unit, Acid, Acid Everywhere, was implemented in 15 school districts across seven states. Although seven science units for high ability learners have been developed through a federally funded project, the student outcome results

Editor's Note: From VanTassel-Baska, J., Bass, G., Ries, R., Poland, D., & Avery, L. (1998). A National Study of Science Curriculum effectiveness with high ability students. *Gifted Child Quarterly*, 42(4), 200–211. © 1998 National Association for Gifted Children. Reprinted with permission.

only from Acid, Acid Everywhere, the most widely replicated unit, are reported here. All units were based on the Integrated Curriculum Model (ICM) developed specifically for gifted learners; the model stresses advanced content, high level process and product, and a concept dimension. Results indicate small, but significant, gains for students in integrated science process skills when compared to equally able students not using the units. Implementation data reflected satisfaction of teachers with the units, especially in terms of student interest and motivation. The effectiveness of this curriculum, designed to align with the new science standards and to be appropriate for gifted students, lends credibility to the argument for using the new content standards as a basis for curriculum development efforts with gifted learners.

G ifted education has reached a difficult crossroads. The field is considered irrelevant by some critics because general reform initiatives promote critical thinking, inter-disciplinary curriculum, and project work for all students, thus hypothetically providing more challenging curricula for gifted students in the regular classroom. The field is also assailed for grouping practices seen as counter to the current interest in inclusion. As questions about what constitutes a defensible gifted program persist, coupled with questions about meaningful settings for delivery, gifted education has been hard-pressed to respond based on existing data. A differentiated curriculum is frequently not a central feature in regular classrooms (Westberg, Archambault, Dobyns, & Slavin, 1993). Yet, if gifted education exists primarily to serve the learning needs of high ability students, then curriculum must be at the center of deliberations on program worth. The nature and extent of student learning become the central concern.

Ongoing longitudinal studies have demonstrated that advanced learning opportunities for the gifted during the K-12 schooling years provide positive pathways for development (Brody & Stanley, 1991; Lubinski & Benbow, 1994; Swiatek & Benbow, 1991) and recent meta-analyses have shown that grouping the gifted only matters if it is linked to differentiated curricula (Kulik & Kulik, 1992). Nevertheless, only a few classroom-based intervention studies have been undertaken to demonstrate the direct impact of differentiated curricula on high end student learning (VanTassel-Baska, 1996).

Correspondingly, in the science education community, there has been concern over student learning and what enhances it. Reports over the past 15 years indicate that students have not been achieving well in science (National Commission on Excellence in Education, 1983); advanced courses were poorly subscribed to and frequently not even offered in many secondary schools (Bybee, 1994; National Science Board Commission on Precollege Education in Mathematics, Science, and Technology, 1983); and girls and minority students were dropping out of the science track as early as possible (Hilton, Hsia, Solorzano, & Benton, 1989). Elementary teachers were not teaching science because they did not know the content or feel secure in the subject area (Rutherford & Ahlgren, 1989); little instructional time in elementary schools was devoted to science (National Assessment of Educational Progress, 1988); and where and when science was taught, it tended to be delivered through basal texts that emphasized reading and canned experiments rather than active learning (Lockwood, 1992a, 1992b).

Putting the Research To Use

This study demonstrates the importance of high-powered curricula in creating defensible programs for gifted learners in schools and illustrating an assessment approach that can be replicated in other programs where the student outcomes focus on enhancing scientific research skills.

The study strongly suggests that the use of the William and Mary problem-based science units enhances learning regardless of grouping patterns employed and contributes positively to student motivation to learn. Careful alignment with national science standards and most state standards allows the curriculum to be used as a fundamental part of any school's curriculum reform agenda.

To address the problems of science learning and teaching, key national groups, including scientists and science educators, collaborated to identify a set of science concepts and processes deemed essential for K-12 learners (Rutherford & Ahlgren, 1989). Other groups, such as the National Science Foundation, the National Academy of the Sciences, and the National Science Teachers Association, have responded through the development of teacher enhancement programs and curriculum development recommendations. Becoming number one in science and mathematics by the year 2000 became a bipartisan national goal (United States Department of Education, 1991). Project 2061, American Association for the Advancement of Science (1993) published benchmarks of science literacy goals that concentrate on a common core of learning. More recently, the National Research Council (1996) also published a set of national science standards.

In a climate of educational reform, the role of exemplary curricula becomes a primary vehicle to improve both gifted and science education. In order to address the issue of world class standards in science, one project initiative, funded by the U.S. Department of Education Javits program, focused on the development and evaluation of curricula appropriate for high ability learners. The National Curriculum Project for High Ability Learners at the College of William and Mary is one model for interpreting world class standards for K-8 students. The assumption was that curriculum, instruction, and materials sufficiently challenging, in-depth, and varied to meet the needs of high ability learners in science at the elementary level would also contain the elements of general curriculum reform. This assumption was tested by examining the relationship of the William and Mary curriculum to the national science recommendations.

An analysis of the relationship of the William and Mary curriculum to the new national science standards and to the benchmarks of scientific literacy revealed considerable congruence. Across grade levels and units, the William and Mary curricula map very consistently on the two national standard sources (see Figures 1 and 2). The William and Mary units focus on the concept of systems, while the national science standards and benchmarks suggest multiple concepts. The content topics treated are comparable to some of the national science standards, but interpreted at a more specific level. For example, physical science is represented in one William and Mary unit through the study of acid-based chemistry. The alignment between the National Science Education standards and the William and Mary units is closest in their review of science as inquiry. In contrast, the Benchmarks of Scientific Literacy emphasize a broader perspective of the habits of mind that undergird the nature of science.

More specifically, the unit used in this study, *Acid, Acid Everywhere*, was examined for its alignment to fourth-grade-level science recommendations. In concept teaching and learning, the William and Mary unit has slightly higher expectations for learning than the National Science Education Standards and significantly higher standards than the Benchmarks'. In terms of content, the William and Mary unit is more specific in its expectations for learners than either of the other documents. Finally, the scientific process component of the William and Mary units requires students to design, conduct, and articulate an experiment in an extended and integrated manner, while the national standards and benchmarks present general expectations for learners in this area and treat the processes of doing sciences as more discrete tasks.

EVALUATION OF SCIENCE CURRICULUM

In the search for evidence of effectiveness, developers of nationally funded science curriculum projects often complained that money was available for project development but not for research to evaluate programs. The largest body of research on effectiveness was done on the science curriculum projects developed in the 1960s: Science, A Process Approach (SAPA); Elementary Science Study (ESS); Science Curriculum Improvement Study (SCIS); and Biological Sciences Curriculum Study (BSCS). These projects were not only the subject of numerous studies by outside researchers, but the studies were also analyzed in several meta-analyses (Bredderman, 1983; Shymanski, Hedges, & Woodward, 1990; Shymanski, Kyle, & Alport, 1983). Studies included in the meta-analyses had comparison groups using traditional curriculum and examined differences in science achievement, attitudes, process skills, creativity, and Piagetian tasks. Mean effect sizes for science process skills favoring Science,

Figure 1   Comparison of Science Standards

Source	Grade Level	Major Concepts	Contents/Topics	Scientific Processes
National Science Education Standards	K-4, 5–8, 9–12	• Systems, Order, & Organization • Evidence, Models, & Explanation • Changes, Constancy, & Measurement • Evolution & Equilibrium • Form & Function	• Physical Science • Life Science • Earth & Space Science • Science in Personal & Social Perspectives • History & Nature of Sciences	Science As Inquiry: Abilities necessary to do scientific inquiry: • framing questions • designing & conducting investigations • using tools & mathematics to improve investigations • using logic & evidence to revise • recognize & analyze alternatives • communicate & defend findings Understand about scientific inquiry: • application of above skills to the world of scientists The Nature of Science: • scientific world of view • scientific inquiry • scientific enterprise Habits of Mind: • values & attributes • computation & estimation • manipulation & observation • communications skills • critical response skills
Benchmarks of Scientific Literacy	K-2, 3–5, 6–8, 9–12	• Systems • Models • Constancy & Change • Scale	• Nature of Mathematics • Nature of Technology • Physical Setting (universe, earth, process that shape the earth, matter, etc.) • Living Environment (diversity, cells, evolution of life, etc.) • Human Organization (human identity, human development, learning, etc.) • Human Society (cultural effects on behavior, group behavior, social change, etc.) • Designed World (agriculture, materials & manufacturing, political systems, etc.) • Historical Perspectives	
William & Mary Curriculum Units	2–8	• Systems	Planet X: Planet physiology, planetary systems, physical features of planets, weather What a Find: Goals, tools, & practice of archaeology Electric City: Definitions, properties, flow of electricity Acid, Acid Everywhere: Acid/base chemistry Hot Rods: Nuclear energy, radioactivity, waste storage Chesapeake Bay: Agriculture, pollution, ecosystems No Quick Fix: Virus transmission, immune systems	Scientific Inquiry through the use of Experimental design: • Explore a new scientific area • Identify meaningful questions within that area • Demonstrate good data handling skills • Analyze any experimental data as appropriate • Evaluate results in light of original problem • Make predictions about similar problems • Communicate understand to others Scientific understanding through problem-based learning

Figure 2   Sample Comparison of Specific Science Standards Drawn from Grade Level 4 to Equate with Acid, Acid Everywhere

Category of Standard	Williams & Mary Unit: Acid, Acid Everywhere	National Science Education Standards	Benchmarks of Scientific Literacy
Concepts	Students will be able to: 1. Analyze systems. 2. Use systems language. 3. Analyze systems interactions. 4. Make predictions based on systems thinking 5. Transfer system concept to new system.	A system is an organized group of related objects or components that form a whole. Systems have boundaries, components, resources flow (input and output) and feedback. The goal of this standard is to think and analyze in terms of systems. Prediction is the use of knowledge to identify and explain observations, or changes in advance.	Systems: 1. Is something that consists of many parts, the parts usually influence one another., 2. Something may not work as well as a part of it is missing, broken, worn out, mismatched, or misconnected.
Content/Topics	Students will be able to: 1. Draw and interpret the pH scale. 2. Identify common acids and bases. 3. Devise safe method for determination of pH of unknown. 4. Neutralize an acid safely. 5. Construct and use a titration curve. 6. Analyze the effect of water dilution on acid. 7. Analyze the effects of acids and bases on living organisms.	Physical Science: 1. Students will develop an understanding of properties of objects and materials. Life Science: 2. Students will develop understandings of organisms and environment. Science in Personal and Social Perspectives: 3. Students will develop an understanding of science and technology in local challenges.	Nature of Mathematics: 1. Mathematical ideas can be represented graphically. Technology & Science: 2. Measuring instruments can be used to gather accurate scientific comparisons. Structure of Matter: 3. When a new material is made by combining two or more materials, it has different properties. Interdependence of Life: 4. Changes in an organism's habitat are sometimes beneficial and sometimes harmful.
Scientific Processes	1. Students will be ale to design, perform, and report on the results of experiments: • Demonstrate data handling • Analyze experimental data • Make predictions to similar problems • Communicate understanding to others 2. Students will be able to identify meaningful scientific problems for investigation	Students will be able to: 1. Ask a question about objects, organisms, and events in the environment. 2. Plan and conduct a simple investigation. 3. Employ simple equipment and tools to gather data and extend the senses. 4. Use data to construct a reasonable explanation. 5. Communicate investigations and explanations.	Students should know that: 1. Scientific investigations may take many different forms. 2. Results of similar investigations seldom turn out the same. 3. Scientists' explanations come from observation and thinking. 4. Claims must be backed up with evidence. 5. Clear communication is an essential part of doing science.

A Process Approach (SAPA) curriculum, one of the leading examples of 1960s curriculum, were .71; affective outcomes favoring the curricula yielded mean effect sizes of .46; and overall mean effect size, based on all outcome areas, was .35. Typically, researchers have argued that effect sizes over .33 have practical significance in generalizing to comparable settings or populations. Significant process skill gains were also found for Elementary Science Study (ESS) and Science Curriculum Improvement Study (SCIS) over more traditional programs. Studies also reported enhanced student performance after teachers received in-service programs. The few follow-up studies reported limited evidence of sustained performance by students after the programs had been discontinued.

During the past five years, a number of relatively new programs have also conducted effectiveness research. The Chemical Education for Public Understanding Program (CEPUP) provides a rare example of a program with clearly stated goals and an evaluation of how those goals were met (Kelly, 1991). Middle School Life Science conducted a comprehensive evaluation of program effectiveness as a requirement for inclusion of the program in the National Diffusion Network (JEFFCO Life Science Program, 1989). The developers of the Teaching Integrated Mathematics and Science (TIMS) program have conducted research on the effectiveness of their program with 5,000 students. They employed a pre-post design (Goldberg & Wagreich, 1989) using an instrument constructed by program developers to measure math and science process skills. The results showed significant improvement in test scores in almost all areas.

Yet, these studies are the exceptions. Most new and old science curricula lack student outcome data and findings about key factors in implementing such curricula. While the 1960s curricula have provided some useful impact and implementation data, and relevant evaluation data are now being collected for individual curricula currently in development, there have been few attempts to study systematically the impact of key components of the new science curricula on student learning and teacher implementation. Since the new science recommendations stress science content and concepts, as well as science process, studies from the 1960s are of limited usefulness. Nor have any studies examined these issues using a national sample of high ability learners. A recent analysis of the NELS data (Hamilton, Nussbaum, Kumpermintz, Kerhoven, & Snow, 1995) found that the instructional variables of working on experiments in class, problem solving, and promoting scientific understanding were the best predictors of achievement in quantitative science by 10th grade. Yet, the authors of this study readily acknowledged the need for understanding how these instructional variables operate in specific school contexts with specific populations of learners. Thus, a need exists to test the assumptions underlying the new science curriculum recommendations through demonstrating learning effects on high ability and, in some contexts, on average learners in schools.

PURPOSE OF THE STUDY

Given the paucity of effectiveness studies based on the use of specialized curriculum or materials in any domain and the lack of systematic implementation data, the purpose of this study was to assess student growth on integrated science process skills after being taught a 20–36 hour science unit designed according to the new science recommendations and to curriculum features appropriate for gifted learners (VanTassel-Baska, 1996; VanTassel-Baska, Bailey, Gallagher, & Fettig 1993). Moreover, the researchers were interested in assessing implementation issues. The study represents a preliminary assessment of these variables. Although the specially designed science units contain goals and outcomes that emphasize science content and the concept of "systems," only science research skills were assessed in this study.

METHOD

Sample

The sample was comprised of 45 classes in 15 school districts in seven states whose teachers had been trained in the use of the selected unit of study and who volunteered to participate in the study. Forty-five experimental and 17 comparison classrooms at grades 4–6 with a total of 1,471 students were identified. Of the 45 experimental classes, 12 were self-contained gifted, 10 were pull-out, 11 were heterogeneous with a gifted cluster, and 12 were heterogeneous. Forty-two teachers completed an implementation questionnaire to assess reactions to the selected unit, Acid, Acid Everywhere, as well as other units in the project.

Gifted students were defined as those already identified by local districts according to ability, achievement, and performance criteria profiles. In addition, demographic information and selection criteria were also collected to ascertain any differences within the student sample.

Instrument

The student outcome measure, the Diet Cola Test (DCT), was originally developed by Fowler (1990) to identify promising science students. The DCT was designed for use on a pre-post basis and provides alternate forms. It is an open-ended test that cues students to demonstrate their ability to design experiments. The National Research Center on the Gifted and Talented at the University of Virginia documented appropriate reliability studies (Adams & Callahan, 1995). Correlation for alternative forms over time was .76, interrater reliabilities ranged from .90–.95. Studies were also conducted on the validity of the DCT as an evaluation tool for science processes (Adams & Callahan), with findings indicating that the DCT was sensitive to differences in student responses. The DCT was also judged by William and Mary project staff to adequately reflect the *Acid, Acid Everywhere* unit objectives to develop student research skills in experimental design. Moreover, it was the only instrument found in a search of the literature to be appropriate in evaluating gifted student outcomes in science at this age range, and with a sufficiently high ceiling.

A teacher questionnaire was constructed for the study, which assessed the extent to which teachers found the curriculum materials appropriate, usable, and effective with students through Likert scales and open-ended items.

Procedure

Using alternative forms for pre and post, the DCT was administered to 1,471 students across 62 classes. The scoring of both pre- and posttest versions of the test was conducted by project staff after training on the protocol. Additionally, each pilot teacher ($N = 42$) completed the implementation questionnaire on the use of the William and Mary science unit.

School districts agreed to participate in the study during the summer training institutes held from 1993–95 at the college of William and Mary. They were provided guidelines for participation which included (a) the designation of an on-site coordinator of data collection and administration; (b) selection of at least one experimental class with directions for setting up a comparison class; (c) a written description of general district demographics and demographics of the students in experimental and comparison classes; and (d) permission to participate from an authorized official of the school district. During the summer institute, trainers provided four to five-day sessions in using the pilot unit of study. In addition, two-day state-wide conferences were held during the same three-year time period throughout the United States; some teachers agreed to participate from these contexts as well. All teachers in the study received at least two days of intensive training in how to implement the selected unit of study. School sites included public urban, suburban, and rural schools in the midwest and southeastern regions.

The unit of study, *Acid, Acid Everywhere*, which was implemented at all sites, was designed to accommodate high ability learners through an emphasis on advanced content, higher order thinking in a problem-based format, research skills in science, and the development of a challenging project demonstrating problem resolution. Through project work (VanTassel-Baska, Bailey, Gallagher, & Fettig, 1993) the unit emphasized factors cited in the National Research Council (1996) science standards:

- learner outcomes of significance;
- authentic assessment;
- emphasis on scientific process and experimental design;
- use of real interdisciplinary problems;
- use of metacognition;
- emphasis on scientific habits of mind;
- collaborative learning; and
- hands-on activities

Table 1   Analysis of Covariance on the Diet Cola Test of Science Process Skills

Classes	n	Means Pretest (SD)	Posttest (SD)	Adjusted	F
Experimental	45	5.19 (1.07)	6.85 (1.08)	6.81	
					32.86*
Comparison	17	5.06 (0.97)	5.37 (1.08)	5.41	

*p < .001

Before it was employed for study purposes, the unit had already been piloted and revised twice based on teacher feedback. Units developed for the National Curriculum Project were designed based on the Integrated Curriculum Model (ICM) developed specifically for use with gifted learners (VanTassel-Baska, 1986, 1992, 1996) by stressing advanced content, high level process and product, and a concept dimension. All seven units were used as a part of the overall data collection effort, but only student outcome results from *Acid, Acid Everywhere* are reported in this paper.

Acid, Acid Everywhere, along with other units, was reviewed by outside groups including the U.S. Department of Education, Eisenhower Program, the National Science Teachers Association, the Department of Research Evaluation and Planning of the third largest school district in the U.S., and curriculum experts in gifted education. The units have received uniformly favorable critiques from all of these sources.

RESULTS

As reported in Table 1, an analysis of covariance on posttest means with the pretest as a covariate showed significant differences between experimental and comparison groups ($F = 32.86$; $p < .001$). The effect size, 1.30, was also found to be high.

Teacher questionnaire data reflected great diversity among the teachers who implemented the curriculum. Of those 42 who returned questionnaires (an 80% response rate), it was found they were generally experienced, with several years of working with both gifted and talented students and in teaching science. The range of years working with gifted students was 1 to 31, with a mean number of 8.3 years. The range of years teaching science for the group was also 1 to 31, with a mean number of 9.9 years.

The teachers also worked with high ability learners in a range of settings, from heterogeneous to self-contained classrooms. The minimum contact time for *Acid, Acid Everywhere* was at least 20 hours of instruction, but several teachers used up to 36 hours to complete the unit. The teachers' weekly scheduling of the unit ranged from one period a week to nine periods a week. Time to complete the unit ranged from 4 to 30 weeks. Consequently, implementation timeframes and the intensity of contact varied considerably across sites.

Moreover, grouping patterns also varied. Students were grouped in one of the following models: self-contained, one-day-per-week pull-out, partial-day pull-out two to three times per week, cluster grouping in the regular classroom, or heterogeneous classroom.

Teacher Questionnaire Ratings

Mean scores for Likert-scale items are reported in Table 2. Teachers gave the highest ratings (above 4.0) to the following five items on the questionnaire:

1. Unit goals and outcomes were appropriate for my students (5.0).

2. Students were actively involved in the unit activities (4.5).

3. Unit exercises and hands-on activities were motivating to my students (4.3).

4. Unit topics were interesting and relevant to my students (4.2).

5. Unit exercises and hands-on activities were appropriate to my students' ability level (4.1).

Less highly rated items were number 3 (3.5) and number 11 (3.2) which asked for teachers' perceptions of the completeness and clarity of unit directions and the assistance in accommodating individual student differences.

Teacher Questionnaire Qualitative Data

In the open-ended portion of the questionnaire, more than half of the teachers cited the hands-on, problem-based and student-centered aspects of the units to be most supportive of their teaching. More than half of the teachers stated that the units generated student enthusiasm, interaction, and involvement to a high degree. Teachers implementing the unit in heterogeneous settings perceived that all students, not just the gifted, learned. Connections to the real world through the use of relevant and local problems were also reported as a powerful aspect of the units.

In response to an open-ended question that probed problems in curriculum implementation, over half of the teachers cited too much paperwork and repetition, noting the numerous exercises, assessments, logs, and worksheets that became tedious for students and teachers.

Thus, it was no surprise that the major areas suggested for improving the units lay in requiring less paperwork of students. Moreover, teachers suggested that educators using the materials in the future should consider adapting them for local contexts. The overall judgment of the units by pilot teachers centered on four main points:

Table 2   Teacher Implementation Questionnaire Rating Results

	Mean Rating
1. Unit goals and outcomes were appropriate for my students.	5.0
2. All necessary instructional materials were listed and adequately described.	3.7
3. Unit directions and explanations were complete and understandable.	3.5
4. Students had inadequate background knowledge in science to learn the specific content outcomes.	2.4
5. Students had insufficient group process skills to learn from the group hands-on experiences.	2.0
6. Students were actively involved in the unit activities.	4.5
7. Unit exercises and hands-on activities were appropriate to my students' ability level.	4.1
8. The hands-on experiences interfered with my monitoring of student learning.	1.4
9. Unit exercises and hands-on activities were motivating to my students.	4.3
10. Unit topics were interesting and relevant to my students.	4.2
11. Unit activities helped me accommodate individual student differences.	3.2
12. Unit topics and activities were too superficial for my students.	2.0
13. Unit activities took too long for the kinds of learning students were able to achieve.	2.8

Note. The values assigned to Likert items were as follows: Never or Almost Never = 1; Seldom = 2; Sometimes = 3; Usually = 4; Always or Almost Always = 5.

- gifted students as well as students at all ability levels benefited from their use;
- the teachers would teach the unit(s) again;
- the units were enjoyable and motivating for both students and teachers; and
- the units were well-designed and documented important curriculum elements for teachers.

Exemplary Student Gains

A great deal of variation among the experimental sample was evident, with posttest scores ranging from 0–16 points, yet with dramatic score increases being documented for individual students. As can be seen from Table 3, individual fifth-grade students increased their understanding of the

Table 3 Sample Fifth-Grade Responses to Fowler (1990) Science Process Test

Student	Pretest Response	Posttest Response

A	First, I would put some earthworms in a container. There would be lights and some dirt. I would put several different earthworms in it. If more earthworms liked the light than that would be right. I would try this with about seven groups and decide if they liked light.
	
	Score: 5
		Materials: Diet Cola, 3 large containers, 3 small containers, 6 bees
		
		Hypothesis: If you give bees diet cola then they will be attracted to it.
		
		1. Gather 6 bees, diet cola, 3 large containers, 3 small containers. 2. Put 2 bees in each large container. 3. Pour 5 ml of diet cola in each small container. 4. Set the small container of diet cola in each large container than has bees in it. 5. Watch and observe to see if the bees are attracted to the diet cola. 6. You should record if the bees like the diet cola on a chart like below.
		
		Bees If they are attracted to Diet Cola
		
		   1
		
		   2
		
		   3 . . .
		
		Score: 11

B	No earthworms don't like light how I know that is because I took a earthworm and put it on some dert and if it liked sun light it would stay on top of the dert but it didn't it went into the dert where it's dark. Score: 4	Title of Experiment is – are bees attracted to diet cola. Materials: a room with nothing in it, 4 bees in a jar, a cup of diet cola, and a pepsi Step by step on how to do the exsperament: First you take the diet cola & put it in the room then you take the pepsi and put it in the room by the diet cola. Then you take the jar of 4 bees and release them in the room & then in about 5 mins. see which one they like better & if they don't like neither of them. How will you know - look in each cup & see how much they drink out of each cup. The data I will be collecting is - how much diet cola & pepsi they drink.

(Continued)

Table 3 Continued

Student	Pretest Response	Posttest Response
C	I don't think earthworms like light, because most of them live underground unless it rains or something and they get washed out of the dirt. I could always do an experiment to make sure, thow. For an experiment, I might taken an earthworm with some kind of light, an dirt, and see if it stays out in the light, or trys to get away from the light by going under the dirt. Score: 5	Data Table Diet ColaPepsi (record information here) Score: 12 Title: "Are bees attracted to diet cola?" Hypothesis: I don't think bees are attracted to diets, just to regular. For example: coke, sprite, Dr. Pepper. Materials: Bee, diet cola, container Description of what I would do: Take one can of diet cola and pour about 1 cup of it into a dish, bowl, etc. Then release a bee about a foot away and see if it moves toward the diet cola. If it does-you know bees like diet cola, but if it moves away from the diet cola, or doesn't respond to it you know bees don't like diet cola. When you are done with your expirament carefully release you bee, pour out your soda, and put back the way you found them. What will you record: If the bees are attracted to the diet cola or if they are attracted to the none diet liquids. Data table: Trys 1 2 3 4 5 6 Reactions: Score: 12

160

initial steps in planning an experiment, as well as their understanding of data collection procedures.

For example, Student A demonstrates noticeable growth from pretest to posttest in the initial layout and design of an experiment. The student provides more detail in the posttest as exhibited by the materials list and hypothesis. Further, the level of detail the student gives in the actual steps of the experiment is considerably more precise in the posttest than in the pretest. Finally, Student A's posttest includes a chart for recording data, not present in the pretest, which indicates increased understanding of data representation.

Similarly, Student B provides a more detailed layout of the experiment in the posttest by including a title and a materials list. Student B's growth in experimental design from pre- to posttest is exhibited through the inclusion of steps for observation, collection, and recording of data.

Student C provides a hypothesis and a sketchy experiment in the pretest, but demonstrates a much stronger understanding of experimental design with the utilization of a title, materials list, hypothesis, detailed experiment, and data collection chart on the posttest. While these increases in learning translated into modest gains of six to eight test score points, they represent substantive increases in the student's understanding of the complexity of conducting research in science.

DISCUSSION

This study represents an initial effort to evaluate the science learning of high ability students using the William and Mary unit, designed to meet science reform specifications and gifted specifications of the ICM model. The findings support the use of one of the units, *Acid, Acid Everywhere*, at grades 4–6 for enhancing student understanding of scientific research and the science process skills that undergird it. Based on teacher perceptions of the unit, additional student benefits lay in motivating students to engage in doing science, a strong feature of the problem-based approach to the curriculum.

However, several issues in interpreting these findings should be discussed. One concern is the limited aspect of learning being measured by the instrument, the DCT, selected for the study. Although the units teach to content, process, and concept outcomes, the results do not reflect potential new learning in either the unit's specialized content or the concept of systems, another major organizing focus of the units. Nor does the instrument tap into the interdisciplinary learning possibly accrued from the use of problem-based learning as an organized feature in the units. Thus, overall learning effects of the unit are probably underrepresented by this study.

While the study demonstrated statistically significant gains on the DCT, it raises questions about how important these gains might be. Total mean gains across all experimental groups from pre- to post-assessment was 1.7 points, on an instrument with a maximum score of 21. That experimental gifted students demonstrated statistically significant gains over their comparison groups may be less important than the fact that the experimental students could and should have performed much better on the tasks assessed. In a content analysis of student performance on the Fowler (1990) instrument, more than 50% of the students responding failed to score points in the following five categories: 1) states plan for interpreting data, 2) states planning for making conclusions based on data, 3) plans to control variables, 4) plans to repeat testing, and 5) safety. These sections represent 8 out of the possible 21 points. The findings may be an indication of students' limited experience in interpreting results and formulating conclusions in true experiments. Such results could suggest that the units do not stress the features of scientific experimentation sufficiently or give students enough practice with designing their own experiments. Since there are six opportunities for such design work by students, it may also suggest that teachers did not fully implement this component of the curriculum.

Teaching scientific research skills is a sophisticated process requiring concentrated time and practice. Earlier science intervention program efforts in gifted education have documented the difficulty in showing short term growth gains on higher level skills like scientific interpretive inquiry (VanTassel-Baska & Kulieke, 1987), critical thinking, or research productivity. Teaching more than one unit in a year or including the scientific research process in a more substantive way in the core science program might result in more enhanced learning.

Another explanation for the modest gains may rest with the teacher variable. As our data indicate, teachers in the pilot study had a broad range of backgrounds in science and science teaching. Even at the middle school level, the range of experience in science teaching was as broad as in the total sample of teachers. Shulman (1987) identified the need for expert teachers to have specific knowledge of the subject matter to be taught and general pedagogical knowledge of how to motivate students, how to manage groups of students in a classroom setting, how to design and administer tests, and so forth. Finally, he noted that expert teachers need pedagogical-content knowledge that includes knowledge of how to explicate particular concepts (e.g., how to explain gravity), how to demonstrate and rationalize procedures and methods (Leinhardt & Greeno, 1986), and how to correct students' naive theories and misconceptions about subject matter (Gardner, 1991). The complexity of the new science curriculum calls for teachers who are expert in exactly these ways. Thus, teachers who will do well with the new science standards and, by implication, with the William and Mary units, will be those who possess these three areas of expertise. That high ability students in this study did not increase their integrated science process skills more on an instrument with plenty of ceiling could be related to the teacher expertise. In a preliminary assessment of teacher knowledge on the same instrument in a summer training institute, teachers achieved a mean score of 8.1, suggesting that teacher content knowledge about scientific research processes may be limited.

CONCLUSION

The use of curriculum designed specifically for gifted students appears to produce significant learning gains, thus lending credibility to the argument for designing into curriculum materials differentiation features appropriate for gifted learners. The study also demonstrates that an interdisciplinary approach to curriculum development can yield powerful effects on student learning through individual curricular components such as demonstrated here with science research skill development. While tailoring existing curriculum works well for accelerative and compacting purposes, new curriculum is necessary to sufficiently address the complexity of curriculum dimensions central to comprehensive differentiation and to new specifications set by the national standards project work.

Limitations of the Study

This study suffers from some of the same problems that plague applied research in general (Snow, 1974), such as lack of random student assignment to experimental and comparison groups. Lack of on-site monitoring of implementation also limits our complete understanding of the fidelity of the intervention. Because we had to rely on teacher volunteerism for site selection, geographic representational considerations, teacher background and experience, type of school setting, and grouping patterns could not be controlled. Variables we were able to control included teacher training on the unit, student population parameters, the specific curriculum unit intervention, minimum contact time for teaching the unit, and the assessment tool.

Implications

As is often the case with broad-based intervention studies, the findings reported and discussed in this study raise questions. We need to explore the effectiveness of the William and Mary curriculum units under more controlled conditions than were possible in this field study. More in-depth qualitative assessments of unit implementation and teacher development are needed to understand the fidelity between teacher training and classroom implementation. Such studies are currently in progress.

We also need to know more about other student outcomes beyond enhanced scientific process skills. Both studies of science-concept learning attributed to the curriculum units and the impact of using problem-based learning need further investigation. Moreover, replications of these study findings are needed in order to substantiate the validity of these initial findings.

The study does, however, provide important insights for practice in gifted education. Improvement in school-based science programs for high ability learners is a worthy goal, and practitioners may wish to profit from what these researchers have learned through the unit implementation data:

- Users of the William and Mary science curriculum units can be assured that the curriculum addresses important and substantive student outcomes aligned with national science standards. Moreover, both students and teachers are motivated and challenged by doing the activities, and student learning in integrated science process skills may be improved by use of the units.
- The DCT may be an excellent assessment tool for evaluating gifted students in scientific research skills. Given a 15-minute administration time, it is relatively unobtrusive and could be used to assess growth in many different science curricula that stress experimental design.
- Teachers of the gifted must develop competency in pedagogical-content knowledge in core domains like science. While research supports teaching higher level skills with substantive content (Perkins & Saloman, 1989), the practice of teaching higher level skills outside of content lingers in the field and contributes to limited application of real-world research skills.
- The impact of grouping appears to be less important if the curriculum being implemented is sufficiently challenging to students. Student gains were robust across various grouping models. Thus, attention to challenging curriculum should be the priority of school-based programs, not the choice of an organizational structure.

Gifted education curriculum practices need to become far more consonant with the national content standards and move into substantive knowledge bases for curriculum offered to these learners. This study is but one indicator of the potential for blending accepted gifted education practices with high level exemplary content. Only through such integration with the subject matter disciplines is the gifted learner likely to thrive in schools.

REFERENCES

Adams, C.M., & Callahan, C.M. (1995). The reliability and validity of a performance task for evaluating science process skills. *Gifted Child Quarterly, 39*(1), 14–20.

Bredderman, T. (1983). Effects of activity-based elementary science on student outcomes: A quantitative synthesis. *Review of Educational Research, 53*(4), 499–518.

Brody, L.E., & Stanley, J.C. (1991). Young college students: Assessing factors that contribute to success. In W.T. Southern & E.D. Jones (Eds.), *Academic acceleration of gifted children* (pp. 102–132). New York: Teachers College Press.

Bybee, R.W. (1994). *Reforming science education: Social perspectives and personal reflections.* New York: Teachers College Press.

Fowler, M. (1990). The diet cola test. *Science Scope, 13*(4), 32–34.

Gardner, H. (1991). *The unschooled mind.* NY: Basic Books.

Goldberg, H., & Wagreich, P. (1989). Evaluation of a model integrated mathematics science program of the elementary school. *International Journal of Educational Research, 14*(2), 193–214.

Hamilton, L.S., Nussbaum, E.M., Kumpermintz, H., Kerhoven, J.I.M., & Snow, R.E. (1995). Enhancing the validity and usefulness of large-scale educational assessments: II. NELS: 88 science achievement. *American Educational Research Journal, 32*(3), 555–581.

Hilton, T.L., Hsia, J., Solorzano, D.G., & Benton, N.L. (1989). *Persistence in science of high-ability minority students.* Princeton, NJ: Educational Testing Service.

JEFFCO Life Science Program. (1989). [Submission to the Program Effectiveness Panel at the U.S. Department of Education]. Golden, CO: Jefferson County Public Schools.

Kelly, P. (1991). *Perceptions and performance: An impact assessment of CEPUP in schools.* Unpublished manuscript, University of California at Berkeley, Lawrence Hall of Science, CEPUP.

Kulik, J.A., & Kulik, C.C. (1992). Meta-analytic findings on grouping programs. *Gifted Child Quarterly, 36*(2), 73–77.

Leinhardt, G., & Greeno, J.G. (1986). The cognitive skill of teaching. *Journal of Education Psychology, 78*(2), 75–95.

Lockwood, A. (1992a). The de facto curriculum? *Focus in Change, 6,* 8–11.

Lockwood, A. (1992b). Whose knowledge do we teach? *Focus in Change, 6,* 3–7.

Lubinski, D., & Benbow, C. (1994). The study of mathematically precocious youth: The first three decades of a planned 50-year study of intellectual talent. In R. Subotnik and K. Arnold (Eds.), *Beyond Terman, contemporary longitudinal studies of giftedness and talent* (pp. 255–281). Norwood, NJ: Ablex.

National Assessment of Educational Progress. (1988). *Science learning matters.* Princeton, NJ: Educational Testing Service.

National Commission on Excellence in Education. (1983). *A nation at risk: The imperative for educational reform.* Washington, DC: U.S. Government Printing Office.

National Research Council. (1996). *National science education standards.* Washington, DC: National Academy Press.

National Science Board Commission on Precollege Education in Mathematics, Science, and Technology. (1983). *Educating Americans for the 21st Century.* Washington, DC: National Science Foundation.

Perkins, D., & Saloman, G. (1989). Are cognitive skills context bound? *Educational Research, 18* (1), 16–25.

Project 2061, American Association for the Advancement of Science. (1993). *Benchmarks for science literacy.* New York: Oxford University Press.

Rutherford, J., & Ahlgren, A. (1989). *Science for all Americans.* Washington, DC: American Association for the Advancement of Science.

Shulman, L.S. (1987). Knowledge and teaching: Foundations of the new reform. *Harvard Educational Review, 19*(2), 4–14.

Shymanski, J.A., Hedges, L.V., & Woodward, G. (1990). A reassessment of the effects of inquiry-based science curricula of the 60's on student performance. *Journal of Research in Science Teaching, 27,* 127–144.

Shymanski, J.A., Kyle, W.C., & Alport, J.M. (1983). The effects of new science curricula on student performance. *Journal of Research in Science Teaching, 20,* 387–404.

Snow, R.E. (1974). Representative and quasi-representative designs for research on teaching. *Review of Educational Research, 44,* 265–291.

Swiatek, M.A., & Benbow, C.P. (1991). Ten-year longitudinal follow-up of ability-matched accelerated and unaccelerated gifted students. *Journal of Educational Psychology, 83,* 528–538.

United States Department of Education. (1991). *America 2000: An education strategy.* Washington, DC: Author.

VanTassel-Baska, J. (1986). Effective curriculum and instructional models for talented students. *Gifted Child Quarterly, 30*(4), 164–169.

VanTassel-Baska, J. (1992). *Planning effective curriculum for the gifted.* Denver, CO: Love Publishing.

VanTassel-Baska, J. (1996). The development of talent through curriculum. *Roeper Review, 18*(2), 98–102.

VanTassel-Baska, J., Bailey, J., Gallagher, S., & Fettig, M. (1993). *A conceptual overview of science education for high ability learners.* Williamsburg, VA: The Center for Gifted Education.

VanTassel-Baska, J., & Kulieke, M. (1987). The role of the community in developing scientific talent. *Gifted Child Quarterly, 31*(3), 115–119.

Westberg, K., Archambault, F., Dobyns, S., & Slavin, T. (1993). *An observational study of instructional and curricular practices used with gifted and talented students in regular classrooms.* Storrs, CT: National Research Center on the Gifted and Talented.

Index